The Complete Poems of
JOHN SKELTON
Laureate

ℭSkelton Poeta.

Eterno mansura die dum sidera fulgent
Equora dumq; tument hec laurea nostra virebit.
Hinc nostrum celebre et nomē referetur ad astra.
Vndiq; Skeltonis memorabitur altera donis

The Complete Poems

of

JOHN SKELTON

Laureate

EDITED BY

PHILIP HENDERSON

LONDON: J. M. DENT & SONS LTD
NEW YORK: E. P. DUTTON & CO. INC.

Printed in Great Britain
by
Butler and Tanner Ltd · Frome · Somerset
for
J. M. DENT & SONS LTD
Aldine House · Bedford Street · London
First published 1931
Second revised edition 1948
Third edition 1959
Fourth edition 1964
Reprinted 1966

INTRODUCTION

JOHN SKELTON is still not a very well-known English poet.
His poetical works will not be found among the Oxford
Standard Authors. Nevertheless he is one of the most
delightful and original writers who have ever used the
English tongue. Unlike much of our poetry from Chaucer
onwards, his verse owes practically nothing to foreign influences; his idiom is often straight from the vernacular in a
way that was a scandal to those worthy clerks who still
founded their practice upon the aureate diction of Latin.
Skelton's contemporary reputation—at least, his earlier
reputation as a humanist—was, of course, founded on his
more rhetorical work, and indeed his prose translation of
Diodorus is 'the most extravagant specimen of aureation in
our language.'[1] For what was most admired was the ability
to use many words to say as little as possible. This was
amplificatio and derived from Geoffrey de Vinsauf's *New
Poetics* of 1210, to which Chaucer and all medieval poets
paid homage. This was the 'sweet smoke of rhetoric.'
Although Skelton always remained a rhetorician in the
sense that he was fond of saying the same thing over and over
again in the same poem in different words, the way he said it
was so direct and simple that many of his poems are as fresh
and alive to-day as when they were first written. After he
had divested himself of the aureate singing robes that still ham-
pered his movements in early poems such as the *Northumberland Elegy* and *Knowledge, Acquaintance, Resort, Favour
with Grace*, we find him leaping and darting about in short
lines of two or three accents rhyming in couplets and triplets
—a measure which he made entirely his own. Yet for all
his 'antic disposition' he never deserted the stately rhyme

---

[1] *The Bibliotheca Historica of Diodorus Siculus*, translated by
John Skelton, edited by F. M. Salter and H. L. R. Edwards, two
vols., E.E.T.S., 1956–7.

royal, using it with an offhand elegance in *Speak, Parrot* which reminds one of Byron's similar use of the elaborate Spenserian stanza in *Don Juan*.

Neglected for centuries, Skelton was enthusiastically re-discovered by Robert Graves and others at Oxford shortly after World War I, though actually Graves's well-known poem 'John Skelton' had appeared in *Fairies and Fusiliers* in 1917.[1] It was a period when English poetry, suffering from the aftermath of Victorian romanticism, badly needed revitalizing. It needed naturalness and vigour to help it to escape from lingering Pre-Raphaelite languors, and these are just the qualities in which Skelton excels. 'He is as like a wild beast as a poet laureate can be,' wrote Elizabeth Barrett Browning in her *Book of the Poets*, 'in his wonderful dominion over language; he tears it, as with teeth and paws, ravenously, savagely. It is the very *sans-culottism* of eloquence.' Echoes of this *sans-culottism* can be heard in the more adventurous verse of the 1920's, in the earlier work of Edith Sitwell, for example, as well as in W. H. Auden and some of the poets of the 1930's. For, as Professor J. Isaacs reminded us in a celebrated broadcast lecture, the rediscovery of Skelton coincided with the rediscovery of Donne and Gerard Manley Hopkins, both poets who in their use of the rhythms of ordinary speech have had an enormous influence on the development of contemporary techniques.

Possibly the lines *Upon a Deadman's Head* are the earliest example we have of Skeltonic verse, though its earliest extended use may be seen in *Philip Sparrow*, which was the first poem of Skelton's to shock the academic world of his time. All the same, Skelton was very proud of his academic awards—the laurel crown of rhetoric bestowed upon him by Oxford and later confirmed by Cambridge. He was still more proud of the fact that Henry VII had granted him the distinction of wearing the Tudor colours of white and green and a robe embroidered 'CALLIOPE,' the muse of epic poetry,

[1] Graves's 1955 Cambridge lectures on poetry, *The Crowning Privilege*, show that his admiration for his favourite poet has not abated a jot in the interval.

and that when he came to the throne Henry VIII kept on
his old tutor as court poet.   That Skelton was still read and
remembered for some years after his death can be seen from
the appearance in 1568 of the first collected edition of his
poems, Thomas Marshe's *The Pithy, pleasant and profitable
works of Master Skelton, Poet Laureate*.   This edition
described the poems as 'newly collected by I. S.' who may be
John Stow, whose Chaucer had appeared in 1561.   The
volume was prefaced by a long poem by Churchyard, who
tells us that Skelton was 'seldom out of princes' grace.'   In
1586 we find Angel Day, in *The English Secretorie*, quoting
'a pretty jest that I have often heard repeated of pleasant,
well-learned Skelton'—a versified petition written for the
prioress of a nunnery at Margate, which owned a mill,
against the stopping of its watercourse by a neighbouring
abbey.   The prioress had evidently complained that Skelton's
first petition was too verbose, so he determined to show her
that brevity was the soul of wit.

> Humbly complaineth to your high estate
>   The Lady Prioress of Margate,
> For that the Abbot of S. Albones did stop
>   With two stones and a stake her water gap.
>   Help, Lord, for God's sake! [1]

At least the Elizabethans still sometimes referred to Skelton
as pleasant and well learned; but he is chiefly remembered
as a buffoon and coupled with Scogan, another folk figure,
though Jonson introduces him into his masque, *The Fortunate
Isles*, as 'the worshipful poet laureate to King Harry.'

But it was the reissue of Marshe's edition in 1736 which
provoked Pope, in the *Epistle to Augustus*, to call him 'beastly
Skelton,' coupling him with Chaucer for ribaldry.   Skelton
would certainly have felt flattered by the comparison and also
glad that he was still quoted, as Pope says he is, by the 'heads
of houses' at the universities, who then as now enjoyed an
occasional bawdy academic joke.   At the Romantic Revival
Coleridge's remark that *Philip Sparrow* was 'an exquisite

---

[1] Reprinted by G. M. McManaway in *Notes and Queries*, 31st
March 1951.

and original poem' perhaps prompted the Reverend Alexander
Dyce to bring out his great two-volume edition of the poems
in 1843. Then in 1924 came Richard Hughes's charmingly
produced selected edition, still in the original spelling, and
the rehabilitation of Skelton as both a brilliantly original
poet and a learned man began.

Born about 1460—though there is little to support this
date—Anthony Wood says in his *Athenae Oxoniensis* that
Skelton 'was originally, if not nearly, descended from the
Skeltons of Cumberland,' and Wordsworth tells us that he
was 'certain of having read somewhere that Skelton was
born at Branthwaite Hall.' [1] But the name Skelton was
common enough in the sixteenth century. There were
numerous Skeltons living in Westminster, where the poet
himself lived for at least part of his life, and there was even
a John Skelton, not the poet, appointed to the rectory of
Shelton in Norfolk in 1518! Professor Edwards, who has
probably devoted more research than anyone to the problem,
sums up as follows: 'The Skelton family, quite distinct from
the Norfolk Sheltons, originated in the north, in Cumberland and Yorkshire. By the fifteenth century members
were scattered over the whole island, and ranged from sheriffs
and gentlemen, vicars and maltmen, to university bigwigs,
cooks, whores, and pirates. Regarding Skelton himself,
facts are non-existent and tradition is almost useless, depending
as it does upon accident, whim, and actual error.' [2]

'*Alma parens, O Cantabrigensis!*' cries Skelton, in *A
Replication*, and the William Ruckshaw respectfully addressed
in the *tetrastichon* following the *Northumberland Elegy*
(Appendix, p. 431) may well have been his tutor in theology
at Peterhouse, though by the time the elegy was written
Ruckshaw had left Cambridge for the service of the Percys.
At Peterhouse too there was a William Skelton who became

[1] Grossart, *Prose Works*, iii. 334.

[2] 'John Skelton: a Genealogical Study,' *Review of English
Studies*, xi, 1935. Since then Edwards has produced his *Skelton:
The Life and Times of an Early Tudor Poet*, 1949, which so far
represents the last word on the subject.

vicar of Cherry Hinton in 1500. As it was customary in those days to attend several universities, at some unspecified date Skelton evidently left Cambridge without taking a degree, as far as we know, and went to Oxford. By 1490, as we learn from Caxton's address to him in the prologue to his *Boke of the Eneydos*, he had been 'late created poet laureate in the university of Oxenford.' By this time Skelton was probably about thirty and had translated the *Bibliotheca Historica* of Diodorus from the Latin of Poggio Bracciolini, the Epistles of Tully, and a number of other Latin classics into English, 'not in rude and old language,' says Caxton, 'but in polished and ornate terms craftily, for he hath read Virgil, Ovid, Tully, and all the other noble poets and orators to me unknown. Also he hath read the Nine Muses and understands their musical sciences. . . . I suppose he hath drunken of Elicon's well.' The *Boke of the Eneydos*, however, was a French romance, ultimately based on Virgil.

The ceremony of Skelton's laureation at Oxford was evidently attended by Henry VII, for as he tells us:

> A king to me mine habit gave:
> At Oxforth the university
> Avanced I was to that degree;
> By whole consent of their senate
> I was made poet laureate.

Edwards points out that this ceremony probably took place in the summer of 1488, when the king was in the neighbourhood of Oxford. With his laureation and the granting of the white and green habit embroidered 'CALLIOPE,' Skelton's career as a court poet began. It was at this time, probably, that he wrote his hearty songs *My Darling Dear, my Daisy Flower* and *Mannerly Margery Milk and Ale*, set to music by William Cornish, who entered the royal household about 1492, also his beautiful and moving hymn *Woefully arrayed* and the three very medieval hymns to the Trinity. In 1493 he appears to have been laureated by both Louvain and Cambridge universities. Early in 1498 he took holy orders and at some time after that was appointed tutor to the Duke of York at Eltham.[1]   Edwards has pointed out that he must have been chosen for this post by the king's mother, the pious and learned Lady Margaret Beaufort, Countess of Richmond and Derby, who was in charge of the Duke of York's education.

As Prince Arthur was heir to the throne, Henry was at first intended for the Church and his father hoped that he would one day become Archbishop of Canterbury!   That Skelton should have been chosen for his tutor seems at first sight a little surprising, in view of his later reputation, and Agnes Strickland, in her *Lives of the Queens of England*, supposes that 'the corruption imparted by this ribald and ill-living wretch laid the foundations of his royal pupil's grossest crimes.'   There is, to say the least, no sort of justification for such a supposition.   As royal tutor Skelton took his duties very seriously, compiling a Latin grammar and little books of moral maxims for his young pupil 'to bear in his hand.'   The only one of these to survive is the *Speculum Principis*, dated 'Eltham, 28th August 1501,' a blameless work which sought to inculcate such principles as 'Choose a wife for yourself: prize her always and uniquely.'

'The honour of England I learned to spell,' Skelton boasts during his 'flyting' with Garnish, and clearly he was now a man of considerable standing at court.   It was as such that John Suckling, Master of Godshouse, Cambridge, entertained him at dinner and supper on a Tuesday after Pentecost 1495, when he came to London to settle a Town and Gown dispute.   'Item Tuesday for dinner and supper with Master Skelton,' he entered in his expense account, 'because he was with the bishop of Sarum'—that is to say, John Blythe, who was both Bishop of Salisbury and Chancellor of Suckling's University.   On the following Saturday Suckling took Skelton out to lunch at Simpson's in Fleet Street, and when he came to Westminster on the same business during the Hilary Term of 1501 he had breakfast with

[1] 'At Marlborough, in the same month of March, a brilliant young Oxonian named Thomas Wolsey was also entering the priesthood.'   Edwards, *Skelton*, p. 57.

Skelton and supper on four separate occasions. For their
last meeting 'in our room' at Westminster they ordered a
gallon of strong ale, which cost the university twopence.
Skelton, it seems, was in demand on this occasion because
he had the ear of Lady Margaret Beaufort, who finally
settled the Town and Gown dispute, being regarded as 'the
king's mother's poet.'[1]

> The debt that ancient Greece
> To Homer owed, to Virgil Mantua,
> That debt to Skelton owes Britannia,
> For he from Latium all the muses led
> And taught them to speak English words instead
> Of Latin, and with Skelton England tries
> With Roman poets to contend the prize.[2]

So sang Erasmus when he visited England as a poor young
man in search of patronage in 1499, and Skelton was glad to
repeat his tribute in the envoy to *The Garland of Laurel* in
1523. Unfortunately Erasmus could not read a word of
English, and his praise of 'Stelkon,' as he calls him, seems to
have been part of an exchange of complimentary verses. But
in his *Description of Britain* he goes out of his way to write
of the excellence of the royal tutor: 'Skelton, that incomparable light and ornament of British letters.'

When Skelton commenced royal tutor Prince Henry
could not have been much more than six years old. But
he remained at Eltham until 1502, when the death of Prince
Arthur necessitated a reorganization of the royal household.
He was paid off in the last week in April—'Item to the duc
of york's scolemaster 40s.' The entry may still be seen in
the account book for 15–18 Henry VII at the Public Record
Office. Then, evidently in recognition of services past, he

---

[1] Account book of John Heron, H.M. Treasurer of the Chamber,
in an entry for 3rd–4th December 1497, recording a present
to Skelton of 66s. 8d. Public Record Office. Perhaps this was
for his translation of Guillaume de Guileville's *Pèlérinage de
la vie humaine*, which he tells us that he undertook for 'my lady's
grace.'

[2] Preserved Smith, *Erasmus*, p. 50.

was rewarded with the living of Diss, on the borders of Suffolk and Norfolk, a living in the gift of the Lady Margaret.

At Diss, Wood tells us, Skelton 'was esteemed more fit for the stage, than the pew or pulpit,' and according to *The Merry Tales* he was soon at loggerheads with his parishioners. They had complained to the Bishop of Norwich that he 'kept a fair wench in his house' and that she was now delivered of a baby. So next Sunday Skelton devoted his sermon to reproving them for their unreasonableness. He was a priest, he could not marry, but he was also a man, so what else did they expect? 'I do tell you, if you had fair wives, if were somewhat to help me at need; I am a man as you be; you have foul wives, I have a fair wench, of the which I have begotten a fair boy, as I do think, and as you shall all see.' Skelton then told his wife to come forward with their child and, holding it up naked before all the parish, he went on: 'How say you, neighbours all? Is not this child as fair as is the best of yours? It hath nose, eyes, hands, and feet, as well as any of yours: it is not like a pig, nor a calf, nor like no fowl nor no monstrous beast. If I had, said Skelton, brought forth this child without arms or legs, or that it were deformed, being a monstrous thing, I would never have blamed you to have complained to the bishop of me; but to complain without a cause, I say, as I said before in my anthem, *vos estis*, you be, and have been, and will and shall be knaves, to complain of me without a cause reasonable. For you be presumptuous and do exalt yourselves, and therefore you shall be made low.' Surely one of the most original sermons ever preached in an English parish church! Such behaviour must have made Skelton irresistible as a rector.

The hilarious epitaphs on some of his parishioners which followed were in the same spirit—for instance, the *Epitaph for Adam Udersall* and *A Devout Trental for Old John Clarke* (1506). Then there was the 'parson beneficed' who exercised his hawks in Diss Church, a scandalous incident which gave rise to that remarkable poem *Ware the Hawk*, which is just as full of unholy glee as the epitaphs.

It may have been something to do with the bracing effect

of the East Anglian air, but it is from the time of his removal
to Diss in 1503–4 that Skelton first appears in his true colours.
It is not without reason that he claims in the cipher of *Ware
the Hawk* to be unique, the phoenix of England.   He was.
It is true that *The Bouge of Court*, written before he left
Eltham and published anonymously in 1499, shows considerable originality in its handling of the old rhyme royal stanza.
It is typical of Skelton that when he introduces his conven-
tional medieval dream allegory, instead of falling asleep in
a bower surrounded by spring flowers and to the sound of
blissful birds he should drop off in a pub at Harwich.   Dread
finds favour at court because of his learning, but he soon
becomes disgusted with the time-servers and place-hunters
and all their petty intrigue.   Nevertheless *The Bouge of
Court* is not an original poem like *Philip Sparrow*, which is
written in a new kind of verse form altogether.   It was no
use, Skelton evidently felt, perpetuating the old forms, which
might be courtly and dignified, but were dead.   The new
age demanded something new.   Besides, the language itself
was changing so rapidly that the old forms had become
awkward and cumbersome.

So, in the spirit of the goliards with their masses of birds,
lovers, and drunkards, Skelton celebrates a mock-mass over
a dead sparrow, Jane Scrope's pet killed by the cat at Carrow
Abbey by Norwich.   He had a weakness for young girls;
he also evidently loved birds, for in this poem all the birds
from the marshes of East Anglia gather for the obsequies of
Jane's 'sparrow white as milk.'   The light, whimsical move-
ment of the verse is full of their chatter and the flicker of
their wings as they gather about the little hearse in response
to the charming invocation, which follows Jane's delightful
exclamatio : 'On all the whole natíon/Of cattès wild and tame.'
They are joined by two exotics not to be found in a wild state
in Norfolk—the parrot and the phoenix, for Skelton shared
the medieval weakness for making catalogues.   There is
some good literary criticism too as Jane recites all the books
she has read.   The poem concludes with a long, a very long,
section called 'The Commendations,' in which the poet sings

the praises of Jane herself, sometimes rather archly. Judging by the Latin epigraph to the poem, either Jane or her family—for the Scropes were local gentry of high standing—resented this as a piece of impertinence, though Skelton is all mock-innocence, pretending not to understand why anybody can take exception to anything he has written. But it was not only the Scrope family who disliked *Philip Sparrow*. This wonderfully lucid, effortless, witty poem aroused the ire of scholars and churchmen alike, in spite of the fact that composers were setting the mass to the tune of popular love songs, as in Taverner's marvellous *Western Wynde* mass. *The Tunning of Elinour Rumming* is simply the reverse side of the medal. At first sight nothing could be more different with its 'drunken, squalid, dirty women prodigal of words,' but it too is in the tradition of the goliards and their humorous vilification of women. In the list of his works in *The Garland of Laurel*, Skelton deliberately classes *Elinour Rumming* with *Colin Clout*, a purely political poem, remarking disarmingly that 'To make such trifles it asketh some conning,/In honest mirth, pardee, requireth no lack;/The white appeareth the better for the black.' This, however, does not necessarily mean that it was written at the same time as *Colin Clout* and the other attacks on Wolsey.

On Henry VIII's accession to the throne in 1509 Skelton made a determined attempt to reinstate himself at court. He hastened to celebrate the event with *A Laud and Praise Made for Our Sovereign Lord the King*, the manuscript of which is also at the Records Office. At the same time he got his name included in the general amnesty with which each new reign began. Here he is described as 'John Skelton, of London, clerk, poet laureate, *alias* late of Diss, Norf. poet laureate and rector of Diss. 21 Oct.' The description 'late of Diss' and also 'rector of Diss' probably means that he was temporally settled in Westminster, where he may already have had his house within the sanctuary on the south side of the Great Belfry. Many other Skeltons also lived in Westminster, including Sir Roger Skelton, vicar of St. Stephens, as well as William Cornish, the musician, and

Pietro Carmeliano, the king's Latin secretary. But he was back at Diss by December 1509, when he cited one of his parishioners, Thomas Pickerell, to appear before the Norwich episcopal court 'to answer certain interrogatories concerning the health of his soul.' Two years later Bishop Nick appointed him one of the arbiters in an ecclesiastical case. Evidently, therefore, though somewhat eccentric in his habits, the rector of Diss was considered a thoroughly responsible member of the Church. There might have been some question of the rector's morals; there was none of his orthodoxy and that is what really mattered.[1]

But he was still hoping to have his old position at court reaffirmed. Instead he had the doubtful pleasure of seeing Thomas Wolsey appointed Royal Almoner and Counsellor to the king. As a reminder, therefore, that he had a prior claim, Skelton presented the king with a carefully written out copy of the *Speculum Principis*, which he had given him as a boy, and two poems in his praise all bound up together in a little leather volume. Under each of the poems he wrote 'Jupiter Feretrius grant that I waste no more time beside Eurotas!' The book closes with the complaint of 'Skelton Laureate, once royal tutor, in mute soliloquy with himself, as a man wholly given over to oblivion. Shall I impute to so mighty and generous a king the conspicuous blemish of inadequate liberality?' Then, with a jealous eye on Wolsey, he adds: 'Rule, be not ruled! Hark to Samuel; read Daniel. Banish Ishmael!'[2] It is not altogether surprising that the king failed to respond.

Early next year, in 1512, Skelton returned to the attack and presented Henry with a tattered and enthusiastically annotated manuscript of the *Chronique de Rains* [Reims],[3] dealing with the life of Richard Cœur de Lion, inscribed in

[1] In July 1511 we find him dining at Westminster with William Mane, the prior. The menu consisted of plaice, soles, salt fish, and 'congger snekes.' Westminster Abbey, *Muniments*, 33325. f. 17*b*.

[2] Edwards, *Skelton*, pp. 129–30.

[3] This manuscript is now in the library at Corpus Christi, Cambridge.

his own peculiarly large and florid Gothic hand. 'Go, my book,' he wrote, 'prostrate yourself before the king and commend me to him, his humble poet Skelton. Above all, recount to his majesty the famous battles waged by England's greatest hero, Richard, first of our race.' As a result of this final appeal the old royal tutor was reinstated at court, as *orator regius*, a title with which he now begins to sign all his poems. As *orator regius*, Skelton composed epitaphs of Henry VII and of his mother, the Lady Margaret, which were inscribed on parchment and hung above their tombs in the miraculous new Lady Chapel at Westminster, now almost completed under the care of his friend, Abbot John Islip. He celebrated the Battle of the Spurs on 16th August 1513 with a *Chorus de Diss* and the defeat of the Scots at Flodden by another Chorus, followed by a truculent and rather unpleasant poem *Against the Scots*.

After Henry VIII's return from France, Skelton evidently left Diss for good, employing a deputy to carry out his duties there. His next commission was to engage in a slanging match with Sir Christopher Garnish, a young court gallant, or rutterkin. But Garnish proved no match for the *orator regius* and called in 'a scribe' who Skelton addresses as 'Gorbellied Godfrey'—possibly Stephen Hawes. If so, one wonders why he missed the obvious chance of a pun on his name. Garnish, a favourite of Henry VIII, was also a protégé of Wolsey, now Bishop of Lincoln and Tournai. Meanwhile Skelton watched Wolsey's phenomenal rise to power with a cold eye. In this summer of 1514 Bainbridge, Cardinal Archbishop of York, was poisoned at Rome, at the instigation, it was whispered, of a great English cleric. Soon after Wolsey was installed in the See of York he began to urge the Pope to make him *legate*. In September he got the cardinal's hat and next year replaced Warham as Lord Chancellor. The king spent his time 'in accomplishments and amusements day and night,' wrote the Italian ambassador, 'leaving business to the Cardinal.'

'The first poetic result of Skelton's hostility to Wolsey,' as Edwards calls it, is the poem *Against Venomous Tongues*, which apparently began as an apology for some satirical remark about the liveries of Wolsey's retinue, which were embroidered 'T' and 'C'—Thomas Cardinalis. Skelton is surprised to find so many 'well-lettered men' among the illiterate! This was followed by the interlude *Magnificence*, written expressly to warn the king against extravagance and evil counsellors. The play is chiefly remarkable for its brilliant use of a variety of verse forms for the different characters, an example followed by T. S. Eliot in *Murder in the Cathedral*, where Skelton's influence is evident in the First Tempter's speech. *The Manner of the World Now-adays*, which may or may not be his, is another bitter commentary on the manners of the time.

But all Skelton's political and social criticism comes to a head in the brilliant series of poems *Speak, Parrot, Colin Clout*, and *Why come ye not to Court?* which he began writing in the early 1520's. It is in *Colin Clout* and *Why come ye not?* that his peculiar idiom is seen at its most powerful. Indeed there could hardly be a more effective idiom for polemical verse than the headlong rush of his lines which, in the manner of an impassioned political speech, constantly recur to the same charges again and again with an annihilating effect. At first the indictment is against the bishops in general, but as the charges accumulate, all corruption in Church and State is seen as embodied in Wolsey, who though not actually named is clearly indicated, until in *Why come ye not?* the great cardinal becomes a figure of nightmare horror. 'Why come ye not to court?' Skelton asks, and replies bitingly: 'To which court? To the king's court or to Hampton Court?' Such a satire as *Colin Clout* was all the more effective because Skelton merely claims to be repeating, through the mouth of the average labourer of the day, what he overhears people saying everywhere as he wanders about the country. The poem might therefore be considered an early example of proletarian literature. But so hilarious is the general effect and so dazzling the verbal fireworks that for all its breathless indignation, one cannot help feeling that Skelton thoroughly enjoyed writing it, while in *Why come*

xviii INTRODUCTION

ye not to Court? he flung at Wolsey some of the most scandalous lines ever addressed to any statesman.

Speak, Parrot, with its array of humanist learning and packed contemporary allusions, is a very different matter and one of the most difficult and obscure poems in the language. In the beautiful introductory stanzas the poet himself comes before us, half bird of paradise, half clown, a position which he had evidently come to occupy in his age. As king's orator Skelton was very much the popinjay royal. The origin of Parrot himself, William Nelson points out,[1] is to be found in Boccaccio's *Geneologia Deorum*. Here it is related that Psyttacus, the son of Deucalion and Pyrrha, is venerated for his wisdom and virtue by the Ethiopians, among whom he lived. In old age the gods, at his entreaty, transformed him into the bird that bears his name. In the course of the poem Parrot becomes not only a symbol of the soul, but of the poetic faculty itself. 'Parrot is my own dear heart, my own dear darling,' Skelton tells us. 'I pray you, let Parrot have liberty to speak.'

In writing these poems, says Skelton, he is following the example of Juvenal, who did not spare to castigate the vices of his age. But he knew that he was playing a dangerous game. After all, his friend Cornish had been clapped into the Fleet in 1504 for his satires on the hated lawyer Empson. To satirize Wolsey, the man who was supreme in both Church and State, demanded far more courage. Skelton may have been living in sanctuary at Westminster, but should Wolsey ever succeed in abolishing the right of sanctuary, as he had already tried to do, then the popinjay royal would have found himself completely at the mercy of a man notorious for his choleric and irascible temper.

We do not know exactly what happened, but the next thing we find is that Skelton has apologized and even been promised a prebend! As we have seen, *The Garland of Laurel* refers to *Colin Clout* as a trifle of honest mirth, though at the close of the same poem Skelton confesses to living '"Tween hope and drede,' and in a respectful address to both

[1] *John Skelton Laureate*, pp. 182-3.

the king and the cardinal asks the latter to give him grounds
'to hope for his protection.' Next in *A Replication* he liter-
ally struggles with superlatives in his efforts to express his
allegiance to 'the most honourable, most mighty, and by far
the most reverend father in Christ and in the Lord, Thomas'
—who had now commissioned him to write against the
young Cambridge heretics Bilney and Arthur.

Skelton's sudden change of front has caused astonishment
to scholars reading his poems in the seclusion of college
libraries. But it does not need very much imagination to
see that the only alternative to making his peace with Wolsey
was the Little Ease or the rack, even though Wolsey could
not get so staunch a defender of the Church for heresy. But
something of the spirit in which Skelton finally made his
submission survives, perhaps, in the *Merry Tales*, with their
account of how Wolsey asked his old enemy to write an epitaph for his tomb—an unlikely request, surely! 'If it shall
like your Grace to creep into this tomb whiles you be alive,'
Skelton is made to reply, 'I can make an epitaph, for I am
sure that when you be dead you shall never have it!' And
how right he was! The magnificent sarcophagus Wolsey
had commissioned from Benedetto da Rovezzano was
ultimately utilized for Nelson. He never occupied it. In
1530, by a sudden turn of Fortune's wheel, he fell from
favour as rapidly as he had risen.

Skelton's last long poem, *The Garland of Laurel*, was
written in honour of himself, and to set forth his claims to be
remembered among the English poets after his death. It
is a sort of *Apologia pro Vita Sua* and was composed early in
1523 while he was a guest of the Countess of Surrey at Sheriff
Hutton Castle. In it he makes a list of his works, many of
which have been lost. With the exception of the enchanting
little lyrics addressed to the Countess of Surrey's young ladies
who are weaving the chaplet of laurel with which he is finally
crowned in the Temple of Fame, with loud cries of 'Triumpha! Triumpha!' from all the poets of the world, ancient
and modern, it is a return to the aureate medieval mode, a
deliberate archaism in compliment to his aristocratic audience.

The scene of such a formal and ceremonious poem as this is found again in the Flemish tapestries of the period, notably the Hampton Court series known as 'Petrarch's Triumphs.' But *A Replication*, his defence of orthodoxy against the Lutheran heresy, is remarkable for its claims for poetry as an independent science and its clear statement of his belief in the Platonic theory of inspiration—a passage which is the answer to those who deny Skelton a place among the humanists— while the prose passages suggest nothing so much as the Elizabethan euphuists, Lyly and Greene.

The Renaissance in England is usually dated from Torrigiano's tomb of Henry VII. But the shrine in which it is placed is, like Skelton, still essentially Gothic. For his poetry coincides, as Mr John Harvey remarks in his *Gothic England*, with the last great flowering of our native school of architecture, which, in the traceries of its fan vaulting and filigree elaboration, introduced a new lightness and exuberance that is reflected in the poetry, music, and fashion of the period. If Skelton is approached, as he should be, through Chaucer, Gower, and Lydgate, and not through Spenser, Keats, and Tennyson, he will be seen for what he is—the last and peculiarly brilliant representative of a great tradition, before the Renaissance brought with it the flood of foreign influences that has resulted in the neglect of our earlier poets, and the underestimation of our great medieval culture— which in fact, the new age was already doing its best to stamp out.

What concerned Skelton most was the remaking of the English language as a literary instrument. *The New English Dictionary* credits him with the first use of hundreds of words, and it is this passion for words that one feels behind his verbal cataracts. At times it seems as if he were positively drunk with English words, as he sets his poetry dancing and jigging to its mad morris. But he whom poetry had made so breathless breathed his last on Midsummer Day, 21st June 1529, at about the age of seventy. He was buried before the high altar at St Margaret's, Westminster, where he had lived so long, with an inscription on alabaster, *Ioannes Skeltonus vates*

Pierius Hic Situs Est—Here Lies John Skelton, Pierian Bard. A special knell was rung for him by 'Our Lady' Brotherhood and his estate was administered by William Mott, curate of St Margaret's. What became of his wife and children is not known. Nor do we know if there was any money left over for masses to help his soul in its flight across the Stygian flood, to be received into the Temple of Fame by all the poets who had so triumphantly acclaimed him in *The Garland of Laurel*. Let us hope that he appeared to them in a form as eternally youthful as that in which he stands, armed with a whole branch of laurel, at the beginning of that edition of *The Garland* of six years before.

PHILIP HENDERSON.

1958.

BIBLIOGRAPHY

Here begynneth a lytell treatyse named the bowge of courte. (Anon.). Emprynted at Westminster by me Wynkyn the Worde. Two issues, one before and one after 1500.

Here folwyth divers Balettys and dyties solacyous devisyd by Master Skelton, Laureat. (Without printer's name, but evidently from the press of Pynson or Rastell [1523–30].)

Skelton Laureate agaynste a comely Coystrowne that curyowsly chawntyd And curryshly cowntred, And madly in hys Musykks mokkyshly made, Against the ix. Musys of polytyke Poems and Poettys matryculat. (Pynson?) Contains also: *Upon a Dead Man's Head* and *Womanhood. Wanton, ye Want.* [1523–30.]

A ryght delectable tratyse upon a goodly Garland or Chapelet of Lawrell, etc. . . . Imprynted by me Rycharde faukes dwelling in dura rent or els in Powlis chyrche yarde at the sygne of the A.B.C. The yere of our lorde god, 1523.

A replycacion agaynst certayne yong scolers, abiured of late, etc. . . . Imprinyed by Richard Pynson, printer to the kynges most noble grace. *c.* 1528.

Magnyfycence. A goodly interlude and a mery devysed and made by mayster Skelton, poete laureate late deceasyd. [Rastell?] [1529–32.]

Also a reprint of Rastell's edition, 1821 (Roxburghe Club); and E.E.T.S. edition, by Robert L. Ramsay, 1908.

Here after foloweth the boke of Phyllyp Sparowe compyled by mayster Skelton, Poete Laureate. Prynted at London at the poultry by Rychard Kele. [1542–6.]

Also editions by John Wyght, 1552; Antony Kitson, 1565; Abraham Veale, and John Walley.

Here after foloweth certaine bokes cōpyled by mayster Skeltō, whose names here after shall appere:
    Speake, Parot.

The death of the noble Prynce, Kynge Edwarde the fourth.

A treatyse of the Scottes.

Ware the Hawke.

The Tunnynge of Elynoure Rummyng.

Imprynted at London, in Crede Lane, by John King and Thomas Marche. [1554.] Also editions by Richard Lant and J. Day. [1565.]

Here after followeth a lytell boke called Colyn Cloute compyled ... etc. Imprinted at London by me Richard Kele dwelling in the powltry at the long shop under saynt Myldredes chyrche. [1532–7.]

Other editions by Thomas Godfrey, Wyghte, Veale, and Kytson.

Here after foloweth a lytell boke, which hath to name, Why come ye nat to courte, compiled, etc., . . . Richard Kele. [1545.]

Other editions by Wyght, Veale, John Wallye, and Robert Toy, 1552; Kyston, 1565.

Pithy pleasaunt and profitable workes of maister Skelton, Poete Laureate. Now collected and newly published. Anno 1568. Imprinted at London in Fletestreate, neare unto saint Donstones churche by Thomas Marshe. Described on reverse of title-page as 'newly collected by I. S.' [? John Stow]. Reprinted 1736.

Elynor Rumming. For J. Busbie and G. Loftis. 1609.

Elynour Rummin: the famous ale-wife of England. For S. Sand, 1629.

Also edition of 1718. Printed for Isaac Dalton. Reprinted in Chalmers's *English Poets*, 1810.

The Tunning of Elynour Rumming, with decorations by Pearl Binder, Fanfrolico Press, London, 1928.

The Manner of the World now a dayes. Imprinted Copland.

Also in *Old Ballads*, Collier, 1840.

Select Poems of John Skelton, edited by E. Sandford, 1819.

The poetical Works of John Skelton, with Notes and Some Account of the Author and his writings. By the Rev. Alexander Dyce. Two vols., Thomas Rodd, 1843 (standard edition).

The Poetical Works of John Skelton . . . principally according to the edition of A. Dyce. Three vols., Boston, Mass., 1856.

A Selection from the Poetical Works of John Skelton (a reprint of portions of Dyce), by W. H. Williams, 1902.

Poems by John Skelton (a selection), edited by Richard Hughes, 1924.

John Skelton (Laureate), a selection and extracts, edited and modernized by Robert Graves, *Augustan Books of English Poetry*, 1927.

Poems (a selection), edited by Roland Gant, Gray Walls Press, 1949.

John Skelton: A Selection from his Poems, edited by Vivian de Sola Pinto, 1950.

The Bibliotheca Historica of Diodorus Siculus, translated by John Skelton. Edited by F. M. Salter and H. L. R. Edwards. Two vols., 1956–7.

Manuscripts

Of the death of the noble prince, King Edwarde the forth. Eg. 29,729, Harl. 4011, B.M.

Upon the doulourus dethe and much lamentable chaunce of the most honourable Erle of Northumberland. Reg. 18 D. ii. fol. 165, B.M.

Manerly Margery Milk and Ale. Fairfax Add. 5465, fol. 109, B.M.

Wofully araid. Fairfax Add. 5465, fols. 76 and 86, B.M. Also Harl. 4012. A copy in a very old hand on the fly-leaves of *Boetius de Discip. Schol.*, etc., 1496 (Heber collection), supplied Dyce with several new stanzas.

Jolly Rutterkin, Fairfax, 5465.

Poems against Garnesche. Harl. 367, fol. 101.

I, liber, et propera, regem tu pronus adora, etc. Corpus Christi College, Cam., No. 432. (Nasmith's *Catal.*, p. 400 (vol. i, 141).)

Salve plus decies quam sunt momenta dierum, etc. Add. 4787, fol. 224 (vol. i, 177), B.M.

Verses on Time. Eg. 2642, B.M.

Garlande of Laurell. Cott. Vit. E. x., fol. 200.

Speake, Parrot. Harl. 2252, fol. 133.

Colyn Cloute. Harl. 2252, fol. 147.

Fragment of above. Rawlinson. C. 813, Bodleian.

Diodorus Siculus translated into English by Skelton, poet-laureat [from the Latin version of Poggio, 1472]. Corpus Christi College, Cam., No. 357.

Speculum Principis (B.M. Add. 26,787).

To the Trinity (B.M. Add. 20,059).

A Laud and Praise Made for Our Sovereign Lord the King. Books of the Treasury of the Receipts of the Exchequer, B. 2.8.

CRITICAL AND BIOGRAPHICAL STUDIES

J. Bale, *Scriptorum Britanniae Catalogus* (1557–9); *Merie Tales of Skelton* (1567); *Athenae Oxoniensis*, ed. by P. Bliss (1813); E. B. Browning, *The Book of the Poets* (1866); F. Brie, 'Skelton-Studien' in *Englische-Studien*, vol. xxxvii, pp. 1–86 (1907); J. M. Berdan, *Early Tudor Poetry* (1920); W. H. Auden in *The Great Tudors*, ed. by K. Garvin (1935); L. J. Lloyd, *John Skelton* (1938); W. Nelson, *John Skelton, Laureate*, New York (1939); I. A. Gordon, *John Skelton, Poet Laureate*, Melbourne (1943); H. L. R. Edwards, *Skelton: The Life and Times of an Early Tudor Poet* (1949); E. M. Forster, *Two Cheers for Democracy* (1951); C. S. Lewis, *English Literature in the Sixteenth Century* (1954); N. C. Carpenter, 'Skelton and Music: "Roty Bully Joys"' in *Review of English Studies*, N.S., vol. vi, pp. 379–84 (1955); J. Holloway, *The Charted Mirror* (1960); Peter Green, *John Skelton*, 'Writers and Their Work,' No. 128 (1960); Robert Graves, *Oxford Addresses on Poetry* (1962); Maurice Pollet, *John Skelton* (1962).

CONTENTS

The poems are arranged in the chronological order first established
by Dr. I. A. Gordon, with the exception of *Colin Clout*, which Dr.
Nelson has shown to have been written 'in the spring or summer
of 1522.' H. L. R. Edwards places *Elinour Rumming* in the same
year. Brie's ascription of the lines 'To Mistress Anne' to Skelton
is now generally disputed.

ON THE DEATH OF THE NOBLE PRINCE,
KING EDWARD THE FOURTH

Miseremini mei, ye that be my friendès!
  This world hath conforméd me downè to fall.
How may I endure, when that every thing endès?
  What crèature is born to be eternall?
  Now there is no morè but 'Pray for me all!'
Thus say I, Edward, that late was your king,
  And twenty two yearès ruled this imperiall,
Some unto pleasure, and some to no likíng.
Mercy I askè of my misdoíng:
  What availeth it, friendès, to be my foe,
Sith I cannot resist, nor amend your complainíng?
  Quia, ecce, nunc in pulvere dormio!

I sleep now in mould, as it is naturall
  That earth unto earth hath his reverture.
What ordainéd God to be terrestriall
  Without recourse to the earth of natúre?
  Who to live ever may himself assure?
What is it to trust on mutability,
  Sith that in this world nothing may endure?
For now am I gone, that late was in prosperity:
To presume thereupon it is but a vanity,
  Not certain, but as a cherry-fair full of woe:
Reignéd not I of late in great felicity?
  Et, ecce, nunc in pulvere dormio!

Where was in my life such one as I,
  While Lady Fortune with me had continuance?
Granted not she me to have victory,
  In England to reignè, and to contribute France?
  She took me by the hand and led me a dance,

And with her sugréd lippés on me she smiled;
 But, what for her dissembléd countenance,
I could not beware till I was beguiled:
Now from this world she hath me exiled
 When I was lothest hence for to go,
And I am in age but, as who saith, a child,
  Et, ecce, nunc in pulvere dormio!

I see well they live that double my yearés:
 Thus dealéd this world with me as it list,
And hath me made, to you that be my peerés,
 Example to think on, had I wist.
 I storéd my coffers and alsó my chest
With taskés taking of the commonalty;
 I took their treasure, but of their prayerés missed;
Whom I beseech with pure humility
For to forgive and have on me pitý:
 I wás your king, and kept you from your foe.
I would now amend, but that will not be,
  Quia, ecce, nunc in pulvere dormio!

I had enough, I held me not content,
 Without remembráncé that I should die;
And more ever to increasé was mine intent,
 I knew not how longé I should it occupy.
 I made the Tower strongé, I wist not why;
 I knew not to whom [1] I purchased Tattershall;
 I amended Dover on the mountain high,
And London I provokéd to fortify the wall;
I made Nottingham a place full royall,
 Windsór, Eltham, and many other mo:
Yet, at the last, I went from them all,
  Et, ecce, nunc in pulvere dormio!

Where is now my conquest and victory?
 Where is my riches and my royal array?

    [1] i.e. for whom.

Where be my coursers and my horses high?
   Where is my mirth, my solace, and my play?
As vanity, to nought all is witheréd away.
O Lady Bess, long for me may ye call!
   For I am departed till doomés day;
But love ye that Lord that is sovereign of all.
Where be my castles and buildíngs royall?
   But Windsór alone,[1] now I have no mo,
And of Eton the prayers perpetuall,
    Et, ecce, nunc in pulvere dormio!

Why should a man be proud or presume high?
   Saint Bernard thereof nobly doth treat,
Saith a man is but a sack of stercory,
   And shall return unto wormés meat.
   Why, what came of Alexander the Great?
Or else of strongé Sampson, who can tell?
   Were not wormés ordainéd their flesh to frete?
And of Salomon, that was of wit the well?
Absolon profferéd his hair for to sell,
   Yet for all his beauty wormés eat him alsó;
And I but late in honour did excel,
    Et, ecce, nunc in pulvere dormio!

I have played my pageant, now am I passed;
   Ye wot well all I was of no great eld:
Thus all thing concluded shall be at the last:
   When Death approacheth, then lost is the field.
   Then sithen this world me no longer upheld,
Nor nought would conserve me here in my place,
   In manus tuas, Domine, my spirit up I yield,
Humbly beseeching thee, God, of thy grace!
O ye courteous commons, your heartés unbrace
   Benignly now to pray for me alsó:
For right well you know your king I was,
    Et, ecce, nunc in pulvere dormio!

       [1] Edward IV was buried at Windsor.

B

UPON THE DOLOROUS DEATH AND MUCH LAMENTABLE CHANCE OF THE MOST HONOURABLE EARL OF NORTHUMBERLAND

I WAIL, I weep, I sob, I sigh full sore
    The deadly fate, the doleful destiny
Of him that is gone, alas, without restore,
    Of the blood royall descending nobelly;
    Whose lordship doubtless was slain lamentably
Thorough treason again him compasséd and wrought,
True to his prince in word, in deed, and thought.

Of heavenly poets, O Clio called by name,
    In the College of Muses goddess historial,
Address thee to me which am both halt and lame
    In elect utterance to make memorial!
    To thee for succour, to thee for help I call,
Mine homèly rudeness and dryness to expel
With the freshè waters of Heliconès well.

Of noble actès anciently enrolled
    Of famous princes and lordès of estate,
By thy report are wont to be extolled,
    Registering truely every former date;
    Of thy bounty after the usual rate
Kindle in me such plenty of thy noblesse
These sorrowful ditties that I may shew express.

In seasons passed, who hath heardè or seen
    Of former writing by any precedent
That villein hastardès in their furious tene,
    Fulfilléd with malice of froward intent,
    Confetteréd together of common consent
Falsely to slay their most singular good lord?
It may be registeréd of shameful record.

4

So noble a man, so valiant lord and knight,
    Fulfilléd with honour, as all the world doth ken;
At his commandment which had both day and night
    Knightès and squires, at every season when
    He called upon them, as menial household men:
Were not these commons uncourteous carls of kind
To slay their own lord?   God was not in their mind!

And were not they to blame, I say, alsó,
    That were about him, his own servants of trust,
To suffer him slain of his mortál foe?
    Fled away from him, let him lie in the dust;
    They bode not till the reckoning were discussed.
What should I flatter? what should I glose or paint?
Fie, fie for shame, their heartès were too faint!

In England and France which greatly was redoubted,
    Of whom both Flanders and Scotland stood in drede,
To whom great estates obeyéd and lowted,
    A meiny of rude villeins made him for to bleed;
    Unkindly they slew him, that holp them oft at need:
He was their bulwark, their paves, and their wall,
Yet shamefully they slew him: that shame may them befall!

I say, ye commoners, why were ye so stark mad?
    What frantic frenesy fell in your brain?
Where was your wit and reason ye should have had?
    What wilful folly made you rise again
    Your natural lord? alas, I cannot feign:
Ye arméd you with will, and left your wit behind:
Well may you be calléd commons most unkind!

He was your chieftain, your shield, your chief defence,
    Ready to assist you in every time of need;
Your worship depended of his excellence:
    Alas, ye madmen, too far ye did exceed;
    Your hap was unhappy, too ill was your speed.
What movéd you again him to war or to fight?
What ailéd you to slay your lord again all right?

The ground of his quarrel was for his sovereign lord,
  The well concerning of all the whole land,
Demanding such duties as needės must accord
    To the right of his prince, which should not be withstand;
    For whose cause ye slew him with your ownė hand.
But had his noblemen done well that day
Ye had not been able to have said him nay.

But there was false packing, or else I am beguiled!
  How be it, the matter was evident and plain,
For if they had occupied their spear and their shield
    This nobleman doubtless had not been slain.
    But men say they were linkėd with a double chain,
And held with the commons under a cloak,
Which kindled the wild fire that made all this smoke.

The commons reniėd their taxes to pay,
  Of them demanded and askėd by the king;
With one voice impórtune they plainly said nay;
    They buskt them on a bushment themselves in bale to
      bring,
    Again the king's pleasure to wrestle or to wring;
Bluntly as beastės with boast and with cry.
They said they forsed not, nor carėd not to die.

The nobleness of the north, this valiant lord and knight,
  As man that was innocent of treachery or train,
Pressed forth boldly to withstand the might,
    And, like martial Hector, he fought them again,
    Vigorously upon them with might and with main,
Trusting in noblemen that were with him there:
But all they fled from him for falsehood or fear.

Barons, knightės, squires, one and all,
  Together with servantės of his family,
Turnėd their backs, and let their master fall,

Of whose life they counted not a fly:
Take up who would, for there they let him lie.
Alas, his gold, his fee, his annual rent
Upon such a sort was ill bestowed and spent!

He was environed about on every side
    With his enemies, that were stark mad and wood;
Yet while he stood he gave them woundès wide.
    Alas for ruth! what though his mind were good,
    His corage manly, yet there he shed his blood:
All left alone, alas, he fought in vain!
For cruelly among them there he was slain.

Alas for pity! that Percy thus was spilt,
    The famous Earl of Northumberland!
Of knightly prowess the sword, pommel, and hilt,
    The mighty lion doubted by sea and land:
    O dolorous chance of Fortune's froward hand!
What man, rememb'ring how shamefully he was slain,
From bitter weeping himself can restrain?

O cruel Mars, thou deadly god of war!
    O dolorous Tuèsday, dedicate to thy name,
When thou shook thy sword so noble a man to mar.
    O ground ungracious, unhappy be thy fame,
    Which wert endyéd with red blood of the same
Most noble earl!   O foul mysuréd ground
Whereon he gat his final deadly wound!

O Atropos, of the fatal sisters three,
    Goddess most cruel unto the life of man,
All merciless, in thee is no pitie!
    O homicide, which slayest all that thou can,
    So forcibly upon this earlè thou ran
That with thy sword, enharpéd of mortal dread,
Thou cut asunder his perfite vital thread!

My words unpolished be, naked and plain,
  Of aureat poems they want illumining;
But by them to knowledge ye may attain
  Of this lord's death and of his murdering;
  Which whiles he lived had foison of everything,
Of knights, of squires, chief lord of tower and town,
Till fickle Fortune began on him to frown.

Paregal to dukes, with kings he might compare,
  Surmounting in honour all earlès he did exceed;
To all countries about him report me I dare;
  Like to Aeneas benign in word and deed,
  Valiant as Hector in every martial need,
Provident, discreet, circumspect, and wise,
Till the chance ran again him of Fortune's double dice.

What needeth me for to extol his fame
  With my rude pen encankeréd all with rust,
Whose noble acts shew worshiply his name,
  Transcending far mine homely Muse, that must
  Yet somewhat write, surprised with hearty lust,
Truly reporting his right noble estate,
Immortally which is immaculate?

His noble blood never distainéd was,
  True to his prince for to defend his right,
Doubleness hating false matters to compáss,
  Traitory and treason he banished out of sight,
  With truth to meddle was all his whole delight,
As all his country can testify the same.
To slay such a lord, alas, it was great shame!

If the whole choir of the Muses nine
  In me all only were set and comprised,
Enbreathéd with the blast of influence divine,
  As perfitely as could be thought or devised:
  To me alsó although it were promísed
Of laureat Phoebus wholly the eloquence,
All were too little for his magnificence.

O youngè lion, but tender yet of age,
    Grow and increase, remember thine estate;
God thee assist unto thine heritage,
    And give thee grace to be more fortunate!
    Again rebellions arm thee to make debate;
And, as the lion, which is of beastès king,
Unto thy subjects be courteous and benign.

I pray God send thee prosperous life and long,
    Stable thy mind constant to be and fast,
Right to maintain, and to resist all wrong:
    All flattering faytors abhor and from thee cast;
    Of foul detraction God keep thee from the blast!
Let double dealing in thee have no place,
And be not light of credence in no case.

With heavy cheer, with dolorous heart and mind,
    Each man may sorrow in his inward thought
This lordès death, whose peer is hard to find,
    Algife England and France were thorough sought.
    All kings, all princes, all dukes, well they ought,
Both temporal and spiritual, for to complain
This nobleman, that cruelly was slain.

More specially barons, and those knightès bold,
    And all other gentlemen with him entertained
In fee, as menial men of his househóld,
    Whom he as lord worshiply maintained:
    To sorrowful weeping they ought to be constrained,
As oft as they call to their remembránce
Of their good lord the fate and deadly chance.

O peerless Prince of heaven imperiall,
    That with one word forméd all things of nought!
Heaven, hell, and earth obey unto thy call;
    Which to thy resemblance wondrously hast wrought
    All mankind, whom thou full dear hast bought,
With thy blood precious our finance thou did pay,
And us redeeméd from the fiendès prey;

To thee pray we, as Prince incomparable,
　　As thou art of mercy and pity the well,
Thou bring unto thy joy interminable
　　The soul of this lordè from all danger of hell,
　　In endless bliss with thee to bide and dwell
In thy paláce above the orient,
Where thou art Lord and God omnipotent.

O Queen of Mercy, O Lady full of grace,
　　Maiden most pure, and Goddès Mother dear,
To sorrowful heartès chief comfort and soláce,
　　Of all women O flower withouten peer!
　　Pray to thy Son above the starès clear,
He to vouchsafe, by thy mediatíon,
To pardon thy servant, and bring to salvatíon.

In joy triumphant the heavenly hierarchy,
　　With all the whole sortè of that glorious place,
His soul may receive into their company,
　　Thorough bounty of Him that forméd all soláce:
　　Well of pitý, of mercy, and of grace,
The Father, the Son, and the Holy Ghost,
In Trinitate one God of mightès most!

WOEFULLY ARRAYED

Woefully arrayed,
    My blood, man,
    For thee ran,
It may not be nay'd:
    My body blo and wan,
Woefully arrayed.

Behold me, I pray thee, with all thy whole reason,
And be not so hard-hearted, and for this encheason,
Sith I for thy soul sake was slain in good season,
Beguiled and betrayéd by Judas' false treason:
    Unkindly entreated,
    With sharp cord sore freted,
    The Jewès me threted:
  They mowéd, they grinnéd, they scornéd me,
  Condemnéd to death, as thou mayest see,
    Woefully arrayed.

Thus naked am I nailéd, O man, for thy sake!
I love thee, then love me; why sleepest thou? awake!
Remember my tender heart-root for thee brake,
With painès my veinès constrainéd to crake:
    Thus tuggéd to and fro,
    Thus wrappéd all in woe,
    Whereas never man was so,
  Entreated thus in most cruel wise,
  Was like a lamb offered in sacrifice,
    Woefully arrayed.

Of sharp thorn I have worn a crown on my head,
So painéd, so strainéd, so rueful, so red,
Thus bobbéd, thus robbéd, thus for thy love dead,
Unfeignéd I deignéd my blood for to shed:

My feet and handès sore
The sturdy nailès bore:
What might I suffer more
Than I have done, O man, for thee?
Come when thou list, welcome to me,
    Woefully arrayed.

Of recórd thy good Lord I have been and shall be:
I am thine, thou art mine, my brother I call thee.
Thee love I entirelý—see what is befall'n me!
Sore beating, sore threating, to make thee, man, all free:
    Why art thou unkind?
    Why hast not me in mind?
    Come yet and thou shalt find
Mine endléss mercy and grace—
See how a spear my heart did race,
    Woefully arrayed.

Dear brother, no other thing I of thee desire
But give me thine heart free to reward mine hire:
I wrought thee, I bought thee from éternál fire:
I pray thee array thee toward my high empíre
    Above the orient,
    Whereof I am regent,
    Lord God omnipotent,
With me to reign in endless wealth:
Remember, man, thy soulès health.

    Woefully arrayed,
      My blood, man,
      For thee ran,
    It may not be nay'd:
      My body blo and wan,
    Woefully arrayed.

PRAYER TO THE FATHER OF HEAVEN

O RADIANT Luminary of light intermináble,
　　Celestial Father, potential God of might,
Of heaven and earth O Lord incomparáble,
　　Of all perfections the Essential most perfite!
　　O Maker of mankindè, that forméd day and night,
Whose power imperial comprehendeth every place!
　　Mine heart, my mind, my thought, my whole delight
Is, after this life, to see thy glorious Face.

Whose Magnificence is incomprehensible,
　　All arguments of reason which far doth exceed,
Whose Deity doubtless is indivisible,
　　From whom all goodness and virtue doth proceed,
　　Of thy support all créatures have need.
Assist me, good Lord, and grant me of thy grace
　　To live to thy pleasure in word, thought, and deed,
And, after this life, to see thy glorious Face.

TO THE SECOND PERSON

O BENIGN Jesu, my sovereign Lord and King,
  The only Son of God by filiatíon,
The Second Person withouten beginníng,
  Both God and man our faith maketh plain relatíon,
  Mary thy mother, by way of incarnatíon,
Whose glorious passion our soulès doth revive!
  Again all bodily and ghostly tribulatíon
Defend me with thy piteous woundès five.

O peerless Prince, painéd to the death,
  Ruefully rent, thy body wan and blo,
For my redemptíon gave up thy vital breath,
  Was never sorrow like to thy deadly woe!
  Grant me, out of this world when I shall go,
Thine endless mercy for my preservative:
  Against the world, the flesh, the devil alsó,
Defend me with thy piteous woundès five.

TO THE HOLY GHOST

O fiery Fervence, inflaméd with all grace,
    Enkindling hearts with brandès charitáble,
The endless reward of pleasure and soláce,
      To the Father and the Son thou are communicáble
      In unitate which is inseparáble!
O water of life, O well of consolatíon!
    Against all suggestions deadly and damnáble
Rescue me, good Lord, by your preservatíon.

To whom is appropried the Holy Ghost by name,
    The Third Person, one God in Trinity,
Of perfite love thou art the ghostly flame:
      O mirror of meekness, peace, and tranquillity,
      My comfort, my counsel, my perfite charity!
O water of life, O well of consolatíon,
    Against all stormès of hard adversity
Rescue me, good Lord, by thy preservatíon.

VEXILLA REGIS

Now sing we, as we were wont,
Vexilla regis prodeunt.

The King's banner on field is splayed,
The cross's myst'ry cannot be nay'd,
To whom our Saviour was betrayed,
   And for our sake.
Thus saith he:
I suffer for thee,
   My death I take,
     Now sing we, as we were wont,
     Vexilla regis prodeunt.

Behold my shanks, behold my knees,
Behold my head, arms, and thees,
Behold of me nothing thou sees
   But sorrow and pine:
Thus was I spilt,
Man, for thy guilt,
   And not for mine.
     Now sing we, as we were wont,
     Vexilla regis prodeunt.

Behold my body, how Jews it dong
With knots of whipcord and scourges strong:
As streams of a well the blood outsprong
   On every side.
The knots were knit
Right well with wit,
   They made woundés wide.
     Now sing we, as we were wont,
     Vexilla regis prodeunt.

Man, thou shalt now understand,
Of my head, both foot and hand,
Are four hundred and five thousand
 Wounds and sixty;
Fifty and seven.
Were told full even
 Upon my body.
  Now sing we, as we were wont,
  Vexilla regis prodeunt.

Sith I for love bought thee so dear,
As thou may see thyself here,
I pray thee with a right good cheer
 Love me again,
That it likes me
To suffer for thee
 Now all this pain.
  Now sing we, as we were wont,
  Vexilla regis prodeunt.

Man, understand now thou shall,
Instead of drink they gave me gal,
And eisel mingled therewithal,
 The Jewès fell.
These pains on me
I suffered for thee
 To bring thee fro hell.
  Now sing we, as we were wont,
  Vexilla regis prodeunt.

Now for thy life thou hast misled,
Mercy to ask be thou not adread:
The least drop of blood that I for thee shed
 Might cleanse thee soon
Of all the sin
The world within
 If thou hadst done.
  Now sing we, as we were wont,
  Vexilla regis prodeunt.

I was more wrother with Judas
For he would no mercy ask
Than I was for his trespass
    When he me sold;
I was ever ready
To grant him mercy,
    But he none wold.
        Now sing we, as we were wont,
        Vexilla regis prodeunt.

Lo, how I hold my arms abroad,
Thee to receive ready y-spread!
For the great love that I to thee had
    Well may thou know.
Some love again
I would full fain
    Thou wouldest to me show.
        Now sing we, as we were wont,
        Vexilla regis prodeunt.

For love I aske nothing of thee
But stand fast in faith, and sin thou flee,
And pain to live in honestie
    Both night and day;
And thou shalt have bliss
That never shall miss
    Withouten nay.
        Now sing we, as we were wont,
        Vexilla regis prodeunt.

Now, Jesu, for thy great goodness,
That for men suffered great hardness,
Save us from the devil's cruelness,
    And to bliss us send,
And grant us grace
To see thy Face
    Withouten end.
        Now sing we, as we were wont,
        Vexilla regis prodeunt.

UPON A DEAD MAN'S HEAD

That was sent to him from an honourable gentlewoman for a token, Skelton, Laureate, devised this ghostly meditation in English, covenable, in sentence, commendable, lamentable, lacrimable, profitable for the soul.

YOUR ugly token
My mind hath broken
From worldly lust:
For I have discust
We are but dust,
And die we must.

    It is general
To be mortal:
I have well espied
No man may him hide
From Death hollow-eyed,
With sinews wyderéd,
With bonés shyderéd,
With his worm-eaten maw,
And his ghastly jaw
Gasping aside,
Naked of hide,
Neither flesh nor fell.

    Then, by my counsel,
Look that ye spell
Well this gospel:
For whereso we dwell
Death will us quell,
And with us mell.

    For all our pampered paunches
There may no fraunchis,
Nor worldly bliss,
Redeem us from this:

Our days be dated
To be checkmated
With draughtès of death
Stopping our breath:
Our eyen sinking,
Our bodies stinking,
Our gummès grinning,
Our soulès brinning.
To whom, then, shall we sue,
For to have rescue,
But to sweet Jesu
On us then for to rue?
  O goodly Child
Of Mary mild,
Then be our shield!
That we be not exiled
To the dyne dale
Of bootless bale,
Nor to the lake
Of fiendès black.
  But grant us grace
To see thy Face,
And to purcháse
Thine heavenly place,
And thy paláce
Full of soláce
Above the sky
That is so high;
Eternally
To behold and see
The Trinity!
  Amen.

[1] *Myrres vous y.*

[1] View yourself therein.

ON TIME

Ye may hear now, in this rime,
How every thing must have a time.

Time is a thing that no man may resist;
 Time is transitory and irrevocable;
Who sayeth the contrary, Time passeth as him list;
 Time must be taken in season covenable:
 Take Time when Time is, for Time is aye mutable;
All thing hath time, who can for it provide;
Bide for Time who will, for Time will no man bide.

Time to be sad, and time to play and sport;
 Time to take rest by way of recreation;
Time to study, and time to use comfort;
 Time of pleasure, and time of consolation:
 Thus Time hath his time of divers manner fashion:
Time for to eat and drink for thy repast;
Time to be liberal, and time to make no waste:

Time to travail, and time for to rest;
 Time for to speak, and time to hold thy peace:
Time would be uséd when Time is best;
 Time to begin, and time for to cease;
 And when time is, to put thyself in press,
And when time is, to hold thyself aback:
For time well spent can never have lack.

The rootes take their sap in time of vere;
 In time of summer flowers fresh and green;
In time of harvest men their corné shere;
 In time of winter the north wind waxeth keen,
 So bitterly biting the flowers be not seen:
The calends of Janus, with his frostes hoar,
That time is when people must live upon the store.

MY DARLING DEAR, MY DAISY FLOWER

WITH lullay, lullay, like a child,
Thou sleepest too long, thou art beguiled.

My darling dear, my daisy flower,
  Let me, quod he, lie in your lap.
Lie still, quod she, my paramour,
  Lie still hardely, and take a nap.
  His head was heavy, such was his hap,
All drowsy dreaming, drowned in sleep,
That of his love he took no keep.
  With hey lullay, lullay, like a child,
  Thou sleepest too long, thou art beguiled.

With ba, ba, ba! and bas, bas, bas!
  She cherished him both cheek and chin,
That he wist never where he was:
  He had forgotten all deadly sin.
  He wanted wit her love to win:
He trusted her payment and lost all his pay;
She left him sleeping and stole away.
  With hey lullay, lullay, like a child,
  Thou sleepest too long, thou art beguiled.

The rivers rough, the waters wan,
  She sparéd not to wet her feet;
She waded over, she found a man
  That halséd her heartily and kissed her sweet:
  Thus after her cold she caught a heat.
My love, she said, routeth in his bed;
Ywis he hath an heavy head.
  With hey lullay, lullay, like a child,
  Thou sleepest too long, thou art beguiled.

What dreamest thou, drunkard, drowsy pate?
  Thy lust and liking is from thee gone;
Thou blinkard blowbowl, thou wakest too late,
  Behold thou liest, luggard, alone!
  Well may thou sigh, well may thou groan,
To deal with her so cowardly:
Ywis, pole hatchet, she bleared thine eye.[1]

       [1] Did you in the eye.

MANNERLY MARGERY MILK AND ALE

Ay, beshrew you! by my fay,
These wanton clerks be nice alway!
Avaunt, avaunt, my popinjay!
What, will ye do nothing but play?
Tilly vally, straw, let be I say!
Gup, Christian Clout, gup, Jack of the Vale!
With Mannerly Margery Milk and Ale.

By God, ye be a pretty pode,
And I love you an whole cart-load.
Straw, James Foder, ye play the fode,
I am no hackney for your rod:
Go watch a bull, your back is broad!
Gup, Christian Clout, gup, Jack of the Vale!
With Mannerly Margery Milk and Ale.

Ywis ye deal uncourteously;
What, would ye frumple me? now fy!
What, and ye shall be my pigesnye?
By Christ, ye shall not, no hardely:
I will not be japéd bodily!
Gup, Christian Clout, gup, Jack of the Vale!
With Mannerly Margery Milk and Ale.

Walk forth your way, ye cost me nought;
Now have I found that I have sought:
The best cheap flesh that ever I bought.
Yet, for His love that all hath wrought,
Wed me, or else I die for thought.
Gup, Christian Clout, your breath is stale!
Go, Mannerly Margery Milk and Ale!
Gup, Christian Clout, gup, Jack of the Vale!
With Mannerly Margery Milk and Ale.

JOLLY RUTTERKIN [1]

HOYDA, jolly rutterkin, hoyda!
Like a rutterkin hoyda.

Rutterkin is come unto our town
In a cloak without coat or gown,
Save a ragged hood to cover his crown,
  Like a rutter hoyda.

Rutterkin can speak no English,
His tongue runneth all on buttered fish,
Besmeared with grease about his dish,
  Like a rutter hoyda.

Rutterkin shall bring you all good luck,
A stoup of beer up at a pluck,
Till his brain be as wise as a duck,
  Like a rutter hoyda.

When rutterkin from board will rise,
He will piss a gallon pot full a-twice,
And the overplus under the table of the new guise,
  Like a rutter hoyda.

[1] From the Fairfax MS. (B.M. 5465), from which also is taken
Woefully Arrayed and *Mannerly Margery*, and the songs set to
music by William Cornysshe of the Chapel Royal. Dyce thought
that 'there is a probability' that this song was composed by Skelton.
In *Magnificence*, Courtly Abusion comes in singing part of it. It
is possible that some of the other songs in this MS. are also by
Skelton—*Margaret Meek*, for instance.

WOMANHOOD, WANTON, YE WANT

Womanhood, wanton, ye want:
  Your meddling, mistress, is mannerless;
Plenty of ill, of goodness scant,
  Ye rail at riot, reckless:
  To praise your port it is needless;
For all your draff yet and your dregs,
As well borne as ye full oft time begs.

Why so coy and full of scorn?
  Mine horse is sold, I ween, you say;
My new furréd gown, when it is worn . . .
  Put up your purse, ye shall not pay!
  By crede, I trust to see the day,
As proud a pea-hen as ye spread,
Of me and other ye may have need!

Though angelic be your smiling,
  Yet is your tongue an adder's tail,
Full like a scorpion stinging
  All those by whom ye have avail.
  Good mistress Anne, there ye do shail:
What prate ye, pretty pigesnye?
I trust to 'quite you ere I die!

Your key is meet for every lock,
  Your key is common and hangeth out;
Your key is ready, we need not knock,
  Nor stand long wresting there about;
  Of your door-gate ye have no doubt:
But one thing is, that ye be lewd:
Hold your tongue now, all beshrewd!

To Mistress Anne, that farly sweet,
That wones at The Key in Thamés Street.

TO MISTRESS ANNE [1]

Mistress Anne,
I am your man,
As you may well espy.
If you will be
Content with me,
I am your man.

But if you will
Keep company still
With every knave that comes by,
Then you will be
Forsaken of me,
That [2] am your man.

But if you fain,
I tell you plain,
If I presently shall die,
I will not such
As loves too much,
That am your man.

For if you can
Love every man
That can flatter and lie,
Then are ye
No match for me,
That am your man.

For I will not take
No such kind of make
(May all full well it try!),
But off will ye cast
At any blast,
That am your man.

[1] First printed by Brie, 'Skelton Studien,' *Englische Studien.*
[2] 'I' in MS.

27

THE ANCIENT ACQUAINTANCE, MADAM, BETWEEN US TWAIN

THE ancient acquaintance, madam, between us twain,
   The familiarity, the former dalliance,
Causeth me that I cannot myself refrain
    But that I must write for my pleasant pastance:
    Remembering your passing goodly countenance,
Your goodly port, your beauteous visage,
Ye may be counted comfort of all corage.

Of all your features favourable to make true description,
   I am insufficient to make such enterprise:
For this dare I say, without contradiction,
    That Dame Menolope was never half so wise.
    Yet so it is that a rumour beginneth for to rise
How in good horsemen ye set your whole delight,
And have forgotten your old true loving knight.

With bound and rebound, bouncingly take up
   His gentle curtal, and set nought by small nags!
Spur up at the hinder girth, with, Gup, morell, gup!
    With, Jayst ye, jennet of Spain, for your tail wags!
    Ye cast all your corage upon such courtly hags.
Have in sergeant farrier, mine horse behind is bare;
He rideth well the horse—but he rideth better the mare.

Ware, ware the mare winceth with her wanton heel!
   She kicketh with her calkins and keyleth with a clench;
She goeth wide behind, and hueth never a deal: [1]
    Ware galling in the withers, ware of that wrench!
    It is parlous for a horseman to dig in the trench.
This grieveth your husband, that right gentil knight,
And so with your servants he fiercely doth fight.

[1] Doesn't blush a bit.

So fiercely he fighteth, his mind is so fell,
  That he driveth them down with dints on their day-
    watch;
He bruiseth their brainpans and maketh them to swell,
  Their browés all to-broken, such clappés they catch;
  Whose jealousy malicious maketh them to leap the hatch,
By their cognizance [1] knowing how they serve a wily pie [2]:
Ask all your neighbours whether that I lie.

It can be no counsel that is criéd at the cross [3]:
  For your gentil husband sorrowful am I;
Howbeit, he is not first hath had a loss.
  Advertising you, madam, to work more secretly,
  Let not all the world make an outcry:
Play fair play, madam, and look ye play clean,
Or else with great shame your game will be seen.

[1] The badge worn by servants.
[2] Double reference to the knight's coat of arms and to the lady.
[3] No secret that is proclaimed in the market-place.

KNOWLEDGE, ACQUAINTANCE, RESORT, FAVOUR WITH GRACE

KNOWLEDGE, acquaintance, resort, favour with grace;
   Delight, desire, respite with liberty;
Corage with lust, convenient time and space;
   Disdains, distress, exiléd cruelty;
   Wordès well set with good hability;
Demure demeanour, womanly of port;
Transcending pleasure, surmounting all disport;

Electuary arrected to redress
   These fervorous axes, the deadly woe and pain
Of thoughtful heartès plungéd in distress;
   Refreshing mindès the April shower of rain;
   Conduit of comfort, and well most sovereign;
Herber enverduréd, continual fresh and green;
Of lusty summer the passing goodly queen;

The topaz rich and precious in virtúe;
   Your ruddies with ruddy rubies may compare;
Sapphire of sadness, enveinéd with Indy blue;
   The polishéd pearl your whiteness doth declare;
   Diamond pointed to rase out heartly care;
'Gain surfeitous suspect the emerald commendable;
Relucent smaragde, object incomparable;

Encircléd mirror and perspective most bright;
   Illuminéd with features far passing my report;
Radiant Hesperus, star of the cloudy night,
   Lodestar to light these lovers to their port,
   'Gain dangerous stormès their anchor of support,
Their sail of solace most comfortably clad,
Which to behold maketh heavy heartès glad.

Remorse have I of your most goodlihood,
   Of your behaviour courteous and benign,
Of your bounty and of your womanhood,
    Which maketh my heart oft to leap and spring,
    And to remember many a pretty thing.
But absence, alas, with trembling fear and dread
Abasheth me, albeit I have no need.

You I assure, absence is my foe,
   My deadly woe, my painful heaviness;
And if ye list to know the cause why so
    Open mine heart, behold my mind express.
    I would ye could! then should ye see, mistress,
How there nis thing that I covet so fain
As to embrace you in mine armés twain.

Nothing earthly to me more desirous
   Than to behold your beauteous countenance:
But, hateful absence, to me so envious,
    Though thou withdraw me from her by long distance,
    Yet shall she never out of remembrance:
For I have gravéd her within the secret wall
Of my true heart, to love her best of all!

GO, PITEOUS HEART, RASÉD WITH DEADLY WOE

Go, piteous heart, raséd with deadly woe,
  Piercéd with pain, bleeding with woundés smart,
Bewail thy fortune, with veinés wan and blo.
  O Fortune unfriendly, Fortune unkind thou art
  To be so cruel and so overthwart,
To suffer me so carefully to endure
That where I love best I dare not discure!

One there is, and ever one shall be,
  For whose sake my heart is sore diseaséd;
For whose love welcome disease to me!
  I am content so all parties be pleaséd:
  Yet, an God would, I would my pain were easéd!
But Fortune enforceth me so carefully to endure
That where I love best I dare not discure!

Skelton, Laureate.
At the instance of a noble lady.

THOUGH YE SUPPOSE ALL JEOPARDIES ARE PASSED

CUNCTA licet cecidisse putas discrimina rerum,
    Et prius incerta nunc tibi certa manent,
Consiliis usure meis tamen aspice caute,
    Subdola non fallat te dea fraude sua:
Saepe solet placido mortales fallere vultu,
    Et cute sub placida tabida saepe dolent;
Ut quando secura putas et cuncta serena,
    Anguis sub viridi gramine saepe latet.

Though ye suppose all jeopardies are passed,
    And all is done that ye lookéd for before,
Ware yet, I rede you, of Fortune's double cast,
    For one false point she is wont to keep in store,
    And under the fell oft festered is the sore:
That when ye think all danger for to pass
Ware of the lizard lieth lurking in the grass.

AGAINST A COMELY COISTROWN

That curiously chanted and currishly countered and madly in his musicks mockishly made against the ix. Muses of politic poems and poets matriculate.

OF all nations under the heaven,
   These frantic foolés I hate most of all;
For though they stumble in the sinnés seven,
   In peevishness yet they snapper and fall,
   Which men the eighth deadly sin call.
This peevish proud, this prendergest,
When he is well, yet can he not rest.

A sweet sugar-loaf and sour bayardés bun
   Be somedele like in form and shape,
The one for a duke, the other for dun,
   A maunchet for morell thereon to snap.
   His heart is too high to have any hap;
But for in his gamut carp that he can,
Lo, Jack would be a gentleman!

With hey trolly lolly, lo, whip here, Jack,
   Alumbek sodildim sillorim ben!
Curiously he can both counter and knack
   Of Martin Swart [1] and all his merry men.
   Lord, how Perkin [2] is proud of his pea-hen!
But ask where he findeth among his monochordés
An holy water clerk a ruler of lordés.

[1] A German nobleman who lead the auxiliaries sent by the Duchess of Burgundy with Lambert Simnel, and who fell fighting at the battle of Stoke.

[2] Perkin Warbeck; the pea-hen is probably his wife, Lady Katherine Gordon.

He cannot find it in rule nor in space:
    He solfas too haute, his treble is too high;
He braggeth of his birth, that born was full base;
    His music without measure, too sharp is his *Mi*;
    He trimmeth in his tenor to counter pardee;
His descant is busy, it is without a mean;
Too fat is his fancy, his wit is too lean.

He lumb'reth on a lewd lute *Roty bully joys*,
    Rumble down, tumble down, hey go, now, now!
He fumbleth in his fingering an ugly good noise,
    It seemeth the sobbing of an old sow!
    He would be made much of, an he wist how;
Well sped in spindles and turning of tavélls;
A bungler, a brawler, a picker of quarréls.

Comely he clappeth a pair of clavichordés;
    He whistleth so sweetly, he maketh me to sweat;
His descant is dashed full of discordés;
    A red angry man, but easy to entreat;
    An usher of the hall fain would I get
To point this proud page a place and a room,
For Jack would be a gentleman, that late was a groom!

Jack would jet, and yet Jill said nay,
    He counteth in his countenance to check with the best:
A malapert meddler that prieth for his prey,
    In a dish dare he rush at the ripést,
    Dreaming in dumpés to wrangle and to wrest:
He findeth a proportíon in his prick-song,
To drink at a draught a large and a long.[1]

Nay, jape not with him, he is no small fool,
    It is a solemn sire and a sullén:
For lords and ladies learn at his school,

[1] Characters in old music: one large=two longs, one long=
two breves.

c

He teacheth them so wisely to solf and to fayne
That neither they sing well prick-song nor plain:
This Doctor Devias commencéd in a cart,
A master, a minstrel, a fiddler, a fart.

What though ye can counter *Custodi nos*?
    As well it becometh you, a parish town clerk,
To sing *Sospitati dedit aegros*.[1]
    Yet bear ye not too bold to brawl nor to bark
    At me, that meddled nothing with your work:
Correct first thyself: walk, and be nought!
Deem what thou list, thou knowest not my thought.

A proverb of old: 'Say well or be still!'
    Ye are too unhappy occasions to find
Upon me to clatter, or else to say ill.
    Now have I shewéd you part of your proud mind:
    Take this in worth, the best is behind!
Written at Croydon by Crowland-in-the-Clay,
On Candlemas even, the calends of May.

        [1] He gave succour to the sick.

THE BOUGE OF COURT [1]

Prologue

In autumn, when the son *in Virgine*
　　By radiant heat enripéd hath our corn;
When Luna, full of mutability,
　　As emperess the diadem hath worn
　　Of our pole arctic, smiling half in scorn
At our folly and our unsteadfastness;
The time when Mars to warré him did 'dress;

I, calling to mind the great authority
　　Of poets old, which full craftily,
Under as covert terms as could be,
　　Can touch a truth and cloak it subtilly
　　With freshé utterance full sententiously,
Diverse in style, some spared not vice to wyte,
Some of morality nobly did endite;

Whereby I rede their renown and their fame
　　May never die, but evermore endure.
I was sore movéd to aforce the same,
　　But Ignorance full soon did me discure,
　　And shewed that in this art I was not sure;
For to illumine, she said, I was to-dull,
Advising me my pen away to pull,

And not to write: for he so will attain
　　Exceeding further than his conning is,
His head may be hard, but feeble is his brain,
　　Yet have I knowen such ere this.
　　But of reproach surely he may not miss
That climbeth higher than he may footing have:
What an he slide down, who shall him save?

[1] Bouche, the Rations or Rewards of Court.

37

Thus up and down my mind was drawn and cast,
   That I ne wist what to do was best;
So sore enwearied, that I was at the last
   Enforced to sleep and for to take some rest,
   And to lie down as soon as I me 'dressed.
At Harwich port slumbering as I lay
In mine hostès house, called Powers Key,

Methought I saw a ship, goodly of sail,
   Come sailing forth into the haven broad,
Her tackling rich and of high appareil:
   She cast an anchor, and there she lay at road.
   Merchants her boarded to see what she had load.
Therein they found royal merchandise,
Fraughted with pleasure of what ye could devise.

But then I thought I would not dwell behind;
   Among all others I put myself in press.
Then there could I none acquaintance find:
   There was much noise; anon one criéd, 'Cease!'
   Sharply commanding each man hold his peace.
'Masters,' he said, 'the ship that ye here see
The Bouge of Court it hight for certainty.

'The owner thereof is lady of estate
   Whose name to tell is Dame Sanspeer;
Her merchandise is rich and fortunate,
   But who will have it must pay therefor dear;
   This royal chaffer that is shippéd here
Is calléd Favour, to stand in her good grace.'
Then should ye see there pressing in apace

Of one and other that would this lady see;
   Which sat behind a traves of silkè fine,
Of gold of tissue the finest that might be,
   In a throne which far clearer did shine
   Than Phoebus in his sphere celestine;
Whose beauty, honour, goodly port
I have too little conning to report.

But of each thing there as I took heed,
   Among all other was written in her throne
In gold letters, these words, which I did read:
   Gardez le fortune, qui est mauvais et bone!
   And, as I stood reading this verse myself alone,
Her chief gentlewoman, Danger by her name,
Gave me a taunt, and said I was to blame

To be so pert to press so proudly up:
   She said she trowed that I had eaten sauce;
She asked if ever I drank of sauce's cup.
   And I then softly answered to that clause,
   That so to say I had given her no cause.
Then asked she me, 'Sir, so God thee speed,
What is thy name?' and I said, it was Drede.

'What movéd thee,' quod she, 'hither to come?'
   'Forsooth,' quod I, 'to buy some of your ware.'
And with that word on me she gave a glum
   With browés bent, and 'gan on me to stare
   Full dainously, and fro me she did fare,
Leaving me standing as a mazéd man,
To whom there came another gentlewoman:

Desire her name was, and so she me told,
   Saying to me, 'Brother, be of good cheer,
Abash you not, but hardely be bold,
   Advance yourself to approach and come near:
   What though our chaffer be never so dear,
Yet I advise you to speak, for any drede:
Who spareth to speak, in faith, he spareth to speed.'

'Mistress,' quod I, 'I have none acquaintance
   That will for me be mediator and mean;
And this another, I have but small substánce.'

'Peace,' quod Desire, 'ye speak not worth a bean!
If ye have not, in faith, I will you lene
A precious jewel, no richer in this land:
Bon Aventure have here now in your hand.

' Shift now therewith, let see, as ye can
    In Bouge of Court chevisaunce to make;
For I dare say that there nis earthly man
    But, an he can Bon Aventure take,
    There can no favour nor friendship him forsake;
Bon Aventure may bring you in such case
That ye shall stand in favour and in grace.

'But of one thing I warn you ere I go:
    She that steereth the ship, make her your friend.'
'Mistress,' quod I, 'I pray you tell me why so,
    And how I may that way and meanès find.'
    'Forsooth,' quod she, 'however blow the wind,
Fortune guideth and ruleth all our ship:
Whom she hateth shall over the seaboard skip;

'Whom she loveth, of all pleasure is rich,
    Whiles she laugheth and hath lust for to play;
Whom she hateth, she casteth in the ditch,
    For when she frowneth, she thinketh to make a fray;
    She cherisheth him, and him she casteth away.'
'Alas,' quod I, 'how might I have her sure?'
'In faith,' quod she, 'by Bon Aventure.'

Thus, in a row, of merchants a great rout
    Suéd to Fortune that she would be their friend:
They throng in fast, and flockéd her about;
    And I with them prayed her to have in mind.
    She promised to us all she would be kind:
Of Bouge of Court she asketh what we would have,
And we askéd Favour, and Favour she us gave.

Thus endeth the Prologue; and beginneth the
Bouge of Court briefly compiled

DREDE

The sail is up, Fortune ruleth our helm,
  We want no wind to pass now over all;
Favour we have tougher than any elm,
  That will abide and never from us fall.
  But under honey ofttime lieth bitter gall:
For, as methought, in our ship I did see
Full subtil persons, in number four and three.

The first was Favell, full of flattery,
  With fables false that well could feign a tale;
The second was Suspect, which that daily
  Misdeemed each man, with face deadly and pale;
  And Harvy Hafter, that well could pick a male,
With other four of their affinity,
Disdain, Riot, Dissimuler, Subtilty.

Fortune their friend, with whom oft she did dance;
  They could not fail, they thought, they were so sure;
And oftentimes I would myself advance
  With them to make soláce and pleasúre.
  But my disport they could not well endure:
They said they hated for to deal with Drede.
Then Favell 'gan with fair speech me to feed.

FAVELL

' No thing earthly that I wonder so sore
  As of your conning, that is so excellent;
Deyntee to have with us such one in store,
  So virtuously that hath his dayés spent;
  Fortune to you gifts of grace hath lent:
Lo, what it is a man to have conníng!
All earthly treasure it is surmountíng.

'Ye be an apt man, as any can be found,
    To dwell with us, and serve my lady's grace;
Ye be to her, yea, worth a thousand pound!
    I heard her speak of you within short space,
    When there were divers that sore did you menace;
And, though I say it, I was myself your friend,
For here be divers to you that be unkind.

'But this one thing—ye may be sure of me;
    For, by that Lord that bought dear all mankind,
I cannot flatter, I must be plain to thee!
    An ye need ought, man, shew to me your mind,
    For ye have me whom faithful ye shall find;
Whiles I have ought, by God, thou shalt not lack,
And if need be, a bold word I dare crack!

'Nay, nay, be sure, whiles I am on your side
    Ye may not fall, trust me, ye may not fail.
Ye stand in favour, and Fortune is your guide,
    And, as she will, so shall our great ship sail:
    These lewd cockwats shall nevermore prevail
Against you hardely, therefore be not afraid.
Farewell till soon, but no word that I said!'

DREDE

Then thanked I him for his great gentleness.
    But, as methought, he ware on him a cloak
That linéd was with doubtful doubleness;
    Methought, of words that he had full a poke;
    His stomach stuffed oft times did reboke.
Suspect, methought, met him at a braid,
And I drew near to hark what they two said.

'In faith,' quod Suspect, 'spake Drede no word of me?'
    'Why? what then? wilt thou let men to speak?

He saith he cannot well accord with thee.'
   'Twyste,' quod Suspect, 'go play! him I ne reke!'
   'By Christ,' quod Favell, 'Drede is sullen freke.
What, let us hold him up, man, for a while?'
'Yea so,' quod Suspect, 'he may us both beguile.'

And when he came walking soberly,
   With hum and ha, and with a crooked look,
Methought his head was full of jealousy,
   His eyen rolling, his handès fast they quoke;
   And to meward the straight way he took.
'God speed, brother!' to me quod he then,
And thus to talk with me he began.

SUSPECT

'Ye remember the gentleman right now
   That communed with you, methought a pretty space?
Beware of him, for, I make God avow,
   He will beguile you and speak fair to your face.
   Ye never dwelt in such another place,
For here is none that dare well other trust—
But I would tell you a thing, an I durst!

'Spake he, i'faith, no word to you of me?
   I wot, an he did, ye would me tell.
I have a favour to you, whereof it be
   That I must shew you much of my counsél.
   But I wonder what the devil of hell
He said of me, when he with you did talk!
By mine advice use not with him to walk.

' The sovranest thing that any man may have
   Is little to say, and much to hear and see;
For, but I trusted you, so God me save,
   I wouldè nothing so plainè be:
   To you onlie, methink, I durst shrive me,
*c

For now am I plenarly disposéd
To shew you things that may not be discloséd.'

DREDE

Then I assuréd him my fidelity
   His counsel secret never to discure,
If he could find in heart to trusté me;
   Else I prayed him, with all my busy cure,
   To keep it himself, for then he might be sure
That no man earthly could him betray,
Whiles of his mind it were locked with the key.

'By God,' quod he, 'this and thus it is . . .'
   And of his mind he shewed me all and some.
'Farewell,' quod he, 'we will talk more of this . . .'
   So he departed where he would be come.
   I dare not speak, I promised to be dumb.
But, as I stood musing in my mind,
Harvy Hafter came leaping, light as lynde.

Upon his breast he bare a versing-box,
   His throat was clear, and lustily could fayne.
Methought his gown was all furréd with fox,
   And ever he sang, '*Sith I am nothing plain* . . .'
   To keep him from picking it was a great pain:
He gazed on me with his goatish beard,
When I looked on him, my purse was half afeard.

HARVY HAFTER

'Sir, God you save! why look ye so sad?
   What thing is that I may do for you?
A wonder thing that ye wax not mad!
   For, an I study should as ye do now,
   My wit would waste, I make God avow!
Tell me your mind: methink ye make a verse;
I could it scan, an ye would it rehearse!

'But to the point shortly to proceed,
    Where hath your dwelling been ere ye came here?
For, as I trow, I have seen you indeed
    Ere this, when that ye made me royal cheer.
    Hold up the helm, look up, and let God steer:
I would be merry, what wind that ever blow!
Heave and ho rumbelow, row the boat, Norman, row!

'*Princes of Youth* can ye sing by rote?
    Or *Shall I sail with you* a fellowship assay?
For on the book I cannot sing a note.
    Would to God, it would please you some day
    A ballad book before me for to lay,
And learn me to sing *re mi fa sol*!
And, when I fail, bob me on the noll.

'Lo, what is to you a pleasure great
    To have that conning and ways that ye have!
By Goddès soul, I wonder how ye gate
    So great pleasúre, or who to you it gave.
    Sir, pardon me, I am an homely knave,
To be with you thus pert and thus bold:
But ye be welcome to our househóld.

'And, I dare say, there is no man therein
    But would be glad of your company.
I wist never man that so soon could win
    The favour that ye have with my ladý.
    I pray to God that it may never die.
It is your fortune for to have that grace—
As I be savéd, it is a wonder case!

'For, as for me, I served here many a day
    And yet unneth I can have my livíng:
But, I require you, no wordè that I say!
    For, an I know any earthly thing
    That is again you, ye shall have weetíng.
And ye be welcome, sir, so God me save!
I hope hereafter a friend of you to have.'

DREDE

With that, as he departed so from me,
    Anon there met with him, as methought,
A man, but wonderly beseen was he.
    He looked haughty; he set each man at nought;
    His gawdy garment with scornės was all wrought;
With indignatíon linéd was his hood:
He frowned, as he would swear by Cockės blood.

He bit the lip, he lookéd passing coy;
    His face was belimmed, as bees had him stung:
It was no time with him to jape nor toy.
    Envy had wasted his liver and his lung,
    Hatred by the heart so had him wrung
That he looked pale as ashes to my sight.
Disdain, I ween, this comerous crab is hight.

To Harvy Hafter then he spake of me,
    And I drew near to hark what they two said.
'Now,' quod Disdain, 'as I shall savéd be,
    I have great scorn, and am right evil apayed.'
    Then quod Harvy Hafter, 'Why art thou so dis-
        mayed?'
'By Christ,' quod he, 'for it is shame to say:
To see yon Johan Dawes, that came but yesterday.

'How he is now taken in conceit,
    This Doctor Dawcock, Drede, I ween, he hight.
By Goddės bones, but if we have some slight
    It is like he will standė in our light.'
    'By God,' quod Harvy, 'and it so happen might.
Let us therefore shortly at a word
Find some means to cast him overboard.'

'By Him that me bought,' then quod Disdain,
    'I wonder sore he is in such conceit!'

'Turd!' quod Hafter, 'I will thee nothing layne,
  There must for him be laid some pretty bait;
  We twain, I trow, be not without deceit:
First pick a quarrel, and fall out with him then,
And so outface him with a card of ten.'

Forthwith he made on me a proud assault,
  With scornful look movéd all in mood;
He went about to take me in a fault;
  He frowned, he stared, he stampéd where he stood.
  I lookéd on him, I wend he had been wood.
He set the arm proudly under the side,
And in this wise he 'gan with me to chide.

DISDAIN

'Rememberest thou what thou said yesternight?
  Wilt thou abide by the words again?
By God, I have of thee now great despite!
  I shall thee angre once in every vein:
  It is great scorn to see such an hayne
As thou art, one that came but yesterday,
With us old servants suché masters to play!

'I tell thee, I am of countenance:
  What weenest I were?   I trow thou know not me!
By Goddés wounds, but for displeasance,
  Of my quarrel soon would I vengéd be.
  But no force, I shall once meet with thee.
Come when it will, oppose thee I shall,
Whatsomever adventure thereof fall.

' Trowest thou, drevil I say, thou gawdy knave,
  That I have deinte to see thee cherished thus?
By Goddés side, my sword thy beard shall shave!
  Well, once thou shalt be charmed, ywis.
  Nay, straw for tales, thou shalt not rule us:
We be thy betters, and so thou shalt us take,
Or we shall thee out of thy clothés shake!'

DREDE

With that came Riot, rushing all at once,
    A rusty gallant, to-ragged and to-rent;
And on the board he whirled a pair of bones,
    Quater trey dews he clatteréd as he went.
    'Now have at all, by Saint Thomas of Kent!'
And ever he threw and cast I wote n'ere what:
His hair was growen thorough out his hat.

Then I beheld how he disguiséd was:
    His head was heavy for watching over night,
His eyen bleered, his face shone like a glass;
    His gown so short that it ne cover might
    His rump, he went so all for summer light.
His hose was garded with a list of green,
Yet at the knee they were broken, I ween.

His coat was checked with patches red and blue;
    Of Kirby Kendal [1] was his short demi;
And aye he sang, *In faith, deacon, thou crew*;
    His elbow bare, he ware his gear so nigh;
    His nose a-dropping, his lippés were full dry;
And by his side his whinard and his pouch,
The devil might dance therein for any crowch.

Counter he could *O lux* upon a pot,
    An ostrich feather of a capon's tail
He set up freshly upon his hat aloft.
    'What revel rout!' quod he, an 'gan to rail
    How oft he had hit Jennet on the tail,
Of Phyllis fetis, and little pretty Kate,
How oft he knockéd at her clicket-gate.

What should I tell more of his ribaldry?
    I was ashaméd so to hear him prate:

[1] Famous for its manufacture of green cloth.

He had no pleasure but in harlotry.
  'Ay,' quod he, 'in the devil's date,
    What art thou? I saw thee now but late.'
'Forsooth,' quod I, 'in this court I dwell now.'
'Welcome,' quod Riot, 'I make God avow.

RIOT

'And, sir, in faith why com'st not us among
  To make thee merry, as other fellows done?
Thou must swear and stare, man, all day long,
  And wake all night, and sleep till it be noon;
  Thou mayest not study, or muse on the moon;
This world is nothing but eat, drink, and sleep,
And thus with us good company to keep.

'Pluck up thine heart upon a merry pin,
  And let us laugh a pluck or twain at nale:
What the devil, man, mirth is here within!
  What, lo man, see here of dice a bale!
  A birdling-cast for that is in thy male!
Now have at all that lieth upon the board!
Fie on these dice, they be not worth a turd!

'Have at the hazard, or at the dozen brown,
  Or else I pass a penny to a pound!
Now, would to God, thou would lay money down!
  Lord, how that I woulde cast it full round!
Ay, in my pouch a buckle I have found,
The arms of Calais, I have no coin nor cross!
I am not happy, I run aye on the loss.

'Now run must I to the stewès side
  To weet if Malkin, my lemman, have got ought:
I let her to hire, that men may on her ride,
  Her armès easy [1] far and near is sought:
  By Goddès side, since I her hither brought
She hath got me more money with her tail
Than hath some ship that into Bordeaux sail.

[1] Easily won favours.

'Had I as good an horse as she is a mare,
    I durst adventure to journey thorough France;
Who rideth on her, he needeth not to care,
    For she is trusséd for to break a lance:
    It is a curtal that well can winch and prance.
To her will I now all my poverty allege,
And, till I come, have here is mine hat to pledge.'

DREDE

Gone is this knave, this ribald foul and lewd.
    He ran as fast as ever that he might.
Unthriftiness in him may well be shewed,
    For whom Tyburn groaneth both day and night.
    And, as I stood and cast aside my sight,
Disdain I saw with Dissimulation
Standing in sadè communicatíon.

But there was pointing and nodding with the head,
    And many wordès said in secret wise;
They wandered aye, and stood still in no stead:
    Methought alway Dissimuler did devise.
    Me passing sore mine heart then 'gan agrise,
I deemed and dread their talking was not good.
Anon Dissimuler came where I stood.

Then in his hood I saw there faces twain:
    That one was lean and like a pinéd ghost,
That other looked as he would me have slain;
    And to meward as he 'gan for to coast,
    When that he was even at me almost,
I saw a knife hid in his one sleeve,
Whereon was written this word, *Mischief.*

And in his other sleeve, methought, I saw
    A spoon of gold, full of honey sweet,
To feed a fool, and for to prove a daw;
    And on that sleeve these wordès were writ,

A false abstract cometh from a false concrete.
His hood was syde, his cope was russet gray:
These were the words that he to me did say.

DISSIMULATION

'How do ye, master? ye look so soberly!
    As I be savéd at the dreadful day,
It is a perilous vice, this envý.
    Alas, a conning man ne dwellé may
    In no place well, but foolé with him fray.
But as for that, conning hath no foe
Save him that nought can, Scripture saith so.

'I know your virtue and your literature
    By that little conning that I have:
Ye be malignéd sore, I you ensure;
    But ye have craft yourself alway to save.
    It is great scorn to see a misproud knave
With a clerké than conning is to prate:
Let them go louse them, in the devil's date!

'For albeit that this 'long not to me,
    Yet on my back I bear such lewd dealíng:
Right now I spake with one, I trow, I see—
    But what—a straw!   I may not tell all thing!
    By God, I say there is great heart-burníng
Between the person ye wot of and you.
Alas, I could not deal so with a Jew!

'I would each man were as plain as I!
    It is a world, I say, to hear of some:
I hate this feigning, fie upon it, fie!
    A man cannot wot where to be come.
    Ywis I could tell—but humlery, hum!
I dare not speak, we be so laid await,
For all our courte is full of deceit.

'Now by Saint Francis, that holy man and friar,
   I hate these ways again you that they take!
Were I as you, I woulde ride them full near,
   And, by my troth, but if an end they make,
   Yet will I say some wordes for your sake
That shall them angre, I hold thereon a groat:
For some shall, I ween, be hangéd by the throat!

'I have a stopping oyster in my poke,
   Trust me, an if it come to a need!
But I am loath for to raise a smoke,
   If ye could be otherwise agreed.
   And so I would it were, so God me speed,
For this may breed to a confusíon
Without God make a good conclusíon.

Nay, see where yonder standeth t'other man!
   A flattering knave and false he is, God wot;
The drevil standeth to harken, an he can.
   It were more thrift he bought him a newe coat;
   It will not be, his purse is not on float:
All that he weareth, it is borrowed ware,
His wit is thin, his hood is threadebare.

'More could I say, but what this is enow:
   Adew till soon, we shall speak more of this.
Ye must be ruled as I shall tell you how;
   Amends may be of that is now amiss.
   And I am yours, sir, so have I bliss,
In every point that I can do or say.
Give me your hand, farewell, and have good-day!'

DREDE

Suddenly, as he departed me fro,
   Came pressing in one in a wonder array.
Ere I was ware, behind me he said, 'BO!'
   Then I, astoniéd of that sudden fray,
   Start all at once, I likéd nothing his play:

For, if I had not quickly fled the touch,
He had plucked out the nobles of my pouch.

He was trusséd in a garment strait:
   I have not seen such another page,
For he could well upon a casket wait;
    His hood all pouncéd and garded like a cage;
    Light lime-finger! he took none other wage.
'Hearken,' quod he, 'lo here mine hand in thine!
To us welcome thou art, by Saint Quintine.'

DECEIT

'But, by that Lord that is one, two, and three,
   I have an errand to round in your ear . . .
He told me so, by God, ye may trust me,
    Parde, remember when ye were there,
    There I winkéd on you—wot ye not where?
In A loco, I mean *juxta B*:
Who is him that is blind and may not see!

'But to hear the subtilty and the craft,
   As I shall tell you, if ye will hark again!
And, when I saw the whoreson would you haft,
    To hold mine hand, by God, I had great pain:
    For forthwith there I had him slain,
But that I drede murder would come out:
Who dealeth with shrews hath need to look about!'

DREDE

And as he rounded thus in mine ear
   Of false collusion confetteréd by assent,
Methought I see lewd fellows here and there
    Come for to slay me of mortal intent.
    And, as they came, the shipboard fast I hent,
And thought to leap, and even with that woke,
Caught pen and ink, and wrote this little book.

I would therewith no man were miscontent,
    Beseeching you that shall it see or read
In every point to be indifferent,
    Sith all in substance of slumbering doth proceed.
    I will not say it is matter indeed,
But yet oft-time such dreams be found true.
Now construe ye what is the residue!

EPITAPH FOR ADAM UDERSALL

THIS treatise devised it is
Of two knaves sometime of Diss.
Though these knaves be dead,
Full of mischief and queed,
Yet, wheresoever they lie,
Their names shall never die.

Compendium de duobus versipellibus, John Jayberd, et Adam
all a knave, *deque illorum notissima vilitate.*

A DEVOUT TRENTAL FOR OLD JOHN CLARKE, SOMETIME THE
HOLY PATRIARCH OF DISS

Sequitur trigintale
Tale quale rationale,
Licet parum curiale,
Tamen satis est formale,
Joannis Clerc, hominis
Cujusdam multinominis,
Joannes Jayberd qui vocatur,
Clerc cleribus nuncupatur.
Obiit sanctus iste pater
Anno Domini MD. sexto.
In parochia de Dis
Non erat sibi similis;
In malitia vir insignis,
Duplex corde et bilinguis;
Senio confectus,
Omnibus suspectus,
Nemini dilectus,
Sepultus est among the weeds:
God forgive him his misdeeds!

55

Dulce melos
Penetrans coelos.

Carmina cum cannis
cantemus festa Joannis:
Clerk obiit vere,
Jayberd nomenque dedere:
Dis popula natus,
Clerk cleribus estque vocatus.
Hic vir Chaldaeus,
nequam vir, ceu Jebuaesus,
In Christum Domini
fremuit de more cameli,
Rectori proprio
tam verba retorta loquendo
Unde resultando-
que Acheronta boando tonaret.
Nunquam sincere
solitus sua crimina flere;
Cui male lingua loquax-
que dicax mendaxque, fuere
Et mores tales
resident in nemine quales;
Carpens vitales
auras, turbare sodales
Et cives socios,
asinus, mulus velut, et bos.
Omne suum studium
rubeum pictum per amictum
Discolor; et victum
faciens semper maledictum
Ex intestinis ovium-
que boumque caprorum;
Tendens adque forum,
fragmentum colligit horum,
Dentibus exemptis
mastigat cumque polentis
Lanigerum caput aut ovis

aut vaccae mugientis.
Quid petis, hic sit quis?
John Jayberd, incola de Dis;
Cui, dum vixerat is,
sociantur jurgia, vis, lis.
  Jam jacet hic stark dead,
Never a tooth in his head.
Adieu, Jayberd, adieu,
In faith, deacon thou crew!
Fratres, orate
For this knavatė,
By the holy rood,
Did never man good:
I pray you all,
And pray shall,
At this trental
On knees to fall
To the football;
With, 'Fill the black bowl
For Jayberd's soul.'
  Bibite multum:
Ecce sepultum
Sub pede stultum,
Asinum, et mulum!
The devil kiss his *culum*!
With, 'Hey, ho, rumbelow!'
Rumpopulorum,
Per omnia secula seculorum!   *Amen.*

Requiem, etc.

Per Fredericum Hely,
Fratrem de Monte Carmeli,
Qui condunt sine sale
Hoc devotum trigintale.
Vale Jayberd, valde male!

Adam Uddersall,
Alias dictus Adam all
a knave, his
Epitaph followeth devoutly;
He was sometime the holy
Bailiff of Diss.

Of Diss.
Adam degebat:
dum vixit, falsa gerebat,
Namque extorquebat
quicquid nativus habebat,
Aut liber natus;
rapidus lupus inde vocatus:
Ecclesiamque satus
de Belial iste Pilatus
Sub pede calcatus
violavit, nunc violatus:
Perfidus, iratus,
numquam fuit ille beatus:
Uddersall stratus
benedictis est spoliatus,
Improbus, inflatus,
maledictis jam laceratus:
Dis, tibi bacchatus
ballivus praedominatus:
Hic fuit ingratus,
porcus velut insatiatus,
Pinguis, crassatus;
velut Agag sit reprobatus!
Crudelisque Cacus
barathro, peto, sit tumulatus!
Belsabub his soul save,
Qui jacet hic, like a knave!
Jam scio mortuus est,
Et jacet hic, like a beast.
   Anima ejus
   De malo in pejus.   *Amen.*

De Dis haec semper erit camena,
Adam Uddersall sit anathema!

Auctore Skelton, rectore de Dis.

Finis, etc. Apud Trumpinton scriptum per curatum ejusdem,
quinto die Januarii Anno Domini, secundum computat.
Angliae, MDVII.

Adam, Adam, ubi es? Genesis. (Res.) *Ubi nulla requies, ubi*
nullus ordo, sed sempiternus horror inhabitat. Job.

PHILIP SPARROW

Pla ce bo! [1]
Who is there, who?
Di le xi! [2]
Dame Margery.
Fa, re, my, my.
Wherefore and why, why?
For the soul of Philip Sparrow
That was late slain at Carrow,[3]
Among the Nunès Black.
For that sweet soulès sake,
And for all sparrows' souls
Set in our bead-rolls,
Pater noster qui,
With an *Ave Mari,*
And with the corner of a Creed,
The more shall be your meed.

    When I remember again
How my Philip was slain,
Never half the pain
Was between you twain,
Pyramus and Thisbe,
As then befell to me.
I wept and I wailéd,
The tearès down hailéd,
But nothing it availéd
To call Philip again,
Whom Gib, our cat, hath slain.

[1] The beginning of the Office for the Dead. This word and others below are broken up to correspond with plainsong notes, which Skelton meant the reader to intone.

[2] Ps. cxiv. 1, Vulg.: 'I am well pleased [that the Lord hath heard].'

[3] Convent in Norwich, where Joanna was educated.

Gib, I say, our cat
Worrowéd her on that
Which I lovéd best.
It cannot be exprest
My sorrowful heaviness,
But all without redress!
For within that stound,
Half slumbering, in a sound
I fell downé to the ground.

Unneth I cast mine eyes
Toward the cloudy skies.
But when I did behold
My sparrow dead and cold,
No créature but that wold
Have ruéd upon me,
To behold and see
What heaviness did me pang:
Wherewith my hands I wrang,
That my sinews cracked,
As though I had been racked,
So painéd and so strainéd
That no life wellnigh remainéd.

I sighéd and I sobbed,
For that I was robbed
Of my sparrow's life.
O maiden, widow, and wife,
Of what estate ye be,
Of high or low degree,
Great sorrow then ye might see,
And learn to weep at me!
Such painés did me frete
That mine heart did beat,
My visage pale and dead,
Wan, and blue as lead:
The pangs of hateful death
Wellnigh had stopped my breath.

Heu, heu, me,[1]
That I am woe for thee!
Ad Dominum, cum tribularer, clamavi.[2]
Of God nothing else crave I
But Philip's soul to keep
From the marees deep
Of Acheronte's well,
That is a flood of hell;
And from the great Plutó,
The prince of endless woe;
And from foul Alecto,
With visage black and blo;
And from Medusa, that mare,
That like a fiend doth stare;
And from Megaera's adders
For ruffling of Philip's feathers,
And from her fiery sparklings
For burning of his wings;
And from the smokės sour
Of Proserpina's bower;
And from the denės dark
Where Cerberus doth bark,
Whom Theseus did affray,
Whom Hercules did outray,
As famous poetės say;
From that hell-hound
That lieth in chainės bound,
With ghastly headės three;
To Jupiter pray we
That Philip preservéd may be!
Amen, say ye with me!

　Do mi nus,
Help now, sweet Jesus!
Levavi oculos meos in montes.[3]
Would God I had Zenophontes,

[1] Woe, woe is me.
[2] 'In my distress, I cried unto the Lord' (Ps. cxix., Vulg.).
[3] 'I lifted up mine eyes unto the hills' (Ps. cxx. 1, Vulg.).

Or Socrates the wise,
To shew me their device
Moderately to take
This sorrow that I make
For Philip Sparrow's sake!
So fervently I shake,
I feel my body quake;
So urgently I am brought
Into careful thought.
Like Andromach, Hector's wife,
Was weary of her life,
When she had lost her joy,
Noble Hector of Troy;
In like manner alsó
Increaseth my deadly woe,
For my sparrow is go.

It was so pretty a fool,
It would sit on a stool,
And learnéd after my school
For to keep his cut,[1]
With 'Philip, keep your cut!'

It had a velvet cap,
And would sit upon my lap,
And seek after small wormés,
And sometime white bread-crumbés;
And many times and oft
Between my breastés soft
It wouldé lie and rest;
It was proper and prest.

Sometime he would gasp
When he saw a wasp;
A fly or a gnat,
He would fly at that;

[1] Be on his best behaviour.

And prettily he would pant
When he saw an ant.
Lord, how he would pry
After the butterfly!
Lord, how he would hop
After the gressop!
And when I said, 'Phip, Phip!'
Then he would leap and skip,
And take me by the lip.
Alas, it will me slo
That Philip is gone me fro!

Si in i qui ta tes . . .[1]
Alas, I was evil at ease!
De pro fun dis cla ma vi,[2]
When I saw my sparrow die!

Now, after my dome,
Dame Sulpicia at Rome,
Whose name registeréd was
For ever in tables of brass,
Because that she did pass
In poesy to indite
And eloquently to write,
Though she would pretend
My sparrow to commend,
I trow she could not amend
Reporting the virtues all
Of my sparrow royal.

For it would come and go,
And fly so to and fro;
And on me it would leap
When I was asleep,
And his feathers shake,
Wherewith he would make
Me often for to wake,

[1] 'If [thou shouldest mark] iniquities . . .' (Ps. cxxix. 3, Vulg.).
[2] 'Out of the depths have I cried [unto thee, O Lord]' (Ps. cxxix. 1, Vulg.).

And for to take him in
Upon my naked skin.
God wot, we thought no sin:
What though he crept so low?
It was no hurt, I trow
He did nothing, perde,
But sit upon my knee.
Philip, though he were nice,
In him it was no vice.
Philip had leave to go
To pick my little toe,
Philip might be bold
And do what he wold:
Philip would seek and take
All the fleas black
That he could there espy
With his wanton eye.

   O pe ra.[1]
La, sol, fa, fa,
Confitebor tibi, Domine, in toto corde meo! [2]
Alas, I would ride and go
A thousand mile of ground!
If any such might be found
It were worth an hundred pound
Of King Croesus' gold,
Or of Attalus the old,
The rich prince of Pergame,
Whoso list the story to see.
Cadmus, that his sister sought,
An he should be bought
For gold and fee,
He should over the sea
To weet if he could bring
Any of the offspring,
Or any of the blood.
But whoso understood

[1] 'The works [of the Lord are great]' (Ps. cx. 2, Vulg.).   [2] 'I will confess to thee, Lord, with my whole heart' (Ps. cx. 1, Vulg.).

Of Medea's art,
I would I had a part
Of her crafty magíc!
My sparrow then should be quick
With a charm or twain,
And play with me again.
But all this is in vain
Thus for to complain.

    I took my sampler once
Of purpose, for the nonce,
To sew with stitches of silk
My sparrow white as milk,
That by representatíon
Of his image and fashíon
To me it might import
Some pleasure and comfórt,
For my solace and sport.
But when I was sewing his beak,
Methought my sparrow did speak,
And opened his pretty bill,
Saying, 'Maid, ye are in will
Again me for to kill,
Ye prick me in the head!'
With that my needle waxéd red,
Methought, of Philip's blood;
Mine hair right upstood,
I was in such a fray
My speech was taken away.
I cast down that there was,
And said, 'Alas, alas,
How cometh this to pass?'
My fingers, dead and cold,
Could not my sampler hold:
My needle and thread
I threw away for dread.
The best now that I may
Is for his soul to pray:

A porta inferi . . .[1]
Good Lord, have mercy
Upon my sparrow's soul,
Written in my bead-roll!

   Au di vi vo cem,[2]
Japhet, Ham, and Shem,
Ma gni fi cat,
Shew me the right path
To the hills of Armony,
Whereon the boards yet lie
Of your father's boat,
That was sometime afloat,
And now they lie and rot;
Let some poetės write
Deucalion's flood it hight.
But as verily as ye be
The natural sonnės three
Of Noė the patriarch,
That made that great ark,
Wherein he had apes and owls,
Beasts, birds, and fowls,
That if ye can find
Any of my sparrow's kind
(God send the soul good rest!)
I would have yet a nest
As pretty and as prest
As my sparrow was.
But my sparrow did pass
All sparrows of the wood
That were since Noė's flood,
Was never none so good.
King Philip of Macedony
Had no such Philip as I,
No, no, sir, hardėly!

[1] 'From the gate of hell.' A versicle in the Absolutions for the Dead.
[2] Another antiphon: 'I heard a voice [from heaven say unto me,
Write, Blessed are the dead]' (Rev. xiv. 13).

D

That vengeance I ask and cry,
By way of exclamation,
On all the wholè natíon
Of cattès wild and tame:
God send them sorrow and shame!
That cat specíally
That slew so cruelly
My little pretty sparrow
That I brought up at Carrow.

O cat of carlish kind,
The fiend was in thy mind
When thou my bird untwined!
I would thou hadst been blind!
The léopards savàge,
The lions in their rage
Might catch thee in their paws,
And gnaw thee in their jaws!
The serpents of Libany
Might sting thee venomously!
The dragons with their tongues
Might poison thy liver and lungs!
The manticors of the mountaíns
Might feed them on thy brains!

Melanchaetes, that hound
That pluckéd Actaeon to the ground,
Gave him his mortal wound,
Changéd to a deer,
The story doth appear,
Was changéd to an hart:
So thou, foul cat that thou art,
The selfsame hound
Might thee confound,
That his own lordè bote,
Might bite asunder thy throat!

Of Ind the greedy grypes
Might tear out all thy tripes!
Of Arcady the bears
Might pluck away thine ears!
The wild wolf Lycaon
Bite asunder thy backbone!
Of Etna the burning hill,
That day and night burneth still,
Set in thy tail a blaze
That all the world may gaze
And wonder upon thee,
From Ocean the great sea
Unto the Isles of Orcady,
From Tilbury Ferry
To the plain of Salísbury!
So traitorously my bird to kill
That never ought thee evil will!

Was never bird in cage
More gentle of coráge
In doing his homáge
Unto his sovereígn.
Alas, I say again,
Death hath departed us twain!
The false cat hath thee slain:
Farewell, Philip, adew!
Our Lord, thy soul rescue!
Farewell, without restore,
Farewell, for evermore!

An it were a Jew,
It would make one rue,
To see my sorrow new.
These villainous false cats
Were made for mice and rats,
And not for birdès smale.
Alas, my face waxeth pale,

Telling this piteous tale,
How my bird so fair,
That was wont to repair,
And go in at my spair,
And creep in at my gore
Of my gown before,
Flickering with his wings!
Alas, my heart it stings,
Remembering pretty things!
Alas, mine heart it sleth,
My Philip's doleful death!
When I remember it,
How prettily it would sit,
Many times and oft,
Upon my finger aloft!
I played with him tittle-tattle,
And fed him with my spittle,
With his bill between my lips,
It was my pretty Phips!
Many a pretty kiss
Had I of his sweet muss!
And now the cause is thus,
That he is slain me fro,
To my great pain and woe.

Of fortune this the chance
Standeth on variance:
Oft time after pleasánce,
Trouble and grievánce.
No man can be sure
Alway to have pleasúre:
As well perceive ye may
How my disport and play
From me was taken away
By Gib, our cat saváge,
That in a furious rage
Caught Philip by the head
And slew him there stark dead!

Kyrie, eleison,
Christe, eleison,
Kyrie, eleison!
For Philip Sparrow's soul,
Set in our bead-roll,
Let us now whisper
A *Paternoster.*

Lauda, anima mea, Dominum! [1]
To weep with me look that ye come
All manner of birdės in your kind;
See none be left behind.
To mourning lookė that ye fall
With dolorous songės funerall,
Some to sing, and some to say,
Some to weep, and some to pray,
Every birdė in his lay.
The goldfinch, the wagtail;
The jangling jay to rail,
The fleckéd pie to chatter
Of this dolorous matter;
And robin redbreast,
He shall be the priest
The requiem mass to sing,
Softly warbeling,
With help of the reed sparrow,
And the chatteringė swallow,
This hearsė for to hallow;
The lark with his long toe;
The spink, and the martinet alsó;
The shoveller with his broad beak;
The dotterel, that foolish peke,
And also the mad coot,
With baldė face to toot;
The fieldfare and the snite;
The crow and the kite;
The raven, called Rolfė,

[1] 'Praise the Lord, O my soul!' (Ps. cxlv. 1, Vulg.).

His plain-song to sol-fa;
The partridge, the quail;
The plover with us to wail;
The woodhack, that singeth 'chur'
Hoarsely, as he had the mur;
The lusty chanting nightingale;
The popinjay to tell her tale,
That toteth oft in a glass,
Shall read the Gospel at mass;
The mavis with her whistle
Shall read there the Epistle.
But with a large and a long
To keep just plain-song,
Our chanters shall be the cuckoo,
The culver, the stockdowe,
With 'peewit' the lapwing,
The Versicles shall sing.

The bittern with his bumpè,
The crane with his trumpè,
The swan of Maeander,
The goose and the gander,
The duck and the drake,
Shall watch at this wake;
The peacock so proud,
Because his voice is loud,
And hath a glorious tail,
He shall sing the Grail; [1]
The owl, that is so foul,
Must help us to howl;
The heron so gaunt,
And the cormorant,
With the pheasant,
And the gaggling gant,
And the churlish chough;
The knot and the ruff;

[1] The *Graduale*.

The barnacle, the buzzard,
With the wild mallard;
The divendop to sleep;
The water-hen to weep;
The puffin and the teal
Money they shall deal
To poorè folk at large,
That shall be their charge;
The seamew and the titmouse;
The woodcock with the longè nose;
The throstle with her warbling;
The starling with her brabling;
The rook, with the osprey
That putteth fishes to a fray;
And the dainty curlew,
With the turtle most true.

At this *Placebo*
We may not well forgo
The countering of the coe;
The stork alsó,
That maketh his nest
In chimneys to rest;
Within those walls
No broken galls
May there abide
Of cuckoldry side,
Or else philosophy
Maketh a great lie.

The ostrich, that will eat
An horseshoe so great,
In the stead of meat,
Such fervent heat
His stomach doth frete;
He cannot well fly,
Nor sing tunably,
Yet at a brayd
He hath well assayed

To sol-fa above E-la.
Fa, lorell, fa, fa!
Ne quando
Male cantando,[1]
The best that we can,
To make him our bell-man,
And let him ring the bells.
He can do nothing else.

   Chanticleer, our cock,
Must tell what is of the clock
By the astrology
That he hath naturally
Conceived and caught,
And was never taught
By Albumazer
The astronomer,
Nor by Ptolomy
Prince of astronomy,
Nor yet by Haly;
And yet he croweth daily
And nightly the tides
That no man abides,
With Partlot his hen,
Whom now and then
He plucketh by the head
When he doth her tread.

   The bird of Araby,
That potentially
May never die,
And yet there is none
But one alone;
A phoenix it is
This hearse that must bless
With aromatic gums
That cost great sums,

[1] Lest ever by singing badly.

The way of thurification
To make a fumigation,
Sweetè of reflarè,
And redolent of airè,
This corsè for to cense
With greatè reverence,
As patriarch or pope
In a blackè cope.
Whiles he censeth the hearse,
He shall sing the verse,
Libera me,[1]
In de la, sol, re,
Softly B molle
For my sparrow's soul.
Pliny sheweth all
In his *Story Natural*
What he doth find
Of the phoenix kind;
Of whose incineratíon
There riseth a new creatíon
Of the same fashíon
Without alteratíon,
Saving that oldè age
Is turnéd into corage
Of freshè youth again;
This matter true and plain,
Plain matter indeed,
Who so list to read.

But for the eagle doth fly
Highest in the sky,
He shall be the sub-dean,
The choir to demean,
As provost principal,
To teach them their Ordinal;
Also the noble falcon,
With the ger-falcon,

[1] 'Deliver me'—the opening of the Responsory.

*D

The tarsel gentil,
They shall mourn soft and still
In their amice of gray;
The saker with them shall say
Dirige [1] for Philip's soul;
The goshawk shall have a roll
The choristers to control;
The lanners and the merlions
Shall stand in their mourning-gowns;
The hobby and the musket
The censers and the cross shall fet;
The kestrel in all this wark
Shall be holy water clerk.

And now the dark cloudy night
Chaseth away Phoebus bright,
Taking his course toward the west,
God send my sparrow's soul good rest!
Requiem aeternam dona eis, Domine! [2]
Fa, fa, fa, mi, re, re,
A por ta in fe ri,
Fa, fa, fa, mi, mi.

Credo videre bona Domini, [3]
I pray God, Philip to heaven may fly!
Domine, exaudi orationem meam! [4]
To heaven he shall, from heaven he came!
    Do mi nus vo bis cum!
Of all good prayers God send him some!
          Oremus,
Deus, cui proprium est misereri et parcere, [5]
On Philip's soul have pity!

[1] 'Direct [my steps]'—another antiphon.
[2] 'Grant them eternal rest, O Lord!'
[3] 'I believe to see the goodness of the Lord' (Ps. xxvi. 13, Vulg.).
[4] 'Lord, hear my prayer!' (Ps. ci. 2, Vulg.).
[5] 'O God, whose property it is to be merciful and to spare.'

For he was a pretty cock,
And came of a gentle stock,
And wrapt in a maiden's smock,
And cherishéd full daintily,
Till cruel fate made him to die:
Alas, for doleful destiny!
But whereto should I
Longer mourn or cry?
To Jupiter I call,
Of heaven imperial,
That Philip may fly
Above the starry sky,
To tread the pretty wren,
That is our Lady's hen.
Amen, amen, amen!

Yet one thing is behind,
That now cometh to mind;
An epitaph I would have
For Philippés grave:
But for I am a maid,
Timorous, half afraid,
That never yet assayed
Of Heliconés well,
Where the Muses dwell;
Though I can read and spell,
Recount, report, and tell
Of the *Tales of Canterbury*,
Some sad stories, some merry;
As Palamon and Arcet,
Duke Theseus, and Partelet;
And of the Wife of Bath,
That worketh much scath
When her tale is told
Among housewivés bold,
How she controlled
Her husbands as she wold,

And them to despise
In the homeliest wise,
Bring other wives in thought
Their husbands to set at nought.
And though that read have I
Of Gawain and Sir Guy,
And tell can a great piece
Of the Golden Fleece,
How Jason it wan,
Like a valiant man;[1]
Of Arthur's Round Table,
With his knights commendable,
And Dame Gaynour, his queen,
Was somewhat wanton, I ween;
How Sir Lancelot de Lake
Many a spear brake
For his lady's sake;
Of Tristram, and King Mark,
And all the whole wark
Of Belle Isold his wife,
For whom was much strife;
Some say she was light,
And made her husband knight
Of the common hall,
That cuckolds men call;
And of Sir Lybius,
Named Dysconius [2];
Of Quater Fylz Amund,[3]
And how they were summoned
To Rome, to Charlemagne,
Upon a great pain,
And how they rode each one
On Bayard Mountalbon;
Men see him now and then
In the forest of Ardén.

[1] *A Book of the Whole Life of Jason* (Caxton).
[2] *Lybeau's Disconus* (*Le beau desconnu*) in Ritson's *Met. Rom.* ii.
[3] *The Four Sons of Aymon* (Caxton).

What though I can frame
The stories by name
Of Judas Maccabeus,
And of Caesar Julius;
And of the love between
Paris and Vienne;
And of the duke Hannibal,
That made the Romans all
Fordread and to quake;
How Scipion did wake
The city of Carthage,
Which by his unmerciful rage
He beat down to the ground.
And though I can expound
Of Hector of Troy,
That was all their joy,
Whom Achilles slew,
Wherefore all Troy did rue;
And of the love so hot
That made Troilus to dote
Upon fair Cresseid;
And what they wrote and said,
And of their wanton willës
Pander bare the billës [1]
From one to the other;
His master's love to further,
Sometime a precious thing,
A brooch or else a ring;
From her to him again
Sometime a pretty chain,
Or a bracelet of her hair,
Prayed Troilus for to wear
That token for her sake;
How heartily he did it take,
And much thereof did make;
And all that was in vain,
For she did but feign;

[1] i.e. *billets-doux.*

The story telleth plain,
He could not obtain,
Though his father were a king,
Yet there was a thing
That made the male to wring; [1]
She made him to sing
The song of lover's lay;
Musing night and day,
Mourning all alone,
Comfort had he none,
For she was quite gone.
Thus in conclusion,
She brought him in abusion;
In earnest and in game
She was much to blame;
Disparaged is her fame,
And blemishéd is her name,
In manner half with shame;
Troilus alsó hath lost
On her much love and cost,
And now must kiss the post;
Pandarus, that went between,
Hath won nothing, I ween,
But light for summer green;
Yet for a special laud
He is named Troilus' bawd;
Of that name he is sure
Whilès the world shall 'dure.

Though I remember the fable
Of Penelope most stable,
To her husband most true,
Yet long-time she ne knew
Whether he were live or dead;
Her wit stood her in stead,

[1] Wrung his withers.

That she was true and just
For any bodily lust
To Ulysses her make,
And never would him forsake.

Of Marcus Marcellus [1]
A process I could tell us;
And of Antiochus,
And of Josephus
De Antiquitatibus;
And of Mardocheus, [2]
And of great Ahasuerus,
And of Vesca his queen,
Whom he forsook with teen,
And of Esther his other wife,
With whom he led a pleasant life;
Of King Alexander;
And of King Evander;
And of Porsena the great,
That made the Romans to sweat.

Though I have enrolled
A thousand new and old
Of these historious tales,
To fill budgets and males
With books that I have read,
Yet I am nothing sped,
And can but little skill
Of Ovid or Virgil,
Or of Plutarch,
Or Francis Petrarch,
Alcaeus or Sappho,
Or such others poets mo,
As Linus and Homerus,
Euphorion and Theocritus,

[1] M. Claudius Marcellus, conqueror of Syracuse in the second
Punic war, and slain by Hannibal.
[2] Mordecai.

Anacreon and Arion,
Sophocles and Philemon,
Pindarus and Simonides,
Philistion and Pherecydes;
These poets of anciente,
They are too diffuse for me:

For, as I tofore have said,
I am but a young maid,
And cannot in effect
My style as yet direct
With English words elect.
Our natural tongue is rude,
And hard to be ennewed
With polished termes lusty;
Our language is so rusty,
So cankered, and so full
Of frowards, and so dull,
That if I would apply
To write ornately,
I wot not where to find
Terms to serve my mind.

Gower's English is old,
And of no value told;
His matter is worth gold,
And worthy to be enrolled.

In Chaucer I am sped,
His *Talès* I have read:
His matter is delectable,
Solacious, and commendable;
His English well allowed,
So as it is enprowed,
For as it is employed,
There is no English void,
At those days much commended;
And now men would have amended

His English, whereat they bark,
And mar all they wark.
Chaucer, that famous clerk,
His termés were not dark,
But pleasant, easy, and plain;
No word he wrote in vain.

  Also John Lydgate
Writeth after an higher rate;
It is diffuse to find
The sentence of his mind,
Yet writeth he in his kind,
No man that can amend
Those matters that he hath penned;
Yet some men find a faute,
And say he writeth too haut.

  Wherefore hold me excused
If I have not well perused
Mine English half abused;
Though it be refused,
In worth I shall it take,
And fewer wordés make.

  But, for my sparrow's sake,
Yet as a woman may,
My wit I shall assay
An epitaph to write
In Latin plain and light,
Whereof the elegy
Followeth by and by:
Flos volucrum formose, vale!
Philippe, sub isto
Marmore jam recubas,
Qui mihi carus eras.

Semper erunt nitido
Radiantia sidera cœlo;
Impressusque meo
Pectore semper eris.[1]

Per me laurigerum
Britonum Skeltonida Vatem
Haec cecinisse licet
Ficta sub imagine texta.
Cujus eris volucris,
Praestanti corpore virgo:
Candida Nais erat,
Formosior ista Joanna est;
Docta Corinna fuit,
Sed magis ista sapit.

Bien m'en souvient.

THE COMMENDATIONS

Beati immaculati in via,[2]
O gloriosa femina!
Now mine whole imagination
And studious meditation
Is to take this commendation
In this consideration;
And under patient toleration
Of that most goodly maid
That *Placebo* hath said,
And for her sparrow prayed
In lamentable wise,
Now will I enterprise,
Thorough the grace divine
Of the Muses nine,
Her beauty to commend,
If Arethusa will send

[1] Farewell, sweet bird.   Philip, beneath that marble you lie, you who were dear to me.   So long as the stars shine in the sky, will your image be graven on my heart.

[2] *Ordo Commendationis Animae* (Ps. cxviii. 1, Vulg.).

Me influence to indite,
And with my pen to write;
If Apollo will promíse
Melodiously to it devise
His tunable harp strings
With harmony that sings
Of princes and of kings
And of all pleasant things,
Of lust and of delight,
Thorough his godly might;
To whom be the laud ascribéd
That my pen hath imbibéd
With the aureate droppés,
As verily my hope is,
Of Tagus, that golden flood,
That passeth all earthly good;
And as that flood doth pass
All floods that ever was
With his golden sandés,
Whoso that understandés
Cosmography, and the streamés
And the floods in strangé reamés,
Right so she doth exceed
All other of whom we read,
Whose fame by me shall spread
Into Persia and Mede,
From Britons' Albion
To the Tower of Babylon.

I trust it is no shame,
And no man will me blame,
Though I register her name
In the court of Fame;
For this most goodly floure,
This blossom of fresh colóur,
So Jupiter me succóur,
She flourisheth new and new
In beauty and virtúe:

Hac claritate gemina,
O gloriosa femina,
Retribue servo tuo, vivifica me! [1]
Labia mea laudabunt te. [2]

But enforcéd am I
Openly to ascry,
And to make an outcry
Against odious Envý,
That evermore will lie,
And say cursedly;
With his leather eye,
And cheekės dry;
With visage wan,
As swart as tan;
His bonės crake,
Lean as a rake;
His gummės rusty
Are full unlusty;
His heart withal
Bitter as gall;
His liver, his lung
With anger is wrung;
His serpent's tongue
That many one hath stung;
He frowneth ever;
He laugheth never,
Even nor morrow,
But other men's sorrow
Causeth him to grin
And rejoice therein;
No sleep can him catch,
But ever doth watch,
He is so bete
With malice, and frete

---

[1] 'Deal bountifully with thy servant, that I may live' (Ps. cxviii. 17, Vulg.).   [2] 'My lips shall praise thee' (Ps. lxii. 4, Vulg.).

With anger and ire,
His foul desire
Will suffer no sleep
In his head to creep;
His foul semblant
All displeasant;
When others are glad,
Then is he sad,
Frantic and mad;
His tongue never still
For to say ill,
Writhing and wringing,
Biting and stinging;
And thus this elf
Consumeth himself,
Himself doth slo
With pain and woe.
This false Envý
Sayeth that I
Use great follý
For to indite,
And for to write,
And spend my time
In prose and rime,
For to express
The nobleness
Of my mistress,
That causeth me
Studious to be
To make a relation,
Of her commendation.
And there again
Envy doth complain,
And hath disdain;
But yet certaín
I will be plain,
And my style 'dress
To this procéss.

Now Phoebus me ken
To sharp my pen,
And lead my fist
As him best list,
That I may say
Honour alway
Of womankind!
Truth doth me bind
And loyalty
Ever to be
Their true bedell,
To write and tell
How women excel
In nobleness;
As my mistress,
Of whom I think
With pen and ink
For to compile
Some goodly style;
For this most goodly floure,
This blossom of fresh colóur
So Jupiter me succóur,
She flourisheth new and new
In beauty and virtúe:
Hac claritate gemina,
O gloriosa femina,
Legem pone mihi, domina, viam justificationum
      tuarum! [1]
Quemadmodum desiderat cervus ad fontes aquarum. [2]

How shall I report
All the goodly sort
Of her featurès clear,
That hath none earthly peer?

[1] Teach me, O lady, to justify Thy ways (Cf. Ps. cxviii. 33, Vulg.).   Here and later Skelton blasphemously substitutes *domina* (lady) for *dominus* (Lord)—Jane Scrope for God.
[2] 'As the hart panteth after the water-brooks' (Ps. xli, Vulg.).

The favour of her face
Ennewéd all with grace,
Comfort, pleasure, and soláce.
Mine heart doth so enbrace,
And so hath ravished me
Her to behold and see,
That in wordés plain
I cannot me refrain
To look on her again.
Alas, what should I feign?
It were a pleasant pain
With her aye to remain.

Her eyen grey and steep
Causeth mine heart to leap;
With her browés bent
She may well represent
Fair Lucres, as I ween,
Or else fair Polexene,
Or else Calliope,
Or else Penelope;
For this most goodly floure,
This blossom of fresh colóur,
So Jupiter me succóur,
She flourisheth new and new
In beauty and virtúe:
Hac claritate gemina,
O gloriosa femina,
Memor esto verbi tui servo tuo! [1]
Servus tuus sum ego. [2]

The Indy sapphire blue
Her veinés doth ennew;
The orient pearl so clear,
The whiteness of her lere;

[1] 'Remember thy word unto thy servant' (Ps. cxviii. 49, Vulg.).
[2] 'I am thy servant' (Ps. cxviii. 125, Vulg.).

Her lusty ruby ruddės
Resemble the rose buddės;
Her lippės soft and merry
Enbloomėd like the cherry:
It were an heavenly bliss
Her sugared mouth to kiss.

Her beauty to augment,
Dame Nature hath her lent
A wart upon her cheek,—
Whoso list to seek
In her viságe a scar,—
That seemeth from afar
Like to the radiant star,
All with favour fret,
So properly it is set!
She is the violet,
The daisy delectable,
The columbine commendable,
The jelofer amiable:
For this most goodly floure,
This blossom of fresh colóur,
So Jupiter me succóur,
She flourisheth new and new
Hac claritate gemina,
O gloriosa femina,
Bonitatem fecisti cum servo tuo, domina,[1]
Et ex praecordiis sonant praeconia! [2]

And when I perceivéd
Her wart and conceivéd,
It cannot be denay'd
But it was well conveyed
And set so womanly,
And nothing wantonly,

[1] Thou hast dealt bountifully with thy servant, lady.
[2] And from his heart ring out thy praises!

But right conveniently,
And full congruently,
As Nature could devise,
In most goodly wise!
Whoso list behold,
It maketh lovers bold
To her to sue for grace,
Her favour to purcháse;
The scar upon her chin,
Enhatchéd on her fair skin,
Whiter than the swan,
It would make any man
To forget deadly sin
Her favour to win!
For this most goodly floure,
This blossom of fresh colóur,
So Jupiter me succóur,
She flourisheth new and new
In beauty and virtúe:
Hac claritate gemina,
O gloriosa femina,
Defecit in salutatione tua anima mea; [1]
Quid petis filio, mater dulcissima? babae! [2]

Soft, and make no din,
For now I will begin
To have in remembránce
Her goodly dalliance,
And her goodly pastánce:
So sad and so demure,
Behaving her so sure,
With wordės of pleasúre
She would make to the lure [3]
And any man convert
To give her his whole heart.

---

[1] 'My soul fainteth after thy salvation' (Ps. cxviii. 81, Vulg.).
[2] What seek you for your son, sweetest mother? Bless my soul!
[3] Attract—a metaphor from falconry.

She made me sore amazed
Upon her when I gazed,
Methought mine heart was crazed,
My eyen were so dazed!
For this most goodly floure,
This blossom of fresh colóur,
So Jupiter me succóur,
She flourisheth new and new
In beauty and virtúe:
Hac claritate gemina,
O gloriosa femina,
Quomodo dilexi legem tuam, domina! [1]
Recedant vetera, nova sunt omnia. [2]

And to amend her tale,
When she list to avail,
And with her fingers smale,
And handès soft as silk,
Whiter than the milk,
That are so quickly veinéd,
Wherewith my hand she strainéd,
Lord, how I was painéd!
Unneth I me refrainéd,
How she me had reclaiméd,
And me to her retainéd,
Embracing therewithall
Her goodly middle small
With sidès long and strait!
To tell you what conceit
I had then in a trice,
The matter were too nice—
And yet there was no vice,
Nor yet no villany,
But only fantasy.
For this most goodly floure,
This blossom of fresh colóur,

[1] 'O how I love thy law, O lady!' (Ps. cxviii. 97, Vulg., adapted).
[2] 'Old things are passed away, all things are new' (2 Cor. v. 17).

So Jupiter me succóur,
She flourisheth new and new
In beauty and virtúe:
Hac claritate gemina,
O gloriosa femina,
Iniquos odio habui! [1]
Non calumnientur me superbi. [2]

But whereto should I note
How often did I toot
Upon her pretty foot?
It raséd mine heart-root
To see her tread the ground
With heelés short and round!
She is plainly express
Egeria, the goddess,
And like to her imáge,
Emporturéd with corage,
A lover's pilgrimage;
There is no beast saváge,
Ne no tiger so wood,
But she would change his mood,
Such relucent grace
Is forméd in her face.
For this most goodly floure,
This blossom of fresh colóur,
So Jupiter me succóur,
She flourisheth new and new
In beauty and virtúe:
Hac claritate gemina,
O gloriosa femina,
Mirabilia testimonia tua! [3]
Sicut novellae plantationes in juventute sua. [4]

---

[1] 'I hate vain thoughts' (Ps. cxviii. 113, Vulg.).
[2] 'Let not the proud oppress me' (Ps. cxviii. 122, Vulg.).
[3] 'Wonderful are thy testimonies' (Ps. cxviii. 129, Vulg.).
[4] 'As plants grown up in their youth' (Ps. cxliii. 12, Vulg.).

So goodly as she dresses,
So properly she presses
The bright golden tresses
Of her hair so fine,
Like Phoebus' beamés shine.
Whereto should I disclose
The gartering of her hose?
It is for to suppose
How that she can wear
Gorgeously her gear;
Her fresh habiliments
With other implements
To serve for all intents,
Like Dame Flora, queen
Of lusty summer green:
For this most goodly floure,
This blossom of fresh colóur,
So Jupiter me succóur,
She flourisheth new and new
In beauty and virtúe:
Hac claritate gemina,
O gloriosa femina,
Clamavi in toto corde, exaudi me! [1]
Misericordia tua magna est super me. [2]

Her kirtle so goodly lacéd,
And under that is bracéd
Such pleasures that I may
Neither write nor say!
Yet though I write with ink,
No man can let me think, .
For thought hath liberty,
Thought is frank and free;
To think a merry thought
It cost me little nor nought.

[1] 'I have cried with my whole heart, hear me!' (Ps. cxviii. 145, Vulg.).
[2] 'Great is thy mercy towards me' (Ps. lxxxv. 13, Vulg.).

Would God mine homely style
Were políshéd with the file
Of Cicero's eloquence,
To praise her excellence!
For this most goodly floure,
This blossom of fresh colóur,
So Jupiter me succóur,
She flourisheth new and new
In beauty and virtúe:
Hac claritate gemina,
O gloriosa femina,
Principes persecuti sunt me gratis! [1]
Omnibus consideratis,
Paradisus voluptatis
Haec virgo est dulcissima. [2]

My pen it is unable,
My hand it is unstable,
My reason rude and dull
To praise her at the full;
Goodly Mistress Jane,
Sober, demure Diane;
Jane this mistress hight,
The lode-star of delight,
Dame Venus of all pleasure,
The well of worldly treasure!
She doth exceed and pass
In prudence Dame Pallás;
For this most goodly floure,
This blossom of fresh colóur,
So Jupiter me succóur,
She flourisheth new and new
In beauty and virtúe:

[1] 'Princes have persecuted me without cause' (Ps. cxviii. 161, Vulg.).

[2] All things considered, this sweetest of girls is a paradise of delights.

Hac claritate gemina,
O gloriosa femina!

    Requiem aeternam dona eis, Domine![1]
With this psalm, *Domine, probasti me,*[2]
Shall sail over the sea,
With *Tibi, Domine, commendamus,*[3]
On pilgrimage to Saint Jamès,
For shrimpès, and for prawnès,
And for stalking cranès.
And where my pen hath offended,
I pray you it may be amended
By discreet consideration
Of your wise reformation.
I have not offended, I trust,
If it be sadly discust.
It were no gentle guise
This treatise to despise
Because I have written and said
Honour of this fair maid.
Wherefore should I be blaméd,
That I Jane have naméd,
And famously proclaiméd?
She is worthy to be enrolled
With letters of gold.
       Car elle vaut.

Per me laurigerum Britonum Skeltonida vatem
Laudibus eximiis merito haec redimita puella est.
Formosam cecini, qua non formosior ulla est;
Formosam potius quam commendaret Homerus.

[1] 'Give them eternal rest, O Lord.'
[2] 'O Lord, thou hast searched me' (Ps. cxxxviii. 1, Vulg.).
[3] 'We commend ourselves to thee, O Lord,' the final oration of the *Ordo Commendationis.*

Sic juvat interdum rigidos recreare labores,
Nec minus hoc titulo tersa Minerva mea est.

Rien que plaisir.

Thus endeth the Book of Philip Sparrow, and here
followeth an addition made by Master Skelton.

The guise nowadays
Of some jangling jays
Is to discommend
That they cannot amend,
Though they would spend
All the wits they have.
  What ails them to deprave
Philip Sparrow's grave?
His *Dirige*, her Commendation
Can be no derogation,
But mirth and consolation
Made by protestation,
No man to miscontent
With Philip's interêment.
  Alas, that goodly maid,
Why should she be afraid?
Why should she take shame
That her goodly name,
Honourably reported,
Should be set and sorted,
To be matriculate
With ladies of estate?
  I conjure thee, Philip Sparrow,
By Hercules that hell did harrow,
And with a venomous arrow
Slew of the Epidaurs
One of the Centaurs,
Or Onocentaurs,
Or Hippocentaurs;

By whose might and main
An hart was slain
With hornés twain
Of glittering gold;
And the apples of gold
Of Hesperides withhold,
And with a dragon kept
That nevermore slept,
By martial strength
He won at length;
And slew Geryon
With three bodies in one;
With mighty couráge
Adaunted the rage
Of a lion savage;
Of Diomedes' stable
He brought out a rabble
Of coursers and rounces
With leapés and bounces;
And with mighty lugging,
Wrestling and tugging,
He pluckéd the bull
By the hornéd skull,
And offered to Cornucopia---
And so forth *per cetera*.

Also by Hecate's bower,
In Pluto's ghastly tower;
By the ugly Eumenides,
That never have rest nor ease;
By the venomous serpént,
That in hell is never brent,
In Lerna the Greekés' fen,
That was engendered then;
By Chimera's flames,
And all the deadly names
Of infernal posty,
Where soulés fry and roasty;

By the Stygian flood,
And the streamès wood
Of Cocytus' bottomless well;
By the ferryman of hell,
Charon with his beard hoar,
That roweth with a rude oar
And with his frowncéd foretop
Guideth his boat with a prop;
I conjure Philip, and call
In the same of King Saul;
Primo Regum express,
He bad the Pythoness
To witchcraft her to 'dress,
And by her abusions
And damnable illusions
Of marvellous conclusions,
And by her superstitions,
And wonderful conditions,
She raiséd up in that stead
Samuel that was dead;
But whether it were so,
He were *idem in numero*,
The self-same Samuel,
Howbeit to Saul he did tell
The Philistines should him ascry,
And the next day he should die,
I will myself discharge
To lettered men at large.

But, Philip, I conjure thee
Now by these namès three,
Diana in the woodès green,
Luna that so bright doth shine,
Proserpina in hell,
That thou shortly tell,
And show now unto me
What the cause may be
Of this perplexity!

E

Inferias, Philippe, tuas Scroupe puchra Joanna
Instanter petiit: cur nostri carminis illam
Nunc pudet? est sero; minor est infamia vero.[1]

Then such as have disdainéd
And of this work complainéd,
I pray God they be painéd
No worse than is containéd
In verses two or three
That follow as you may see.

Luride, cur, livor, volucris pia funera damnas?
Talia te rapiant rapiunt quae fata volucrem!
Est tamen invidia mors tibi continua.[2]

---

[1] Philip, your obsequies the fair Joanna Scroupe ardently longed for: why is she now ashamed of our song? It is too late; shame is less than truth. This 'addition' was evidently written considerably later (as it also appears as part of *The Garland of Laurel*, though it is not repeated there in this edition), after Jane Scrope had become Mistress Brews of Topcroft Hall, Norfolk, and the manor-house, Little Wenham, Suffolk, where she may be seen lying beside her husband, Thomas, on a memorial brass in the church (Edwards, *Skelton*, pp. 113–14). These lines, however, appear at the end of all existing editions of *Philip Sparrow*.

[2] Why, Green Envy, do you condemn the sacred funeral rites of a sparrow? May the fate which overtook my bird seize upon thee. Yet is malice a perpetual death to thee.

WARE THE HAWK

Prologus Skeltonidis Laureati super Ware the Hawk

THIS work deviséd is
For such as do amiss;
And specially to control
Such as have cure of soul,
That be so far abuséd
They cannot be excuséd
By reason nor by law;
But that they play the daw,
To hawk, or else to hunt
From the altar to the font,
With cry unreverent,
Before the sacrament,
Within holy church's boundès,
That of our faith the ground is.
That priest that hawkès so
All grace is far him fro;
He seemeth a schismatic,
Or else an heretic,
For faith in him is faint.
Therefore to make complaint
Of such misadviséd
Parsons and disguiséd,
This book we have deviséd,
Compendiously compriséd,
No good priest to offend,
But such daws to amend,
In hope that no man shall
Be miscontent withal.

I shall you make relation,
By way of apostrophation,

Under supportation
Of your patient toleration,
How I, Skelton Laureate,
Devised and also wrate
Upon a lewd curáte,
A parson beneficéd,
But nothing well advised.
He shall be as now nameless,[1]
But he shall not be blameless,
Nor he shall not be shameless;
For sure he wrought amiss
To hawk in my church of Diss.
This fond frantic falconer,
With his polluted pawtener,
As priest unreverent,
Straight to the sacrament
He made his hawk to fly,
With hugeous shout and cry.
The high altar he stripped naked;
Thereon he stood and crakéd;
He shook down all the clothès,
And sware horrible oathès,
Before the face of God,
By Moses and Aaron's rod,
Ere that he hence yede
His hawk should pray and feed
Upon a pigeon's maw.
The blood ran down raw
Upon the altar-stone;
The hawk tiréd on a bone;
And in the holy place
She dungéd there a chase
Upon my corporas'[2] face.
Such *sacrificium laudis*
He made with such gambadés.

[1] Rector of Whipstock.   See Latin lines in Appendix.

[2] The corporal, a square of linen on which the host and chalice
are placed during Mass.

OBSERVATE

His second hawk waxéd gery,
And was with flying weary;
She had flowen so oft,
That on the rood-loft
She perchéd her to rest.
The falconer then was prest,
Came running with a dow,
And cried 'Stow, stow, stow!'
But she would not bow.
He then, to be sure,
Calléd her with a lure.
Her meat was very crude,
She had not well endued;
She was not clean ensaiméd,[1]
She was not well reclaiméd:
But the falconer unfainéd
Was much more feebler brainéd.
The hawk had no list
To come to his fist;
She lookéd as she had the frounce;
With that he gave her a bounce
Full upon the gorge.
I will not feign nor forge—
The hawké with that clap
Fell down with evil hap.
The church doors were sparréd,
Fast bolted and barréd,
Yet with a pretty gin
I fortuned to come in,
This rebel to behold,
Whereof I him controlled.
But he saidé that he would,
Against my mind and will,
In my church hawké still.

[1] Purged from her grease.

CONSIDERATE

On Saint John decollation [1]
He hawkéd in this fashion,
Tempore vesperarum,
Sed non secundum Sarum,[2]
But like a March harum
His brainés were so *parum.*
He said he would not let
His houndés for to fet,[3]
To hunt there by liberty
In the despite of me,
And to halloo there the fox.
Down went my offering-box,
Book, bell, and candle,
All that he might handle—
Cross, staff, lectern, and banner,
Fell down in this manner.

DELIBERATE

With troll, citrace, and trovy,
They rangéd Hankin Bovy [4]
My churché all about.
This falconer then 'gan shout,
'These be my gospellers,
These be my epistolers,
These be my choristers
To helpé me to sing,
My hawks to matins ring!'
In this priestly gydíng
His hawk then flew upon
The rood with Mary and John.
Dealt he not like a fon?

[1] On the festival of the beheading of St. John.
[2] At the time of vespers, but not according to the ordinals of Osmond, Bishop of Sarum.
[3] That he would fetch his dogs without delay.
[4] A dance called Hankin Booby.

Dealt he not like a daw?
Or else is this God's law,
Decrees or decretáls,
Or holy synodals,
Or else provincials,
Thus within the walls
Of holy Church to deal,
Thus to ring a peal
With his hawkės bells?
Doubtless such losels
Make the church to be
In small authority:
A curate in speciall
To snapper and to fall
Into this open crime!
To look on this were time.

VIGILATE

But whoso that lookės
In the official bookės,
There he may see and read
That this is matter indeed.
Howbeit, maiden Meed
Made them to be agreed,
And so the Scribe was feed,
And the Pharisay
Then durst nothing say,
But let the matter slip,
And madė truth to trip;
And of the spiritual law
They madė but a geegaw,
And took it out in drink,
And thus the cause doth shrink.
The Church is thus abusėd,
Reproachėd and polluted;
Correction hath no place,
And all for lack of grace.

DEPLORATE

Look now in *Exodi* [1]
And *de arca Domini*,
With *Regum* [2] by and by
(The Bible will not lie),
How the Temple was kept,
How the Temple was swept,
Where *sanguis taurorum*, [3]
Aut sanguis vitulorum, [4]
Was offeréd within the wallés,
After ceremonialles;
When it was polluted
Sentence was executed,
By way of expiation
For reconciliation.

DEVINATE

Then much more, by the rood,
Where Christès precious blood
Daily offéred is,
To be polluted thus;
And that he wishéd withall
That the doves dung down might fall
Into my chalice at Mass,
When consecrated was
The blessed Sacrament.
O priest unreverent!
He said that he would hunt
From the altar to the font.

REFORMATE

Of no tyrant I read
That so far did exceed,

[1] The Book of Exodus.
[2] The Book of Kings.
[3] Blood of bulls.
[4] Or blood of calves.

Neither Diocletian,
Nor yet Domitian,
Nor yet crooked Cacus,[1]
Nor yet drunken Bacchus;
Neither Olibrius,[2]
Nor Dionysius,
Neither Phalary [3]
Rehearséd in Valery; [4]
Nor Sardanapall,
Unhappiest of all;
Nor Nero the worst,
Nor Claudius the curst;
Nor yet Egeas,
Nor yet Sir Ferumbras; [5]
Neither Zorobabel,
Nor cruel Jezebel;
Nor yet Tarquinius,
Whom Titus Livius
In writing doth enroll;
I have read them poll by poll; [6]
The story of Aristobel,[7]
And of Constantinople,
Which city miscreants won
And slew many a Christian man;
Yet the Soldan, nor the Turk,
Wrought never such a work,
For to let their hawkės fly
In the Church of Saint Sophý;

---

[1] A cruel giant who ruled in Carthage (Caxton's *Recuyel of the Historyes of Troy*).

[2] Who tortured and beheaded St. Margaret at Antioch.

[3] i.e. Phalaris.

[4] Valerius Maximus.

[5] Saracen giant vanquished by Oliver.

[6] Head by head, one by one.

[7] Aristobulus, high-priest and governor of Judaea, who starved his mother to death and assassinated his brother.

*E

With much matter more,
That I keep in store.

PENSITATE

Then in a table plain
I wrote a verse or twain,
Whereat he made disdain:
The peckish parson's brain
Could not reach nor attain
What the sentence meant.
He said, for a crooked intent,
The wordès were perverted:
And thus he overthwarted.
Of the which procéss
Ye may know more express,
If it please you to look
In the residue of this book.

Hereafter followeth the table.

Look on this table,
Whether thou art able
To read or to spell
What these verses tell.

Sicculo lutureis est colo būraarā
Nixphedras visarum caniuter tuntantes
Raterplas Natābrian umsudus itnugenus.
18. 10. 2. 11. 19. 4. 13. 3. 3. 1. ten *valet.*
Chartula stet, precor, haec nullo temeranda petulco:
  Hos rapiet numeros non homo, sed mala bos.
Ex parte rem chartae adverte asperte, pone Musam Arethusam
  hanc.

Whereto should I rehearse
The sentence of my verse?
In them be no schools
For brain-sick frantic fools.
Construas hoc,

Domine Dawcock!
   Ware the hawk!
Master *sophista,*
Ye *simplex syllogista,*
Ye devilish *dogmatista,*
Your hawk on your fista,
To hawk when you lista
In ecclesia ista,
Domine concupisti,
With thy hawk on thy fisty?
Nunquid sic dixisti?
Nunquid sic fecisti?
Sed ubi hoc legisti,
Aut unde hoc,[1]
Doctor Dawcock?
   Ware the hawk!
Doctor *Dialetica,*
Where find you in *Hypothetica,*
Or in *Categoria,*
Latina sive Dorica,
To use your hawkès *forica* [2]
In propitiatorio,
Tanquam diversorio ? [3]
Unde hoc,
Domine Dawcock?
   Ware the hawk!
Say to me, Jack Harris,
Quare aucuparis
Ad sacramentum altaris? [4]
For no reverence thou sparès
To shake thy pigeon's featherès
Super arcam foederis: [5]

[1] Did you never say so?   Did you never act so?   But where did you gather that, or whence this?

[2] Lavatory.

[3] In the propitiatory, as if it were in the tavern.

[4] Why do you go bird-catching by the sacrament of the altar?

[5] Over the Ark of the Covenant.

Unde hoc,
Doctor Dawcock?
    Ware the hawk!
Sir *Dominus vobiscum,*
Per aucupium [1]
Ye made your hawk to come
Desuper candelabrum
Christi Crucifixi [2]
To feed upon your fisty:
Dic, inimice crucis Christi,
Ubi didicisti
Facere hoc,[3]
Domine Dawcock?
    Ware the hawk!
Apostata Julianus,
Nor yet Nestorianus,
Thou shalt nowhere read
That they did such a deed,
To let their hawkès fly
Ad ostium tabernaculi,
In que est corpus Domine: [4]
Cave hoc,
Doctor Dawcock!
    Ware the hawk!
Thus doubtless ye ravéd,
Diss church ye thus depravéd;
Wherefore, as I be savéd,
Ye are therefore beknavéd:
Quare? quia Evangelia,
Concha et conchylia,
Accipter et sonalia,
Et bruta animalia,
Caetera quoque talia

[1] Sir priest, by fowling.
[2] From above the candlesticks of Christ crucified.
[3] Say, enemy of Christ's cross, where did you learn to do this?
[4] Even to the door of the tabernacle, where the body of the
Lord is:

Tibi sunt aequalia: [1]
Unde hoc,
Domine Dawcock?
Ware the hawk!
Et relis et ralis,
Et reliqualis,
From Granada to Galis,[2]
From Winchelsea to Walès,
Non est brain-sick talès,
Nec minus rationalis,
Nec magis bestialis,[3]
That singès with a chalice:
Construas hic,
Doctor Dawcock!
Ware the hawk!
Mazéd, witless, smeary smith,
Hampar with your hammer upon thy stith,
And make hereof a sickle or a saw,
For though ye live a hundred year, ye shall
die a daw.
Vos valete,
Doctor indiscrete!

---

[1] Why? because the Gospels, holy shells and shell-fish, a hawk and bells and brutish animals, and other such things are all alike to you.

[2] Galicia.

[3] Nor less reasonable, nor more bestial.

THE TUNNING OF ELINOUR RUMMING

TELL you I chill,[1]
If that ye will
Awhile be still,
Of a comely Gill
That dwelt on a hill:
But she is not gryl,
For she is somewhat sage
And well worn in age.
For her viságe
It would assuage
A man's coráge.

Her loathly lere
Is nothing clear,
But ugly of cheer,
Droopy and drowsy,
Scurvy and lowsy,
Her face all bowsy,
Comely crinkléd,
Woundrously wrinkléd,
Like a roast pig's ear,
Bristléd with hair.

Her lewd lippès twain,
They slaver, men sayne,
Lik a ropy rain,
A gummy glair.
She is ugly fair.
Her nose somedele hookéd,
And camously crooked,[2]
Never stopping,
But ever dropping;
Her skin, loose and slack,
Grainéd like a sack;

[1] i.e. Ich will.   [2] Turned up.

With a crooked back.
   Her eyen gowndy
Are full unsowndy,
For they are bleared;
And she gray-haired,
Jawéd like a jetty;
A man would have pity
To see how she is gumméd,
Fingered and thumbéd,
Gently jointed,
Greased and annointed
Up to the knuckles;
The bones of her huckles
Like as they were with buckles
Together made fast.
Her youth is far past.
Footed like a plane,
Leggéd like a crane,
And yet she will jet
Like a jollivet,
In her furréd flocket,
And gray russet rocket,
With simper and cocket.
Her hood of Lincoln green
It had been hers, I ween,
More than forty year;
And so doth it appear,
For the green bare threadés
Look like sere weedés,
Witheréd like hay,
The wool worn away.
And yet, I daré say,
She thinketh herself gay
Upon the holy day
When she doth her array
And girdeth in her geets
Stitched and pranked with pleats;
Her kirtle Bristol-red,

With clothes upon her head
That weigh a sow of lead,
Writhen in wondrous wise
After the Saracen's guise,
With a whim-wham
Knit with a trim-tram
Upon her brain-pan;
Like an Egyptían
Cappéd about.
When she goeth out
Herself for to shew,
She driveth down the dew
With a pair of heelés
As broad as two wheelés;
She hobbles as a goose
With her blanket hose
Over the fallow;
Her shoon smeared with tallow,
Greaséd upon dirt
That baudeth her skirt.

FIT THE FIRST

And this comely dame,
I understand, her name
Is Elinour Rumming,
At home in her wonning;
And as men say
She dwelt in Surrey,
In a certain stead
Beside Leatherhead.
She is a tonnish gib,[1]
The devil and she be sib.

But to make up my tale,
She breweth nappy ale,
And maketh thereof pot-sale

[1] A beery old cat.

To travellers, to tinkers,
To sweaters, to swinkers,
And all good ale-drinkers,
That will nothing spare
But drink till they stare
And bring themselves bare,
With '*Now away the mare!*
And let us slay care.'
As wise as an hare!

Come whoso will
To Elinour on the hill
With 'Fill the cup, fill!'
And sit there by still,
Early and late.
Thither cometh Kate,
Cisly and Sarah,
With their legs barė,
And alsó their feet
Hardely full unsweet;
With their heelės daggéd,
Their kirtles all to-jaggéd,
Their smockės all to-ragged,
With titters and tatters,
Bring dishes and platters,
With all their might running
To Elinour Rumming
To have of her tunning.
She lendeth them on the same,[1]
And thus beginneth the game.
Some wenches come unlacéd,
Some housewives come unbracéd,
With their naked pappės,
That flippės and flappės,
That wiggės and waggės
Like tawny saffron baggės;

[1] i.e. on their clothes.

A sort of foul drabbės
All scurvy with scabbės.
Some be flybitten,
Some skewéd as a kitten;
Some with a shoe-clout
Bind their headės about;
Some have no hair-lace,
Their locks about their face,
Their tresses untrussed
All full of unlust;
Some look strawry,
Some cawry-mawry;
Full untidy teggės,
Like rotten eggės.
Such a lewd sort
To Elinour resort
From tide to tide.
Abide, abide!
And to you shall be told
How her ale is sold
To Maud and to Mold.

FIT THE SECOND

Some have no money
That thither comė
For their ale to pay.
That is a shrewd array!
Elinour swearéd, 'Nay,
Ye shall not bear away
My ale for nought,
By Him that me bought!'
With 'Hey, dog, hey!
Have these hogs away!'
With 'Get me a staff,
The swine eat my draff!

Strike the hogs with a club,
They have drunk up my swilling-tub!'
For, be there never so much press,
These swine go to the high dais,
The sow with her pigs,
The boar his tail wrigs,
His rump alsó he frigs
Against the high bench!
With, 'Fo, there's a stench!
Gather up, thou wench;
Seest thou not what is fall?
Take up dirt and all,
And bear out of the hall:
God give it ill-preving,
Cleanly as evil 'chieving!'

But let us turn plain,
There we left again.
For, as ill a patch as that,
The hens run in the mash-vat;
For they go to roost
Straight over the ale-joust,
And dung, when it comės,
In the ale-tunnės.
Then Elinour taketh
The mash-bowl, and shaketh
The hens' dung away,
And skimmeth it into a tray
Whereas the yeast is,
With her mangy fistės:
And sometime she blens
The dung of her hens
And the ale together,
And sayeth, 'Gossip, come hither,
This ale shall be thicker,
And flower the more quicker;
For I may tell yóu

I learned it of a Jew
When I began to brew,
And I have found it true.
Drink now while it is new:
An ye may it brook,
It shall make you look
Younger than ye be
Yearès two or three,
For ye may prove it by me.
Behold,' she said, 'and see
How bright I am of ble!
Ich am not cast away,
That can my husband say,
When we kiss and play
In lust and in likíng;
He calleth me his whiting,
His mulling and his miting,
His nobbès and his coney,
His sweeting and his honey,
With 'Buss, my pretty bonny,
Thou art worth goods and money!"
Thus make I my fellow fonny,
Till that he dream and drony;
For, after all our sport,
Then will he rout and snort:
Then sweetly together we lie
As two pigs in a sty.'

To cease meseemeth best,
And of this tale to rest,
And for to leave this letter
Because it is no better,
And because it is no sweeter;
We will no further rime
Of it at this time,
But we will turnè plain
Where we left again.

FIT THE THIRD

Instead of coin and money
Some bringė her a coney,
And some a pot with honey,
Some a salt, and some a spoon,
Some their hose, some their shoon;
Some run a good trot
With a skillet or a pot;
Some fill their pot full
Of good Lemster wool:
An housewife of trust,
When she is athirst,
Such a web can spin,
Her thrift is full thin.

Some go straight thither,
Be it slaty or slither:
They hold the highway,
They care not what men say,
Be that as be may.
Some, loth to be espied,
Start in at the backė-side
Over the hedge and pale,
And all for the good ale.
Some runnė till they sweat,
Bring with them malt or wheat,
And Dame Elinour entreat
To birle them of the best.

Then cometh another guest:
She sweareth by the rood of rest
Her lippės are so dry
Without drink she must die,
'Therefore fill it by and by,
And have here a peck of rye.'

Anon cometh another,
As dry as the other,

And with her doth bring
Meal, salt, or other thing,
Her harvest girdle, her wedding-ring,
To pay for her scot
As cometh to her lot.
One bringeth her husband's hood
Because the ale is good;
Another brought her his cap
To offer to the ale-tap,
With flax and with tow;
And some brought sour dough
With 'Hey' and with 'Ho!
Sit we down a row,
And drink till we blow,
And pipe "Tirly Tirlow!"'

Some laid to pledge
Their hatchet and their wedge,
Their heckle and their reel,
Their rock, their spinning-wheel;
And some went so narrow
They laid to pledge their wharrow,
Their ribskin and their spindle,
Their needle and their thimble.
Here was scant thrift
When they made such shift.

Their thirst was so great
They askéd never for meat,
But 'Drink, still drink,
And let the cat wink!
Let us wash our gums
From the dry crumbs!'

FIT THE FOURTH

Some for very need
Laid down a skein of thread,
And some a skein of yarn;
Some brought from the barn

Both beanés and peas;
Small chaffer doth ease
Sometime, now and then;
Another there was that ran
With a good brass-pan,
Her colour was full wan;
She ran in all the haste,
Unbracéd and unlaced;
Tawny, swart, and sallow
Like a cake of tallow.
I swear by all hallow
It was a stale to take
The devil in a brake!

And then came halting Joan,
And brought a gambone
Of bacon that was reasty:
But, Lord, as she was testy,
Angry as a waspy!
She began to gape and gaspy,
And bade Elinour go bet
And fill in good met;
It was dear that was far-fet.

Another brought a spick
Of a bacon flick,[1]
Her tongue was very quick
But she spake somewhat thick.
Her fellow did stammer and stut,
But she was a foul slut,
For her mouth foaméd
And her belly groanéd:
Joan sayn she had eaten a fiest.
'By Christ,' said she, 'thou liest,
I have as sweet a breath
As thou, with shameful death!'
Then Elinour said, 'Ye callets,
I shall break your palates,

[1] Flitch

Without ye now cease!'
And so was made the peace.
    Then thither came drunken Alice,
And she was full of talės,
Of tidings in Walės,
And of Saint James in Galės,
And of the Portingalės,
With 'Lo, gossip, ywis,
Thus and thus it is:
There hath been great war
Between Temple Bar
And the Cross in Cheap,
And there came an heap
Of mill-stones in a rout . . .'
She speaketh thus in her snout,
Snivelling in her nose
As though she had the pose.
'Lo, here is an old tippet,
An ye will give me a sippet
Of your stale ale,
God send you good sale!'
And as she was drinking
She fell in a winking
With a barlichood,
She pissed where she stood.
Then began she to weep,
And forthwith fell asleep.
Elinour took her up
And blessed her with a cup
Of newė ale in cornės:
Alice found therein no thornės,
But supped it up at onės,
She found therein no bonės.

FIT THE FIFTH

    Now in cometh another rabble:
First one with a ladle,

Another with a cradle,
And with a side-saddle:
And there began a fabble,
A clattering and a babble
Of foolish Philly
That had a foal with Willy,
With 'Jast you!' and 'Gup gilly!'
She could not lie stilly.

Then came in a jennet
And swore, 'By Saint Bennet,
I drank not this sennight
A draught to my pay!
Elinour, I thee pray,
Of thine ale let us essay,
And have here a pilch of gray:
I wear skinnès of coney,
That causeth I look so dony!'

Another then did hitch her,
And brought a pottle-pitcher,
A tunnel and a bottle,
But she had lost the stopple:
She cut off her shoe-sole,
And stoppéd therewith the hole.

Amongè all the blommer
Another brought a skommer,
A frying-pan, and a slicer:
Elinour made the pricè
For good ale each wit.

Then start in mad Kit
That had little wit:
She seeméd somedele sick
And brought a penny chick
To Dame Elinour
For a draught of liquor.

Then Margery Milkduck
Her kirtle she did uptuck
An inch above her knee,
Her legs that ye might see;
But they were sturdy and stubbéd,
Mighty pestles and clubbéd,
As fair and as white
As the foot of a kite.
She was somewhat foul,
Crooken-neckéd like an owl;
And yet she brought her fees,
A cantle of Essex cheese,
Was well a foot thick
Full of maggots quick:
It was huge and great,
And mighty strong meat
For the devil to eat:
It was tart and pungete!

Another set of sluts:
Some brought walnuts,
Some apples, some pears,
Some brought their clipping shears,
Some brought this and that,
Some brought I wot ne'er what;
Some brought their husband's hat,
Some puddings and links,
Some tripes that stinks.
But of all this throng
One came them among,
She seeméd half a leech
And began to preach
Of the Tuesday in the week
When the mare doth kick;
Of the virtue of an unset leek,
Of her husband's breek;
With the feathers of a quail
She could to Bordeaux sail;

And with good ale barmé
She could make a charmé
To help withal a stitch:
She seemed to be a witch.

Another brought two goslings
That were noughty frostlings;
She brought them in a wallet,
She was a comely callet:
The goslings were untied;
Elinour began to chide,
'They be wretchocks thou hast brought,
They are sheer shaking nought!'

FIT THE SIXTH

Maud Ruggy thither skippéd:
She was ugly hippéd,
And ugly thick lippéd,
Like an onion sided,
Like tan leather hided.
She had her so guided
Between the cup and the wall
That she was there withal
Into a palsy fall;
With that her head shakéd,
And her handés quakéd,
One's head would have achéd
To see her naked.
She drank so of the dreggés,
The dropsy was in her leggés;
Her face glistering like glass,
All foggy fat she was.
She had alsó the gout
In all her joints about;
Her breath was sour and stale,
And smelléd all of ale:
Such a bedfellaw
Would make one cast his craw.

But yet for all that
She drank on the mash-vat.
    There came an old ribibe:
She halted of a kibe,
And had broken her shin
At the threshold coming in,
And fell so wide open
That one might see her token,
The devil thereon be wroken!
What need all this be spoken?
She yelléd like a calf.
'Rise up, on God's half!'
Said Elinour Rumming,
'I beshrew thee for thy coming!'
And as she at her did pluck,
'Quack, quack!' said the duck
In that lampatram's lap;
With 'Fie, cover thy shap
With some flip flap!
God give it ill hap,'
Said Elinour, 'for shame!'—
Like an honest dame.
Up she start, half lame,
And scantly could go
For pain and for woe.
    In came another dant,
With a goose and a gant:
She had a wide weasant;
She was nothing pleasant,
Neckéd like an elephant;
It was a bulliphant,
A greedy cormorant.

    Another brought her garlic heads,
Another brought her beads
(Of jet or of coal)
To offer to the ale pole.

Some brought a wimble,
Some brought a thimble,
Some brought a silk lace,
Some brought a pincase,
Some her husband's gown,
Some a pillow of down,
Some of the napery
. . . . . [1]
And all this shift they make
For the good ale sake.

'A straw!' said Bely, 'stand utter,
For we have eggs and butter,
. . . . . [2]
And of pigeons a pair.'

Then start forth a fizgig,
And she brought a boar pig,
The flesh thereof was rank,
And her breath strongly stank;
Yet, ere she went, she drank,
And gat her great thank
Of Elinour for her ware
That she thither bare
To pay for her share.
Now truly, to my thinking,
This is a solemn drinking!

FIT THE SEVENTH

'Soft!' quod one hight Sybil,
'And let me with you bibble.'
She sat down in the place
With a sorry face
Whey-wormèd about.
Garnishèd was her snout

[1] A line missing.
[2] A line missing.

With here and there a pustule
Like a scabbéd mussel.
'This ale,' said she, 'is noppy;
Let us suppè and soppy
And not spill a droppy,
For, so may I hoppy,
It cooleth well my croppy.

   'Dame Elinour,' said she,
'Have here is for me—
A clout of London pins!'
And with that she begins
The pot to her pluck
And drank a 'good-luck.'
She swingéd up a quart
At once for her part:
Her paunch was so pufféd,
And so with ale stufféd,
Had she not hied apace
She had defiled the place.

   Then began the sport
Among that drunken sort.
'Dame Elinour,' said they,
'Lend here a cock of hay
To make all thing clean—
Ye wot well what we mean!'

   But, sir, among all
That sat in that hall
There was a prick-me-dainty
Sat like a sainty
And began to painty
As though she would fainty:
She made it as coy
As a *lege de moy*;
She was not half so wise
As she was peevish nice.

She said never a word,
But rose from the board
And callèd for our dame,
Elinour by name.
We supposèd, ywis,
That she rose to piss:
But the very ground
Was for to compound
With Elinour in the spence,
To pay for her expense.
'I have no penny nor groat
To pay,' she said, 'God wote,
For washing of my throat,
But my beads of amber
Bear them to your chamber.'
Then Elinour did them hide
Within her beddès side.

    But some then sat right sad
That nothing had,
There of their own,
Neither gelt nor pawn: [1]
Such were there many
That had not a penny.
But, when they should walk,
Were fain with a chalk
To score on the balk,
Or score on the tail:
God give it ill hail!
For my fingers itch,
I have written too much
Of this mad mumming
Of Elinour Rumming.
Thus endeth the geste
Of this worthy feast.

  [1] Neither money nor pledge.

LAUREATI SKELTONIDIS IN DESPECTU
MALIGNANTIUM DISTICHON

Quamvis insanis, quamvis marcescis inanis,
Invide, cantamus: haec loca plena jocis.

Bien m'en souvient.

Omnes feminae, quae nimis bibulae sunt, vel quae sordida
labe squaloris, aut qua spurca foeditatis macula, aut verbosa
loquacitate notantur, poeta invitat ad audiendum hunc libellum,
etc.

Ebria, squalida, sordida femina, prodiga verbis,
Huc currat, properet, veniat!   Sua gesta libellus
Iste volutabit: Paean sua plectra sonando
Materiam risus cantabit carmine rauco.

Finis.

Quod Skelton, Laureate.

A LAUD AND PRAISE MADE FOR OUR
SOVEREIGN LORD THE KING

THE Rose both White and Red
   In one Rose now doth grow:
Thus thorough every stead
   Thereof the fame doth blow.
   Grace the seed did sow:
England, now gather floures,
Exclude now all doloures.

Noble Henry the Eight,
   Thy loving sovereign lord,
Of kingès line most straight
   His title doth record:
   In whom doth well accord
Alexis young of age,
Adrastus wise and sage,

Astrea, Justice hight,
   That from the starry sky
Shall now come and do right.
   This hundred year scantly
   A man could not espy
That Right dwelt us among,
And that was the more wrong.

Right shall the foxes chare,
   The wolvès, the bearès alsó,
That wrought have muchè care,
   And brought Engeland in woeı
   They shall worry no mo,
Nor root the Rosary
By extort treachery.

Of this our noble king
    The law they shall not break;
They shall come to reckoning;
    No man for them will speak:
    The people durst not creke
Their griefés to complain,
They brought them in such pain.

Therefore no more they shall
    The commons overbace,
That wont were over all
    Both lord and knight to face:
    For now the years of grace
And wealth are come again,
That maketh England fain.

Adonis of fresh colóur,
    Of youth the goodly floure,
Our prince of high honóur,
    Our paves, our succóur,
    Our king, our emperóur,
Our Priamus of Troy,
Our wealth, our worldly joy:

Upon us he doth reign,
    That maketh our heartés glad,
As king most sovereign
    That ever England had;
    Demure, sober, and sad,
And Mars's lusty knight;
God save him in his right!

                        Amen.

THE MANNER OF THE WORLD NOWADAYS[1]

So many pointed caps
Laced with double flaps,
And so gay felted hats,
   Saw I never:
So many good lessons,
So many good sermons,
And so few devotíons,
   Saw I never.

So many gardès worn,
Jaggéd and all to-torn,
And so many falsely forsworn,
   Saw I never:
So few good policies
In townès and cities
For keeping of blind hostries,[2]
Saw I never.

So many good workès,
So few well-learnéd clerkès,
And so few that goodness markès,
   Saw I never:
Such prankéd coats and sleevès,
So few young men that prevès,
And such increase of thieves,
   Saw I never.

So many garded hose,
Such pointed shoes,
And so many envious foes,
   Saw I never:

[1] Sloane MS. 747, fol. 88.   Part of this poem may be by another hand.

[2] Hostelries.

133

So many inquests sit
With men of smalė wit,
And so many falsely quit,
   Saw I never.

So many gay swordės,
So many altered wordės,
And so few covered boardės,
   Saw I never:
So many empty purses,
So few good horses,
And so many curses,
   Saw I never.

Such boasters and braggers,
So new fashioned daggers,
And so many beggers,
   Saw I never:
So many proper knives,
So well apparelled wives
And so ill of their lives,
   Saw I never.

So many cuckold-makers,
So many crakers,
And so many peace-breakers,
   Saw I never:
So much vain clothing
With cutting and jagging,
And so much bragging,
   Saw I never.

So many newės and knackės,
So many naughty packės,
And so many that money lackės,
   Saw I never:

So many maidens with child
And wilfully beguiled,
And so many places untiled,
   Saw I never.

So many women blaméd
And righteously defaméd,
And so little ashaméd,
   Saw I never:
Widows so sooné wed
After their husbands be dead,
Having such haste to bed,
   Saw I never.

So much striving
For goodés and for wiving,
And so little thriving,
   Saw I never:
So many capacities,
Offices and pluralities,
And changing of dignities,
   Saw I never.

So many laws to use
The truth to refuse,
Such falsehood to excuse,
   Saw I never:
Executors having the ware,
Taking so little care
How the soul doth fare,
   Saw I never.

Among them that are rich,
Where friendship is to seek,
Such fair glosing speech,
   Saw I never:

So many poor
Coming to the door,
And so small succóur,
   Saw I never.

So proud and so gay,
So rich in array,
And so scant of monéy,
   Saw I never:
So many bowyers,
So many fletchers,
And so few good archers,
   Saw I never.

So many cheapers,
So few buyers,
And so many borrowers,
   Saw I never:
So many ale-sellers
In bawdy holes and cellars,
Of young folks ill-counsellors,
   Saw I never.

So many pinkers,
So many thinkers,
And so many good ale-drinkers,
   Saw I never:
So many wrongs,
So few merry songs,
And so many ill tongues,
   Saw I never.

So many a vagabond
Through all this land,
And so many in prison bound,
   Saw I never:

So many citations,
So few oblations,
And so many new fashions,
  Saw I never.

So many flying tales,
Pickers of purses and males,
And so many sales,
  Saw I never:
So much preaching,
Speaking fair and teaching,
And so ill believing,
  Saw I never.

So much wrath and envy,
Covetise and gluttony,
And so little charity,
  Saw I never:
So many carders,
Revellers and dicers,
And so many ill-ticers,
  Saw I never.

So many lollers,
So few true tollers,
So many bawds and pollers,
  Saw I never:
Such treachery,
Simony and usury,
Poverty and lechery,
Saw I never.

So new-fashioned jacks,
With broad flaps in the necks,
And so gay new partlets,
  Saw I never.

So many sluttish cooks,
So new-fashioned tucking-hooks,
And so few buyers of books,
   Saw I never.

So many cloisters closéd,
And priests at large loöséd,
Being so evil-disposéd,
   Saw I never:
God save our sovereign lord the King,
And all his royal spring,
For so noble a prince reigning,
   Saw I never.

So many Easterlings,
Lombards and Flemings, [1]
To bear away our winnings,
   Saw I never:
By their subtle ways
All England decays,
For such false Januays, [2]
   Saw I never.

Sometime we sang of mirth and play,
But now our joy is gone away,
For so many fall in decay,
   Saw I never:
Whither is the wealth of England gone?
The spiritual saith they have none,
And so many wrongfully undone,
   Saw I never.

It is great pity that every day
So many bribers go by the way,
And so many extortioners in each countréy,
   Saw I never:

[1] i.e. Flemish wool merchants.
[2] Genoese.

To thee, Lord, I make my moan,
For thou mayst help us every one:
Alas, the people is so woe-begone,
   Worse was it never!

Amendment
Were convenient,
But it may not be:
We have exiled verity.
God is neither dead nor sick;
He may amend all yet,
And trow ye so indeed,
As ye believe ye shall have meed.
After better I hope ever,
For worse was it never.

             Finis.   J. S.

AGAINST THE SCOTS

Against the proud Scots clattering,
That never will leave their tratling:
Won they the field, and lost their king?
They may well say, Fie on that winning!

      Lo, these fond sots
      And tratling Scots,
      How they are blind
      In their own mind,
      And will not know
      Their overthrow
      At Brankston Moor!
      They are so stour,
      So frantic mad,
      They say they had
      And won the field
      With spear and shield.
      That is as true
      As black is blue
      And green is grey!
      Whatever they say,
      Jemmy[1] is dead
      And closed in lead,
      That wás their own king:
      Fie on that winning!
      At Flodden hills
      Our bows, our bills,
      Slew all the floure
      Of their honóur.
      Are not these Scots
      Fools and sots,
      Such boast to make,

[1] i.e. James IV

To prate and crake,
To face, to brace,
All void of grace,
So proud of heart,
So overthwart,
So out of frame,
So void of shame,
As it is enrolled,
Written and told
Within this quaire?
Who list to repair,
And therein read,
Shall find indeed
A mad reckoning,
Considering all thing,
That the Scots may sing
Fie on the winning!

When the Scot Lived

Jolly Jemmy, ye scornful Scot,
Is it come unto your lot
A solemn sumner for to be?
It 'greeth nought for your degree
Our king of England for to cite,[1]
Your sovereign lord, our prince of might:
Ye for to send such a citation,
It shameth all your naughty nation,
In comparison but king Copping
Unto our prince, anointed king!
Ye play Hob Lobbin of Lothian;
Ye shew right well what good ye can;
Ye may be lord of Loch Ryán—
Christ cense you with a frying-pan!
Of Edinburgh and Saint John's town:[2]
Adieu, Sir Sumner, cast off your crown!

[1] James sent his defiance to Henry VIII while the latter was
encamped before Thérouanne.
[2] Perth.

When the Scot was Slain

Continually I shall remember
The merry month of September,
With the ninth day of the same,[1]
For then began our mirth and game;
So that now I have deviséd,
And in my mind I have compriséd,
Of the proud Scot, King Jemmy,
To write some little tragedy,
For no manner consideration
Of any sorrowful lamentation,
But for the special consolation
Of all our royal English nation.

    Melpomene, O muse tragediall,
Unto your grace for grace now I call
To guide my pen and my pen to imbibe!
Illumine me, your poet and your scribe,
That with mixture of aloes and bitter gall
I may compound confectures for a cordiall,
To angre the Scots and Irish keterings[2] withal,
That late were discomfect with battle martiall.

Thalia, my Muse, for you also call I,
To touch them with taunts of your harmony,
A medley to make of mirth with sadness,
The hearts of England to comfort with gladness!
And now to begin I will me address,
To you rehearsing the sum of my process.

    King Jamey, Jemmy, Jocky my jo,
Ye summoned our king,—why did ye so?
To you nothing it did accord
To summon our king, your sovereign lord.
A king, a sumner! it was great wonder:
Know ye not sugar and salt asunder?

[1] 1513. Flodden Field.
[2] Not Irish troops, but Highlanders and Islemen—marauders who carried off corn and cattle (*cataranes*).

Your sumner too saucy, too malapert,
Your herald in arms not yet half expert:
Ye thought ye did yet valiantly,
Not worth three skips of a pie!
Sir Skirgalliard, ye were too skit,
Your will then ran before your wit.

Your alledge ye laid and your allý,
Your frantic fable not worth a fly,
French king, or one or other;
Regarded ye should your lord, your brother.[1]
Trowéd ye, Sir Jemmy, his noble Grace
From you, Sir Scot, would turn his face?
With, Gup, Sir Scot of Galloway,
Now is your pride fall to decay!
Male uréd was your false intent
For to offend your president,
Your sovereign lord most reverent,
Your lord, your brother, and your regént.

In him is figuréd Melchizedek,
And ye were disloyal Amalek.
He is our noble Scipion,
Anointed king; and ye were none,
Though ye untruly your father have slain.[2]
His title is true in France to reign; [3]
And ye, proud Scot, Dundee, Dunbar,
Pardé, ye were his homager,
And suitor to his parliament:
For your untruth now are ye shent.

[1] James married Margaret, sister of Henry VIII.
[2] James III was murdered by an unknown hand in a cottage after his flight from the battle of Sauchieburn, where his son (then seventeen) had appeared in arms against him. James IV was always haunted by remorse for his father's death and wore in penance an iron girdle, the weight of which he every year increased.
[3] Reference to Henry's pretensions to the French crown.

Ye bear yourself somewhat too bold,
Therefore ye lost your copyhold;
Ye were bond tentant to his estate;
Lost is your game, ye are checkmate.

Unto the castle of Norham,
I understand, too soon ye came.
At Brankston Moor and Flodden hills,
Our English bows, our English bills,
Against you gave so sharp a shower
That of Scotland ye lost the flower.
The White Lion,[1] there rampant of mood,
He ragéd and rent out your heart-blood;
He the White, and ye the Red,[2]
The White there slew the Red stark dead.
Thus for your guerdon quit are ye,
Thankéd be God in Trinity,
And sweet Saint George, Our Lady's knight!
Your eye is out: adew, good-night!

Ye were stark mad to make a fray,
His Grace being out of the way:
But, by the power and might of God,
For your own tail ye made a rod!
Ye wanted wit, sir, at a word;
Ye lost your spurs, ye lost your sword.
Ye might have buskéd you to Huntly-banks,
Your pride was peevish to play such pranks.
Your poverty could not attain
With our king royal war to maintain.

Of the king of Navarre ye might take heed,[3]
Ungraciously how he doth speed:

[1] The Earl of Surrey's badge.

[2] The royal arms of Scotland.

[3] A reference to Henry's letter in reply to James. See Hall's *Chronicle* (Henry VIII).

In double dealing so he did dream
That he is king without a ream;
And, for example ye would none take,
Experience hath brought you in such a brake.
Your wealth, your joy, your sport, your play,
Your bragging boast, your royal array,
Your beard so brim as boar at bay,
Your Seven Sisters,[1] that gun so gay,
All have ye lost and cast away.
Thus Fortune hath turnéd you, I dare well say,
Now from a king to a clot of clay.
Out of your robés ye were shakéd,
And wretchedly ye lay stark naked.
For lack of grace hard was your hap:
The Popés curse [2] gave you that clap.

Of the out isles [3] the rough-footed Scots,
We have well-eased them of the bots:
The rude rank Scots, like drunken dranes,
At English bows have fetched their banes.
It is not fitting in tower and town
A sumner to wear a kingés crown:
Fortune on you therefore did frown;
Ye were too high, ye are cast down.
Sir Sumner, now where is your crown?
Cast off your crown, cast up your crown!
Sir Sumner, now ye have lost your crown.

Quod Skelton Laureate, orator to the King's
most royal estate.

Scotia, reducta in formam provinciae,
Regis parebit nutibus Angliae;
Alioquin, per desertum sin, super cherubim,
Cherubim, seraphim, seraphimque, ergo, etc.

[1] Seven huge cannon from Edinburgh Castle.
[2] James died excommunicated for infringing the pacification with England.
[3] The Hebrides.

Unto Divers People that remord this Rhyming against the Scot Jemmy

I am now constrainéd,
With wordès nothing feignéd,
This invective to make,
For some peoples' sake
That list for to jangle
And waywardly to wrangle
Against this my making,
Their males thereat shaking,
At it reprehending,
And venomously stinging,
Rebuking and remording,
And nothing according.

Cause have they none other,
But for that he was brother,
Brother unnatural
Unto our king royal,
Against whom he did fight
Falsely against all right,
Like that untrue rebel
False Cain against Abel.

Whoso thereat picketh mood,[1]
The tokens are not good
To be true English blood;
For, if they understood
His traitorly despite,
He was a recreant knight,
A subtle schismatic,
Right near an heretic,
Of grace out of the state,
And died excommunicate.

And for he was a king,
The more shameful reckoning

[1] Picks a quarrel.

Of him should men report,
In earnest and in sport.
He scantly loveth our king,
That grudgeth at this thing:
That cast such overthwarts
Perchance have hollow hearts.

Si veritatem dico, quare non creditis mihi? [1]

VILISSIMUS SCOTUS DUNDAS ALLEGAT CAUDAS CONTRA
ANGLIGENAS

Caudatos Anglos, spurcissime Scote, quid effers?
Effrons es, quoque sons, mendax, tua spurcaque bucca est.

> *Anglicus a tergo*
> *caudam gerit;*
> *est canis ergo.*
> *Anglice caudate,*
> *cape caudam*
> *ne cadat a te.*
> *Ex causa caudae*
> *manet Anglica*
> *gens sine laude.*

> *Diffamas patriam, qua non*
> *est melior usquam.*
> *Cum cauda plaudis dum*
> *possis, ad ostia pultas*
> *Mendicans; mendicus eris,*
> *mendaxque bilinguis,*
> *Scabidus, horribilis, quem*
> *vermes sexque pedales*
> *Corrodunt misere; miseris*
> *genus est maledictum.*

Skelton, *nobilis poeta.*

[1] If I speak truth, why do you not believe me?

Gup, Scot,
Ye blot:
Laudate
Caudate,
Set in better
Thy pentameter.
This Dundas,
This Scottish ass,
He rhymes and rails
That Englishmen have tails.[1]
Skeltonus laureatus,
Anglicus natus,
Provocat Musas
Contra Dundas
Spurcissimum Scotum,
Undique notum,
Rustice. fotum,
Vapide potum.
Skelton laureate
After this rate
Defendeth with his pen
All English men
Against Dundas,
That Scottish ass.
Shake thy tail, Scot, like a cur,
For thou beggest at every man's door.
Tut, Scot, I say,
Go shake thee, dog, hey!
Dundas of Galoway
With thy versifying rails
How they have tails.
By Jesu Christ,
False Scot, thou liest:
But behind in our hose

[1] A reference to the legend that as a punishment for driving St. Austin out of a certain town in England (for throwing fishes' tails, etc., at him) God caused the children of that town to be born with tails. Cf. *Life of St. Austin—Golden Legend.*

We bear there a rose
For thy Scottish nose,
A spectacle case
To cover thy face,
With trey, deuce, ace!
A toolman to blot
A rough footed Scot!
Dundas, sir knave,
Why dost thou deprave
This royal ream,
Whose radiant beam
And relucent light
Thou hast in despite,
Thou dunghill knight?
But thou lackest might,
Dundas, drunken and drowsy,
Scabbéd, scurvy, and lousy,
Of unhappy generation
And most ungracious nation!
Dundas,
That drunk ass,
That rates and ranks,
That prates and pranks
Of Huntly-banks,
Take this our thanks:—
Dundee, Dunbar,
Walk, Scot,
Walk, sot,
Rail not too far!

POEMS AGAINST GARNESCHE

Skelton Laureate, Defender, against Master Garnesche, Challenger

Sith ye have me challengéd, Master Garnesche,
  Rudely reviling me in the king's noble hall,
Such another challenger could no man wish,
    But if it were Sir Termagant that tourneyed without nall;
    For Sir Frollo de Franko [1] was never half so tall.
But say me now, Sir Satrapas, what authority ye have
In your challenge, Sir Chesten, to call me a knave?

What, have ye kithéd you a knight, Sir Douglas the Doughty,
    So currishly to beknave me in the king's paláce?
Ye strong sturdy stallion, so stern and stouty,
    Ye bear ye bold as Barabas, or Sir Terry of Thrace;
    Ye girn grimly with your gummés and with your grisly face!
But say me yet, Sir Satrapas, what authority ye have
In your challenge, Sir Chesten, to call me a knave?

Ye foul, fierce and fell, as Sir Ferumbras the freke,[2]
    Sir captain of Catywade, catacumbas of Cayre,[3]
Though ye be lusty as Sir Libius [4] lances to break,
    Yet your countenance uncomely, your face is not fair:
    For all your proud pranking, your pride may impair.
But say me yet, Sir Satrapas, what authority ye have
In your challenge, Sir Chesten, to call me a knave?

[1] A Roman knight, governor of Gaul, killed by King Arthur.—Geoffrey of Monmouth.
[2] A Saracen giant vanquished by Oliver.—Caxton's *Life of Charles the Great.*
[3] Cairo.
[4] The romance *Lybeaus Disconus* (*Le beau desconnu*).

Of Mantrible the Bridge,[1] Malchus the Murrion,[2]
  Nor black Balthasar with his basnet rough as a bear,
Nor Lycaon, that loathly lusk, in mine opinion,
  Nor no boar so brimly bristléd is with hair,
  As ye are bristléd on the back for all your gay gear.
But say me yet, Sir Satrapas, what authority ye have
In your challenge, Sir Chesten, to call me a knave?

Your wind-shaken shanks, your long loathly legs,
  Crooked as a camock, and as a cow calfless,
Brings you out of favour with all female tegs:
  That Mistress Punt put you off, it was not all causeless;
  At Orwell her haven your anger was lawless.
But say me yet, Sir Satrapas, what authority ye have
In your challenge, Sir Chesten, to call me a knave?

I say, ye solemn Saracen, all black is your ble;
  As a glede glowing, your eyen glister as glass,
Rolling in your hollow head, ugly to see;
  Your teeth tainted with tawny; your snivelly snout doth
    pass,
  Hookéd as an hawkès beak, like Sir Topas.
Boldly bend you to battle, and busk yourself to save:
Challenge yourself for a fool, call no more knave!

            By the King's most noble commandment.

*Skelton Laureate, Defender, against Master Garnesche, Chal-
lenger, with Greasy, Gorbellied Godfrey*

How may I your mockery meekly tolerate,
  Your groaning, your grunting, your groining like a swine?
Your pride is all to-peevish, your port importunate:
  You manticore, ye malapert, ye can both wince and whine;
  Your loathsome lere to look on, like a greaséd boot doth
    shine.

  [1] Concerning the giant who kept this bridge see Caxton, op. cit.
  [2] Moor.

Ye cappéd Cayface copyus, your paltock on your pate,
Though ye prate like proud Pilate, beware yet of checkmate.

Whole is your brow that ye brake with Durandal [1] your own
    sword;
  Why hold ye on your cap, sir, then? your pardon is
    expiréd:
Ye hobble very homely before the king's board;
  Ye counter umwhile [2] too captiously, and ere ye be desiréd;
  Your moth-eaten mockish manners, they be all to-miréd.
Ye cappéd Cayface copyus, your paltock on your pate,
Though ye prate like proud Pilate, beware of checkmate.

O Gabionite of Gabion, why do ye gane and gasp?
  Huf a gallant Garnesche, look on your comely corse!
Lusty Garnesche, like a louse, ye jet full like a jasp;
  As witless as a wild goose, ye have but small remorse
  Me for to challenge that of your challenge maketh so little
    force.
Ye cappéd Cayface copyus, your paltock on your pate,
Though ye prate like proud Pilate, beware of checkmate.

Sir Guy, Sir Gawain, Sir Cayus,[3] for and Sir Olivere,
  Pyramus, nor Priamus,[4] nor Sir Pyrrus the proud,
In Arthur's ancient actès nowhere is provéd your peer;
  The fashion of your phys'nomy the devil in a cloud;
  Your heart is too haut, ywis, it will not be allowed.
Ye cappéd Cayface copyus, your paltock on your pate,
Though ye prate like proud Pilate, beware of checkmate.

Ye ground you upon Godfrey, that grisly gorgon's face,
  Your standard, Sir Olifaunte,[5] against me for to 'splay:

      [1] Roland's sword.
      [2] Sing some time.
      [3] Foster-brother of King Arthur.
      [4] Who fought with Sir Gawain (*Morte d'Arthur*).
      [5] The giant in Chaucer's *Sir Thopas*.

Baile, baile at you both, frantic fools! follow on the chase!
   Come Garnesche, come Godfrey, with as many as ye may!
   I advise you beware of this war, range you in array.
Ye cappéd Cayface copyus, your paltock on your pate,
Though ye prate like proud Pilate, beware of checkmate.

Gup, gorbellied Godfrey, gup, Garnesche, gawdy fool!
   To tourney or to taunt with me ye are too far to seek:
For these twain whipslovens call for a cuck-stool: [1]
   Thou manticore, ye marmoset, garnished like a Greek,
   Wrangling, wayward, witless, raw, and nothing meek.
Ye cappéd Cayface copyus, your paltock on your pate,
Though ye prate like proud Pilate, beware of checkmate.

Mirres vous y,
Look not too high.

By the King's most noble commandment.

*Skelton Laureate, Defender, against Lusty Garnesche,
Well-beseen Christopher, Challenger*

I have your lewd letter receivéd,
And well I have it perceivéd,
And your skrike I have espiéd,
That your mad mind contrivéd.
Saving your usher's rod,[2]
I cast me not to be odd
With neither of you twain:
Wherefore I write again
How the favour of your face
Is void of all good grace;
For all your carpet cushions,
Ye have knavish conditions.

[1] A stool fixed to a long pole used for punishing scolds by plunging
them into water.
[2] Garnesche was gentleman-usher to Henry VIII.

Gup, marmoset, jast ye, morell!
I am laureate, I am no lorel.
Lewdly your time ye spend
My living to reprehend;
And will never intend
Your own lewdness to amend:
Your English lewdly ye sort,
And falsely ye me report.
Garnesche, ye gape too wide:
Your knavery I will not hide,
For to assuage your pride.

When ye were younger of age
Ye were a kitchen-page,
A dish-washer, a drivel,
In the pot your nose did snivel;
Ye friéd and ye broiléd,
Ye roasted and ye boiléd,
Ye roasted, like a fon,
A goose with the feet upon;
Ye sluffered up souce
In my Lady Bruce's house.
Whereto should I write
Of such a greasy knight?
A bawdy dish-clout
That bringeth the world about
With hafting and with polling,
With lying and controlling.

At Guines when ye were
But a slender spere,
Deckéd lewdly in your gear;
For when ye dwelt there
Ye had a knavish coat
Was scantly worth a groat;
In dud frieze ye were shrinéd
With better frieze linéd;

The outside every day,
Ye might no better a way;
The inside ye did call
Your best gown festivall.
Your drapery ye did want,
The ward with you was scant.
When ye cast a sheepès eye,
. . . .[1] Mistress Andelby,
. . . . Guines upon a gong,
. . . . sat somewhat too long;
. . . . her husband's head
. . . . mall of lead,
. . . . that ye there preachéd,
To her love ye not reachéd:
Ye would have bussed her bum
So that she would have come
Unto your lousy den.
But she of all men
Had you most in despite,
Ye lost her favour quite;
Your pilléd-garlick head [2]
Could occupy there no stead;
She calléd you Sir Guy of Gaunt,
Noséd like an elephaunt,
A pickaxe or a twible;
She said how ye did bridle,
Much like a dromedary;
Thus with you she did wary,
With much matter more
That I keep in store.

Your breath is strong and quick;
Ye are an elder-stick;
Ye wot what I think—
At both ends ye stink.
Great danger for the king,
When his Grace is fastíng,

[1] Manuscript torn here.   [2] i.e. bald, like peeled garlic.

His presence to approach:
It is to your reproach.
It falleth for no swine,
Nor sowters, to drink wine,
Nor such a noddipol
A priest for to control.

    Little wit in your scribès noll,
That scribbléd your fond scroll,
Upon him for to take
Against me for to make,
Like a doctor dawpate,
A laureate poet for to rate.
Your termès are too gross,
Too far from the purpose,
To contaminate
And to violate
The dignity laureate.

    Bold bayard, ye are too blind,
And grow all out of kind,
To occupy so your mind;
For reason can I none find
Nor good rhyme in your matter:
I wonder that ye smatter,
So for a knave to clatter!
Ye would be calléd a maker
And make much like Jake Raker;
Ye are a comely craker,
Ye learnéd of some pie-baker!
Cast up your curious writing,
And your dirty inditing,
And your spiteful despiting,
For all is not worth a miting,
A mackerel nor a whiting:
Had ye gone with me to school

And occupied no better your tool,
Ye should have kowthéd me a fool.

But now, gawdy, greasy Garnesche,
Your face I wis to varnish
So surely it shall not tarnish.
Though a Saracen's head ye bear,
Rough and full of lousy hair,
As every man well seeth,
Full of great knavish teeth,
In a field of green peason,
Is rhyme yet out of reason;
Your wit is so geson
Ye rail all out of season.

Your skin scabbéd and scurvy,
Tawny, tannéd, and shurvy;
Now upon this heat
Rankly when ye sweat,
Men say ye will wax lousy,
Drunken, droopy, drowsy!
Your sword ye swear, I ween,
So trenchant and so keen,
Shall cut both white and green: [1]
Your folly is too great
The king's colours to threat.
Your breath it is so fell
And so puauntly doth smell,
And so heinously doth stink,
That neither pump nor sink
Doth savour half so sour
Against a stormy shower.
O ladies of bright colóur,
Of beauty that beareth the floure,
When Garnesche cometh you among
With his breath so strong,
Without ye have a confectíon
Against his poisoned infectíon,

[1] i.e. the white and green dress that Skelton wore as laureate.

Else with his stinking jaws
He will cause you cast your craws,
And make your stomach seek
Over the perch to preke.

Now, Garnesche, guard thy gums,
My serpentines and my guns
Against ye now I bend;
Thyself therefore defend.
Thou toad, thou scorpion,
Thou bawdy babion,
Thou bear, thou bristléd boar,
Thou Moorish manticore,
Thou rammish stinking goat,
Thou foul churlish parrót,
Thou grisly Gorgon glaimy,
Thou sweaty sloven seimy,
Thou murrion, thou mawment,
Thou false stinking serpent,
Thou mockish marmoset,
I will not die in thy debt!
Tyburn thou me assignéd,
Where *thou* shouldst have been shrinéd;
The next halter there shall be
I bequeath it whole to thee!
Such pilfery thou hast packéd,
And so thyself o'er-watchéd
That there thou shouldst be rackéd,
If thou were meetly matchéd.

Ye may well be bedawéd,
Ye are a fool outlawéd;
And for to tell the ground,
Pay Stokes his five pound.
I say, Sir Dalyrag,
Ye bear you bold and brag

With other mennès charge:
Ye cut your cloth too large:
Such polling pageants ye play,
To point you fresh and gay.

And he that scribbléd your scrollès,
I reckon you in my rollès
For two drunken soulès.
Read and learn ye may
How old proverbès say,
That bird is not honést
That 'fileth his own nest.
If he wist what some wot,
The flesh basting of his coat
Was sowéd with slender threde.
God send you well good speed,
With *Dominus vobiscum*!
Good Latin for Jack-a-Thrum,
Till more matter may come.

By the King's most noble commandment.

*Donum Leaureati Distichon contra Golliardum Garnesche
et Scribam ejus*

*Tu, Garnesche, fatuus, fatuus tuus est mage scriba:
Qui sapuit puer, insanit vir, versus in hydram.*

*Skelton Laureate, Defender, against Lusty Garnesche,
Well-be-seen Christopher, Challenger*

Garnesche, gorgon, ghastly grime,
I have receivéd your second rime.
Though ye can skill of large and long,
Ye sing alway the cuckoo song:
Ye rail, ye rhyme, with 'Hey, dog, hey!'
Your churlish chanting is all one lay.
Ye, sir, rail all in deformity!
Ye have not read the property
Of Nature's workès, how they be

Mixed with some incommodity,
As proveth well in his Rhetorics old
Cicero with his tongue of gold.
That Nature wrought in you and me,
Irrevocable is her decree;
Waywardly wrought she hath in thee,
Behold thyself, and thou mayst see;
Thou shalt behold nowhere a worse,
Thy mirror may be the devil's arse.
With 'Knave, sir knave, and knave again!'
To call me knave thou takest great pain:
The proudest knave yet of us twain
Within thy skin he shall remain;
The starkest knave, and least good can,
Thou art callèd of every man;
The court, the country, village and town,
Saith from thy toe unto thy crown
Of all proud knaves thou bearest the bell,
Loathsome as Lucifer, lowest in hell.
On that side, on this side thou doth gazè,
And thinkest thyself Sir Pierre de Brézé,[1]
Thy caitiff's carcass coarse and crazy,
Much of thy manners I can blazè.

Of Lombardy George Ardeson,
Thou would have scorèd his habergeon;
That gentle George the Januay,
Ye would have enticèd his trull away:
Such pageants with your friends ye play
With treachery ye them betray.
Garnesche, ye got of George with gawdry
Crimson velvet for your bawdry.
Ye have a fantasy to Fenchurch Street,
With Lombards' lemans for to meet,
With 'Buss me, butting, pretty Cis!'
Your loathsome lips love well to kiss,

[1] Grand-seneschal of Anjou, Poitou, and Normandy: a warrior
in the reigns of Charles VII and Lewis XI.

Slavering like a slimy snail—
I would ye had kissed her on the tail!

Also not far from Budgé Row,
Ye pressèd pertly to pluck a crow:
Ye lost your hold, unbend your bow,
Ye won nothing there but a mow;
Ye won nothing there but a scorn;
She would not of it thou had sworn.
She said ye were colourèd with coal-dust;
To dally with you she had no lust.
She said your breath stank like a brock,
With 'Gup, Sir Guy,' ye got a mock!
She swear with her ye should not deal,
For ye were smery, like a seal,
And ye were hairy, like a calf;
She prayed you walk, on Goddès half ! [1]
And thus there ye lost your prey—
Get ye another where ye may.

Disparage ye mine ancestry?
Ye are disposèd for to lie:
I say, thou fell and foul flesh-fly,
In this debate I thee ascry.
Thou claimest thee gentle, thou art a cur;
Heralds they know thy coat armóur:
Though thou be a gentleman born,
Yet gentleness in thee is threadbare worn;
Heralds from honour may thee divorce,
For harlots haunt thine hateful corse.
Ye bear out brothels like a bawd,
And get thereby a slender laud
Between the tappet and the wall—
Fusty bawdias! I say not all.
Of harlots to use such an haras,
Ye breed moths in cloth of Arras.

What aileth thee, ribald, on me to rave?
A king to me mine habit gave:

[1] i.e. to go away, for God's sake.

At Oxford, the university,
Advancéd I was to that degree;
By whole consent of their senate
I was made poet laureate.
To call me lorel ye are too lewd:
Lith and listen, all beshrewd!
Of the Muses nine, Calliope
Hath 'pointed me to rail on thee.
It 'seemeth not thy pilléd pate
Against a poet laureate
To take upon thee for to scrive:
It 'comes thee better for to drive
A dung-cart or a tumbrel
Than with my poems for to mell.

The honour of England I learnéd to spell,
In dignity royal that doth excel.
Note and mark well this parcél:
I gave him drink of the sugared well
Of Helicon's waters crystalline,
Acquainting him with the Muses nine.
It 'cometh thee well me to remord
That creanser was to thy sovereign lord!
It pleaseth that noble prince royall
Me as his master for to call
In his learning primordial.
Avaunt, ribald, thy tongue reclaim!
Me to beknave thou art to blame.
Thy tongue untaught, with poison infect,
Without thou leave thou shalt be checked,
And taken up in such a frame
That all the world will spy your shame.
Avaunt, avaunt, thou sluggish . . .[1]
And say poets no dis[honour]
It is for no bawdy knave
The dignity laureate for to have.

[1] Manuscript illegible.

Thou callest me scalléd, thou callest me mad:
Though thou be pilléd, thou art not sad.[1]
Thou art frantic and lackest wit
To rail with me that thee can hit.
Though it be now full-tide with thee,
Yet there may fall such casualtý,
Ere thou be ware, that in a throw
Thou mayest fall down and ebb full low.
Wherefore in wealth beware of woe,
For wealth will soon depart thee fro.
To know thyself if thou lack grace,
Learn or be lewd, I shrew thy face!

Thou sayest I calléd thee a peacock:
Thou lyest, I calléd thee a woodcock;
For thou hast a long snout,
A seemly nose and a stout,
Prickéd like an unicorn:
I would some man's back ink-horn
Were thy nose spectacle-case,
It would garnish well thy face.

Thou deemest my railing overthwart:
I rail to thee such as thou art.
If thou were acquainted with all
The famous poets satirical,
As Persius and Juvenal,
Horace and noble Martial,
If they were living this day,
Of thee wot I what they would say.
They would thee write, all with one stevin,
The foulest sloven under heaven,
Proud, peevish, lither, and lewd,
Malapert, meddler, nothing well-thewed,
Busy, brainless, to brawl and brag,
Witless, wayward, Sir Wrig-wrag,

[1] Though you are bald you are not grave.

G

Disdainous, double, full of deceit,
Lying, spying by subtlety and sleight,
Fleering, flattering, false, and fickle,
Scornful and mocking over too mickle.

My time, I trow, I should but lese
To write to thee of tragedies,
It is not meet for such a knave.
But now my process for to save,
Inordinate pride will have a fall.
Presumptuous pride is all thine hope:
God guard thee, Garnesche, from the rope!
Stop a tide, and be well ware
Ye be not caught in an hempen snare.
Harken thereto, ye Harvy Hafter,
Pride goeth before and shame cometh after.

Thou writest, I should let thee go play:
Go play thee, Garnesche, garnished gay.
I care not what thou write or say,
I cannot let thee the knave to play,
To dance the hay or run the ray: [1]
Thy fond face can me not fray!
Take this for that, bear this in mind,
Of thy lewdness more is behind;
A ream of paper will not hold
Of thy lewdness that may be told.
My study might be better spent;
But for to serve the king's intent,
His noble pleasure and commandment.
Scribble thou, scribble thou, rail or write,
Write what thou wilt, I shall thee requite!

By the King's most noble commandment.

[1] Names of dances.

MAGNIFICENCE

A Goodly Interlude and a Merry

These be the Names of the Players:

Felicity	Folly
Liberty	Adversity
Measure	Poverty
Magnificence	Despair
Fancy	Mischief
Counterfeit Countenance	Goodhope
Crafty Conveyance	Redress
Cloaked Collusion	Sad Circumspection
Courtly Abusion	Perseverance

Stage I. *Scene* I. PROSPERITY

Felicity. All thing is contrivéd by mannes reasón,
  The world environéd of high and low estate.
Be it early or late, wealth hath a seasón.
  Wealth is of wisdom the very true probate;
  A fool is he with wealth that falleth at debate:
But men nowadays so unhappily be uréd
That nothing than wealth may worse be enduréd.[1]

To tell you the cause meseemeth it no need.
  The amends thereof is far to call again;
For, when men buy wealth, they have little drede
  Of that may come after; experience true and plain,
  How after a drought there falleth a shower of rain,
And after a heat oft cometh a stormy cold.
A man may have wealth, but not, as he wold,

[1] Made to endure.

165

Aye to continue and still to endure.
  But if prudence be provéd with sad circumspectíon
Wealth might be wonné and made to the lure,
  If nobleness were acquainted with sober directíon;
  But will hath reason so under subjectíon,
And so disordereth this worldé over all,
That wealth and felicity is passing small.

But where wons wealth, an a man would weet?
For Wealthful Felicity truly is my name.

Stage 1.   Scene 2

Enter LIBERTY

Lib. Mary, Wealth and I was appointed to meet,
And either I am deceivéd, or ye be the same.
Fel. Sir, as ye say, I have heard of your fame;
Your name is Liberty, as I understand.
Lib. True you say, sir; give me your hand.
Fel. And from whence come ye, an it might be askéd?
Lib. To tell you, sir, I dare not, lest I should be maskéd
In a pair of fetters or a pair of stocks!
Fel. Hear you not how this gentleman mocks!
Lib. Yea, to knacking earnest what an it prove?
Fel. Why, to say what he will Liberty hath leave.
Lib. Yet Liberty hath been lockéd up and kept in the mew.
Fel. Indeed, sir, that liberty was not worth a cue!
Howbeit, Liberty may sometime be too large,
But if reason be regent and ruler of your barge.
Lib. To that ye say I can well condescend.
Show forth, I pray you, herein what you intend.
Fel. Of that I intend to make demonstratíon,
It asketh leisure with good advertence.
First, I say, we ought to have in consideratíon
That Liberty be linkéd with the chain of continence,
Liberty to let from all manner offence;

For Liberty at large is loth to be stoppéd,
But with continence your corage must be croppéd.

Lib. Then thus to you—
Fel.   Nay, suffer me yet further to say
And peradventure I shall content your mind.
Liberty, I wot well, forbear no man there may:
It is so sweet in all manner of kind.
Howbeit, Liberty maketh many a man blind;
By Liberty is done many a great excess;
Liberty at large will oft wax reckléss.
Perceive ye this parcel?
Lib. Yea, sir, passing well.
But an you would me permit
To show part of my wit,
Somewhat I could infer
Your conceit to debar,
Under supportatíon
Of patient toleratíon.
Fel. God forbid ye should be let
Your reasons forth to set;
Wherefore at liberty.
Say what ye will to me.
Lib. Briefly to touch of my purpose the effect:
Liberty is laudable and privilegéd from law;
Judicial rigour shall not me correct—
Fel. Soft, my friend; herein your reason is but raw.
Lib. Yet suffer me to say the surplus of my saw.
What weet ye whereupon I will conclude?
I say there is no wealth whereas Liberty is subdued.
I trow ye cannot say nay much to this:
To live under law it is captivity;
Where dread leadeth the dance, there is no joy nor bliss.
Or how can ye prove that there is felicity
An you have not your own free liberty
To sport at your pleasure, to run, and to ride?
Where Liberty is absent, set wealth aside.

Stage 1.   *Scene* 3

Enter MEASURE

Meas. Christ you assist in your altercatíon!
Fel. Why, have you heard of our disputatíon?
Meas. I perceive well how each of you doth reason.
Lib. Master Measure, you be come in good season.
Meas. And it is wonder that your wild insolence
Can be content with Measure's présence!

> *Fel.* Would it please you then—
> *Lib.* Us to inform and ken—
> *Meas.* Ah, ye be wondrous men!
> Your language is like the pen
> Of him that writeth too fast!
> *Fel.* Sir, if any word have passed
> Me, either first or last,
> To you I arect it, and cast
> Thereof the reformatíon.
> *Lib.* And I of the same fashíon;
> Howbeit, by protestatíon
> Displeasure that you none take;
> Some reason we must make.
> *Meas.* That will not I forsake,
> So it in measure be.
> Come off therefore, let see:
> Shall I begin, or ye?
> *Fel.* Nay, ye shall begin, by my will.
> *Lib.* It is reason and skill
> We your pleasure fulfil.
> *Meas.* Then ye must both consent
> You to hold content
> With my argument;
> And I must you require
> Me patiently to hear.
> *Fel.* Yes, sir, with right good cheer.
> *Lib.* With all my heart entire.

Meas. Horacius to record, in his volumès old,
  With every condition measure must be sought.
Wealth without measure would bear himself too bold;
  Liberty without measure prove a thing of nought.
  I ponder by number; by measure all thing is wrought,
As at the first original, by godly opinion:
Which proveth well that measure should have dominion.

Where measure is master, plenty doth none offence;
  Where measure lacketh, all thing disorderèd is;
Where measure is absent, riot keepeth residence;
  Where measure is ruler, there is nothing amiss.
  Measure is treasure. How say ye, is it not this?
Fel. Yes, questionless, in mine opinion,
Measure is worthy to have dominion.

Lib. Unto that same I am right well agreed,
  So that Liberty be not left behind.
Meas. Yea, Liberty with Measure need never drede.
  Lib. What, Liberty to Measure then would ye bind?
  Meas. What else? for otherwise it were against kind:
If Liberty should leap and runnè where he list
It were no virtue, it were a thing unblessed.

It were a mischief, if Liberty lackèd a rein
  Wherewith to rule him with the writhing of a wrest.[1]
All trebles and tenors be rulèd by a mean.
  Liberty without Measure is accounted for a beast;
  There is no surfeit where Measure ruleth the feast;
There is no excess where Measure hath his health:
Measure continueth prosperity and wealth.

Fel. Unto your rule I will annex my mind.
  Lib. So would I, but I would be loth,
That wont was to be foremost, now to come behind.
  It were a shame, to God I make an oath,
  Without I might cut it out of the broadè cloth,

[1] As on a harp.

As I was wont ever at my free will.
Meas. But have ye not heard say, that will is no skill?

Take sad direction, and leave this wantonness.
  Lib. It is no mastery!
  Fel.   Tush, let Measure proceed,
And after his mind hardely yourself address;
  For, without Measure, Poverty and Need
  Will creep upon us, and us to Mischief lead:
For Mischief will master us if Measure us forsake.
Lib. Well, I am content your ways to take.

Meas. Surely I am joyous that ye be minded thus.
  Magnificence to maintain your promotion shall be.
Fel. So in his heart he may be glad of us.
  Lib. There is no prince but he hath need of us three:
  Wealth with Measure, and pleasant Liberty.
Meas. Now pleaseth you a little while to stand;
Meseemeth Magnificence is coming here at hand.

Stage 1.   Scene 4

Enter MAGNIFICENCE

Magn. To assure you of my noble port and fame,
  Who list to know, Magnificence I hight.
But Measure, my friend, what hight this mannès name?
  Meas. Sir, though ye be a noble prince of might,
  Yet in this man you must set your delight.
And, sir, this other man's name is Liberty.
Magn. Welcome, friends, ye are both unto me.

But now let me know of your conversation.
  Fel. Pleaseth your Grace, Felicity they me call.
Lib. And I am Liberty, made of in every nation.
  Magn. Convenient persons for any prince royall.
  Wealth with Liberty, with me both dwell ye shall,
To the guiding of my Measure you both committing,
That Measure be master, us seemeth it is fitting.

Meas. Whereas ye have, sir, to me them assignéd,
   Such order I trust with them for to take
That Wealth with Measure shall be combinéd,
   And Liberty his large with Measure shall make.
   Fel. Your ordinance, sir, I will not forsake.
Lib. And I myself wholly to you will incline.
Magn. Then may I say that ye be servantés mine,

For by Measure, I warn you, we think to be guided.
   Wherein it is necessary my pleasure you know:
Measure and I will never be divided,
   For no discord that any man can sow;
   For Measure is a mean, neither too high nor too low,
In whose attemperance I have such delight
That Measure shall never departé from my sight.

Fel. Laudable your conceit is to be accounted,
   For Wealth without Measure suddenly will slide.
Lib. As your Grace full nobly hath recounted,
   Measure with nobleness should be allied.
   Magn. Then, Liberty, see that Measure be your guide,
For I will use you by this advertísement.
Fel. Then shall you have with you prosperity resident.

Meas. I trow Good Fortune hath annexéd us together,
   To see how 'greeable we are of one mind;
There is no flatterer, nor losel so lither,
   This linkéd chain of love that can unbind.
   Now that ye have me chief ruler assigned,
I will endeavour me to order every thing
Your nobleness and honour concerníng.

Lib. In joy and mirth your mind shall be enlargéd,
   And not embracéd with pusillanimity:
But plenarly all thought from you must be dischargéd,
   If ye list to live after your free Libertý.
   All delectations acquainted is with me.
By me all persons worké what they list.
Meas. Hem, sir, yet beware of 'Had I wist!'
   *G

Liberty in some cause becometh a gentle mind,
  By cause course of Measure, if I be in the way:
Who counteth without me is cast too far behind
  Of his reckoning, as evidently we may
  See at our eye the worldė day by day.
For default of Measure all thingė doth exceed.
Fel. All that ye say is as true as the Creed.

For howbeit, Liberty to Wealth is convenient,
  And from Felicity may not be forborne,
Yet Measure hath been so long from us absént
  That all men laugh at Liberty to scorn.
  Wealth and wit, I say, be so threadbare worn
That all is without Measure and far beyond the moon.
Magn. Then nobleness, I see well, is almost undone,

But if thereof the sooner amends be made;
  For doubtless I perceive my magnificence
Without Measure lightly may fade,
  Of too much liberty under the offence:
  Wherefore, Measure, take Liberty with you hence,
And rule him after the rule of your school.
Lib. What, sir, would ye make me a popping fool?[1]

Meas. Why, were not yourself agreéd to the same,
  And now would ye swerve from your own ordinance?
Lib. I would be ruléd, an I might for shame!
  Fel. Ah, ye make me laugh at your inconstance!
  Magn. Sir, without any longer dalliance,
Take Liberty to rule, and follow mine intent.
Meas. It shall be done at your commandėment.
                              [*Exit* MEASURE *with* LIBERTY.

Stage 1. Scene 5

Magn. It is a wanton thing, this Libertý!
  Perceive you not how loth he was to abide

---

[1] i.e. like a parrot.

The rule of Measure, notwithstanding we
　　Have deputed Measure him to guide?
　　By measure each thing duly is tried.
Think you not thus, my friend Felicity?
Fel. God forbid that it otherwise should be!

Magn. Ye could not else, I wot, with me endure.
　　Fel. Endure? No, God wot, it were great pain!
But if I were orderéd by just measure
　　It were not possible me long to retain.

Stage 1. Scene 6

Enter FANCY

Fan. Tush, hold your peace, your language is vain.
Please it, your Grace, to take no disdain,
To shew you plainly the truth as I think.
Magn. Here is none forseth whether you float or sink!
Fel. From whence come you, sir, that no man lookéd after?
　　Magn. Or who made you so bold to interrupt my tale?
Fan. Now, *benedicite*, ye ween I were some hafter,
　　Or else some jangling Jack of the Vale;
　　Ye ween that I am drunken, because I look pale.
Magn. Meseemeth that ye have drunken more than ye have
　　bled.
Fan. Yet among noblemen I was brought up and bred.

Fel. Now leave this jangling and to us expound
　　Why that ye said our language was in vain.
Fan. Mary, upon truth my reason I ground,
　　That without Largesse nobleness cannot reign:
　　And that I said once yet I say again.
I say, without Largesse worship hath no place,
For Largesse is a purchaser of pardon and of grace.

Magn. Now, I beseech thee, tell me what is thy name?
　　Fan. Largesse, that all lords should love, sir, I hight.
Fel. But hight you Largesse, increase of noble fame?
　　Fan. Yea, sir, undoubted.

Fel.   Then of very right
  With Magnificence, this noble prince of might,
Should be your dwelling, in my consideration.
Magn. Yet we will therein take good deliberation.

Fan. As in that, I will not be against your pleasure.
  Fel. Sir, hardely remember what may your name advance.
Magn. Largesse is laudable, so it be in measure.
  Fan. Largesse is he that all princes doth advance.
  I report me herein to King Lewis of France.[1]
Fel. Why have ye him named and all other refused?
Fan. For, sith he died, Largesse was little used.

Pluck up your mind, sir; what ailé you to muse?
  Have ye not Wealth here at your will?
It is but a madding, these ways that ye use:
  What availeth Lordship, yourself for to kill
  With care and with thought how Jack shall have Gill?
Magn. What? I have espied ye are a careless page.
Fan. By God, sir, ye see but few wise men of mine age!

But Covertise hath blowen you so full of wind
  That *colica passio* hath gropéd you by the guts.
Fel. In faith, Brother Largesse, you have a merry mind!
  Fan. In faith, I set not by the world two Doncaster cuts!
  Magn. Ye want but a wild flying bolt to shoot at the butts!
Though Largesse ye hight, your language is too large:
For which end goeth forward ye take little charge!

Fel. Let see, this checké if ye voidé can.
  Fan. In faith, else had I gone too long to school,
But if I could know a goosé from a swan!
  Magn. Well, wise men may eat the fish when ye shall
    draw the pole!
  Fan. In faith, I will not say that ye shall prove a fool,
But oft time have I seen wise men do mad deeds.
Magn. Go! shake thee, dog! hey, sith ye will needs!

                    [1] Louis XII.

You are nothing meet with us for to dwell,
 That with your lord and master so pertly can prate:
Get you hence, I say, by my counsell;
 I will not use you to play with me checkmate.
 Fan. Sir, if I have offended your noble estate,
I trow I have brought you such writing of recórd
That I shall have you againé my good lord.

To you recommendeth Sad Circumspectíon,
 And sendeth you this writing closéd under seal.
Magn. This writing is welcome with hearty affectíon.
 Why kept you it thus long? How doth he? Weel?
 Fan. Sir, thankéd be God, he hath his heal.
Magn. Wealth, get you home, and commend me to Measúre;
Bid him take good heed to you, my singular treasure.

Fel. Is there anything else your Grace will commandé me?
 Magn. Nothing but fare you well till soon;
And that he take good keep to Libertý.
 Fel. Your pleasure, sir, shortly shall be done.
 Magn. I shall come to you myself, I trow, this afternoon.
            [*Exit* FELICITY.

I pray you, Largesse, here to remain
Whilest I know what this letter doth contain.

Stage 1. Scene 7

As MAGNIFICENCE *is reading the letter,* COUNTERFEIT
COUNTENANCE *comes in on tiptoe, humming to himself, but,
seeing* MAGNIFICENCE, *withdraws quietly; then, a little later,
he comes back again, hailing* FANCY *from a safe distance.*
FANCY *motions him to keep quiet.*

   C. Count. What! Fancy, Fancy!
   Magn. Who is that that thus did cry?
   Methought he calléd Fancy.
   Fan. It was a Fleming hight Hansy.

Magn. Methought he calléd Fancy me behind.
Fan. Nay, sir, it was nothing but your mind.
But now, sir, as touching this letter—
Magn. I shall look in it at leisure better:
And surely ye are to him behold,
And for his sake right gladly I wold
Do what I could to do you good.
Fan. I pray God keep you in that mood!
Magn. This letter was written far hence.
Fan. By lakin,[1] sir, it hathé cost me pence
And groats many one, ere I came to your presénce!
Magn. Where was it deliveréd you, shew unto me.
Fan. By God, sir, beyond the sea.
Magn. At what place now, as you guess?
Fan. By my troth, sir, at Pontesse:[2]
This writing was taken me there,
But never was I in greater fear.
Magn. How so?
Fan.   By God, at the sea side,
Had I not openéd by pursé wide
I trow, by Our Lady, I had been slain,
Or else I had lost mine earés twain.
Magn. By your sooth?
Fan. Yea, and there is such a watch
That no man can 'scape but they him catch.
They bare me in hand that I was a spy,
And another bade put out mine eye,
Another would mine eye was bleared,
Another bade shave half my beard;
And boys to the pillory 'gan me pluck,
And would have made me Friar Tuck,
To preach out of the pillory hole
Without an anthem or a stole;
And some bade 'Sear him with a mark!'
To get me fro them I had much wark.
Magn. Mary, sir, ye were afrayed!

[1] Ladykin (Our Lady).
[2] Pontoise.

Fan. By my troth, had I not paid and prayed,
And made largesse, as I hight,
I had not been here with you this night;
But surely largesse savéd my life,
For largesse stinteth all manner of strife.
Magn. It doth so, sure, now and then;
But largesse is not meet for every man.
Fan. No, but for you great estates.
Largesse stinteth great debates,
And he that I came fro to this place
Said I was meet for your Grace.
And indeed, sir, I hear men talk
By the way, as I ride and walk,
Say how you exceed in nobleness
If you had with you Largesse.
Magn. And say they so in very deed?
Fan. With yea, sir, so God me speed.
Magn. Yet Measure is a merry mean.
Fan. Yea, sir, a blanchéd almond is no bean!
Measure is meet for a merchant's hall,
But Largesse becometh a state royall.
What, should you pinch at a peck of oats,
Ye would soon pinch at a peck of groats!
Thus is the talking of one and of other,
As men dare speak it hugger-mugger:
A lord, a niggard, it is a shame!
But Largesse may amend your name.
Magn. In faith, Largesse, welcome to me.
Fan. I pray you, sir, I may so be,
And of my service you shall not miss.
Magn. Together we will talk more of this:
Let us depart from hence home to my place.
Fan. I follow even after your noble Grace.

[*Exit* MAGNIFICENCE. COUNTERFEIT COUNTENANCE,
entering, detains FANCY.

C. *Count.* What, I say, hark a word!
Fan. Do away, I say, the devil's turd!

C. Count. Yea, but how long shall I here await?
Fan. By God's body, I come straight!
  I hate this blundering that thou dost make.
                                        [*Exit.*
C. Count. Now, to the devil I thee betake,
For in faith ye be well met!

Stage 2.   Scene 8.   CONSPIRACY

COUNTERFEIT COUNTENANCE *alone in the place*

C. Count. Fancy hath catchéd in a fly-net
This noble man Magnificence,
Of Largesse under the pretence.
They have made me here to put the stone:
But now will I, that they be gone,
In bastard rhyme, after the doggerel guise,
Tell you whereof my name doth rise.

For Counterfeit Countenance known am I,
This world is full of my folly.
I set not by him a fly
That cannot counterfeit a lie,
Swear, and stare, and bide thereby,
And countenance it cleanly,
And defend it mannerly.

A knave will counterfeit now a knight,
A lurdain like a lord to flyte,
A minstrel like a man of might,
A tapster like a lady bright:
Thus make I them with thrift to fight,
Thus at the last I bring him right
To Tyburn, where they hang on hight.

To counterfeit I can by pretty ways:
Of nightés to occupy counterfeit keys,
Cleanly to counterfeit new arrays,
Counterfeit earnest by way of plays:

Thus am I occupiéd at all essays.
Whatsoever I do, all men me praise,
And mickle am I made of nowadays.

Counterfeit matters in the law of the land,
With gold and groats they grease my hand
Instead of right that wrong may stand,
And counterfeit freedom that is bound;
I counterfeit sugar that is but found;
Counterfeit captains by me are manned;
Of all lewdnéss I kindle the brand;

Counterfeit kindness, and think deceit;
Counterfeit letters by the way of sleight;
Subtily using counterfeit weight;
Counterfeit language, *fait bon geyt*.[1]
Counterfeit is a proper bait;
A count to counterfeit in a receipt,—
To counterfeit well is a good conceit.

Counterfeit maidenhood may well be born,
But counterfeit coins is laughing to scorn;
It is evil patching of that is torn,
When the nap is rough, it would be shorn;
Counterfeit halting without a thorn,
Yet counterfeit chaffer is but evil corn;
All thing is worse when it is worn.

What would ye, wives, counterfeit
The courtly guise of the newé jet?
An oldé barn would be underset:
It is much worth that is far-fet.
What, wanton, wanton, now well ymet!
What, Margery Milk Duck, marmoset!
It would be maskéd in my net;

[1] i.e. *geste*—makes a good story.

It would be nice, though I say nay;
By Crede, it would have fresh array,
And therefore shall my husband pay;
To counterfeit she will essay
All the newe guise, fresh and gay,
And be as pretty as she may,
And jet it jolly as a jay.

Counterfeit preaching, and believe the contrary;
Counterfeit conscience, peevish pope holy;
Counterfeit sadness, with dealing full madly;
Counterfeit holiness is calléd hypocrisy;
Counterfeit reason is not worth a fly;
Counterfeit wisdom, and works of folly;
Counterfeit countenance every man doth occupy.

Counterfeit worship outward men may see;
Riches rideth out, at home is poverty;
Counterfeit pleasure is borne out by me.
Coll would go cleanly, and it will not be,
And Annot would be nice, and laughs 'Tehe wehe!'
Your counterfeit countenance is all of necessitý,
A pluméd partridge all ready to fly.

A knuckleboneyard will counterfeit a clerk,
He would trot gently, but he is too stark,
At his cloakéd counterfeiting dogs doth bark;
A carter a courtier, it is a worthy wark,
That with his whip his mares was wont to yark;
A coistrel to drive the devil out of the dark,
A counterfeit courtier with a knavès mark.

To counterfeit thus friars have learnéd me;
Thus nunnès now and then, an it might be,
Would take in the way of counterfeit charity
The grace of God under *benedicite*;
To counterfeit their counsel they give me a fee;
Canons cannot counterfeit but upon three,
Monkès may not for dread that men should them see.

Stage 2.   Scene 9

Enter FANCY, *talking excitedly to* CRAFTY CONVEYANCE

Cr. Con. What, Counterfeit Countenance!

C. Count. What, Crafty Conveyance!

Fan. What, the devil, are ye two of acquaintance?
God give you a very mischance!

Cr. Coun. Yes, yes, sir, he and I have met.

C. Count. We have been together both early and late.
But, Fancy, my friend, where have ye been so long?

Fan. By God, I have been about a pretty prong;
Crafty Conveyance, I should say, and I.

Cr. Con. By God, we have made Magnificence to eat a fly!

C. Count. How could ye do that, an I was away?

Fan. By God, man, both his pageant and thine he can play.

C. Count. Say truth?

Cr. Con.   Yes, yes, by lakin, I shall thee warrant,
As long as I live, thou hast an heir apparent.

Fan. Yet have we pickéd out a room for thee.

C. Count. Why, shall we dwell together all three?

Cr. Con. Why, man, it were too great a wonder
That we three gallants should be long asunder.

C. Count. For Cock's heart, give me thy hand!

Fan. By the mass, for ye are able to destroy an whole land!

Cr. Con. By God, yet it must begin much of thee.

Fan. Who that is ruled by us it shall be long ere he three.

C. Count. But, I say, keepest thou the old name still that
thou had?

Cr. Con. Why, wendest thou, whoreson, that I were so mad?

Fan. Nay, nay, he hath changéd his, and I have changéd
mine.

C. Count. Now, what is his name, and what is thine?

Fan. In faith, Largesse I hight.
And I am made a knight.

C. Count. A rebellion against nature,
So large a man, and so little of stature!
But, sir, how counterfeited ye?

Cr. Con. Sure Surveyance I naméd me.

C. Count. Surveyance! where ye survey
Thrift hath lost her coffer-key!
Fan. But is it not well? how thinkest thou?
C. Count. Yes, sir, I give God a vow,
Myself could not counterfeit it better.
But what became of the letter
That I counterfeited you underneath a shrowd?
Fan. By the mass, oddly well allowed.
Cr. Con. By God, had not I it conveyéd
Fancy had been deceivéd.
C. Count. I wot, thou art false enough for one!
Fan. By my troth, we had been gone.—
And yet, in faith, man, we lackéd thee
For to speak with Liberty.
C. Count. What is Largesse without Liberty?
Cr. Con. By Measure masteréd yet is he.
C. Count. What, is your conveyance no better?
Fan. In faith, Measure is like a tetter
That overgroweth a mannès face,
So he ruleth over all our place.
Cr. Con. Now therefore, whilst we are together,—
Counterfeit Countenance, nay, come hither,—
I say, whilst we are together in same—
C. Count. Tush, a straw, it is a shame
That we can no better than so.
Fan. We will remedy it, man, ere we go:
For, like as mustard is sharp of taste,
Right so a sharp fancy must be found
Wherewith Measure to confound.
Cr. Con. Can you a remedy for a tisic,
That sheweth yourself thus sped in physic?
C. Count. It is a gentle reason of a rake!
Fan. For all these japes yet that ye make—
Cr. Con. Your fancy maketh mine elbow to ache!
Fan. Let see, find you a better way.
C. Count. Take no displeasure of what we say.
Cr. Con. Nay, an you be angry and overthwart,
A man may beshrew your angry heart.

Fan. Tush, a straw, I thought none ill.
C. Count. What, shall we jangle thus all the day still?
Cr. Con. Nay, let us our heads together cast.
Fan. Yea, and see how it may be compássed
That Measure were cast out of the doors.
C. Count. Alas, where is my boots and my spurs?
Cr. Con. In all this haste whither will ye ride?
C. Count. I trow, it shall not need to abide.
Cock's wounds, see, sirs, see, see!

Stage 2. Scene 10

Enter CLOAKÉD COLLUSION, *pacing up and down*
with a lofty air

Fan. Cock's arms, what is he?
Cr. Con. By Cock's heart, he looketh high!
He hawketh, methink, for a butterfly.
C. Count. Now, by Cock's heart, well abidden,
For, had you not come, I had ridden.
Cl. Col. Thy words be but wind, never they have no weight;
Thou hast made me play the jurde hayt.
C. Count. And if ye knew how I have muséd
I am sure ye would have me excuséd.
Cl. Col. I say, come hither: what are these twain?
C. Count. By God, sir, this is Fancy small brain,
And Crafty Conveyance, know you not him?
Cl. Col. 'Know him, sir!' quod he: yes, by Saint Sim!
Here is a leash of ratches to run a hare:[1]
Woe is that purse that ye shall share!
Fan. What call ye him—this?
Cr. Con. I trow what he is—
C. Count. Tush, hold your peace.
See you not how they press
For to know your name?
Cl. Col. Know they not me, they are to blame.
Know you not me, sirs?

[1] i.e. The rache or ratch hunted by scent and was useless against
hares.

Fan. No, indeed.

Cr. Con. Abide, let me see, take better heed;
Cock's heart, it is Cloakéd Collusíon!

Cl. Col. Ay, sir, I pray God give you confusíon!

Fan. Cock's arms, is that your name?

C. Count. Yea, by the mass, this is even the same,
That all this matter must undergrope.

Cr. Con. What is this he weareth—a cope?

Cl. Col. Cap, sir! I say you be too bold.

Fan. See how he is wrappéd for the cold:
Is it not a vestment?

Cl. Col.   Ah, ye want a rope!

C. Count. Tush, it is Sir John Double-Cloak.

Fan. Sir, an if you would not be wroth—

Cl. Col. What sayest?

Fan.   Here was too little cloth!

Cl. Col. Ah, Fancy, Fancy, God send thee brain!

Fan. Yea, for your wit is cloakéd for the rain.

Cr. Con. Nay, let us not chatter thus still.

Cl. Col. Tell me, sirs, what is your will.

C. Count. Sir, it is so that these twain
With Magnificence in household do remain,
And there they woulde have me to dwell,
But I will be ruléd after your counsell.

Fan. Mary, so will we alsó.

Cl. Col. But tell me whereabout ye go.

C. Count. By God, we would get us all thither—
Spell the remnant, and do together.[1]

Cl. Col. Hath Magnificence any treasure?

Cr. Con. Yea, but he spendeth it all in measure.

Cl. Col. Why, dwelleth Measure where ye two dwell?
In faith, he were better to dwell in hell!

Fan. Yet where we won, now there wonneth he.

Cl. Col. And have you not among you Libertý.

C. Count. Yea, but he is in captivity.

Cl. Col. What the devil! how may that be?

C. Count. I cannot tell you: why ask you me?

[1] i.e. put it together.

Ask these two that there doth dwell.
Cl. Col. Sir, the plainness you me tell.
Cr. Con. There dwelleth a master man called Measure—
Fan. Yea, and he hath rule of all his treasure.
Cr. Con. Nay, either let me tell, or else tell ye.
Fan. I care not, I, tell on for me.
C. Count. I pray God let you never to three!
Cl. Col. What the devil aileth you? can you not agree?
Cr. Con. I will pass over the circumstance
And shortly shew you the whole substance.
Fancy and I, we twain,
With Magnificence in household do remain,
And counterfeited our names we have
Craftily all things upright to save,
His name Largesse, Surveyance mine.
Magnificence to us beginneth to incline
Counterfeit Countenance to have alsó,
And would that we should for him go.
C. Count. But shall I have mine old name still?
Cr. Con. Peace, I have not yet said what I will.
Fan. Here is a 'pistle of a postic!
Cl. Col. Tush, fonnish Fancy, thou art frantic!
Tell on, sir—how then?
Cr. Con. Mary, sir, he told us when
We had him found we should him bring,
And that we failéd not for nothing.
Cl. Col. All this ye may easily bring about.
Fan. Mary, the better an Measure were out.
Cl. Col. Why, can ye not put out that foul freke?
Cr. Con. No, in every corner he will peke,
So that we have no libertý,
Nor no man in court but he,
For Liberty he hath in guiding.
C. Count. In faith, and without Liberty there is no biding.
Fan. In faith, and Liberty's room is there but small.
Cl. Col. Hem! that like I nothing at all.
Cr. Con. But, Counterfeit Countenance, go we together,
All three, I say.

C. Count. Shall I go? whither?

Cr. Con. To Magnificence with us twain,
And in his service thee to retain.

C. Count. But then, sir, what shall I hight?

Cr. Con. Ye and I talkéd thereof to-night.

Fan. Yea, my fancy was out of owl-flight,
For it is out of my mindé quite.

Cr. Con. And now it cometh to my remembrance.
Sir, ye shall hight Good Demeanance.

C. Count. By the arms of Calais, well conceivéd!

Cr. Con. When we have him thither conveyéd,
What an I frame such a sleight
That Fancy with his fond conceit
Put Magnificence in such a madness
That he shall have you in the stead of sadness,
And Sober Sadness shall be your name!

Cl. Col. By Cock's body, here beginneth the game!
For then shall we so craftily carry
That Measure shall not there long tarry.

Fan. For Cock's heart, tarry whilst that I come again.

Cr. Con. We will see you shortly one of us twain.

C. Count. Now let us go, an we shall, then.

Cl. Col. Now let see quit you like pretty men.

[*Exeunt* FANCY, CRAFTY CONVEYANCE, *and*
COUNTERFEIT COUNTENANCE.

Stage 2. *Scene* 11

Here CLOAKÉD COLLUSION *promenades*

Cl. Col. To pass the time and order while a man may talk
Of one thing and other to occupy the place;
Then for the season that I here shall walk,
As good to be occupied as up and down to trace
And do nothing. Howbeit, full little grace
There cometh and groweth of my coming,
For Cloakéd Collusíon is a perilous thing.

Double dealing and I be all one,
  Crafting and hafting contrivéd is by me;
I can dissemble, I can both laugh and groan,
  Plain dealing and I can never agree:
  But divisíon, dissensíon, derisíon, these three
And I am counterfeit of one mindė and thought,
By the means of mischief to bring all thingė to nought.

And though I be so odious a guest,
  And every man gladly my company would refuse,
In faith yet am I occupiéd with the best:
  Full few that can themselves of me excuse.
  When other men laugh, then study I and muse,
Devisingė the meanės and ways that I can,
How I may hurtė and hinder every man.

Two faces in a hood covertly I bear,
  Water in the one hand, and fire in the other;
I can feed forth a fool, and lead him by the ear:
  Falsehood-in-Fellowship is my sworn brother.
  By Cloakéd Collusíon, I say, and none other,
Cumberance and trouble in England first began:
From that lord to that lord I rode and I ran,

And flattered them with fables fair before their face,
  And told all the mischief I could behind their back,
And made as I had knowen nothing of the case.
  I would begin all mischief, but I would bear no lack.
  Thus can I learn you, sirs, to bear the devil's sack.
And yet, I trow, some of you be better sped than I
Friendship to feign, and think full litherý.

Paint to a purpose good countenance I can,
  And craftily can I grope how every man is minded;
My purpose is to spy and to pointė every man;
  My tongue is with favell forkéd and tinéd:
  By Cloakéd Collusíon thus many one is beguiléd.
Each man to hinder I gape and I gaspė:
My speech is all pleasure, but I sting like a waspė.

I am never glad but when I may do ill,
   And never am I sorry but when that I see
I cannot mine appetite accomplish and fulfil
   In hinderance of wealth and prosperity.
   I laugh at all shrewdness, and lie at liberty.
I muster, I meddle among these great estates
I sow seditious seeds of discord and debates.

To flatter and to fleerė is all my pretence
   Among all such persons as I well understand
Be light of belief and hasty of credénce;
   I make them to startle and sparkle like a brand,
   I move them, I maze them, I make them so fond
That they will hear no man but the first tale:
And so by these meanės I brewé much bale.

Stage 2.   Scene 12

Enter COURTLY ABUSION, *singing*

Court. Ab. Huffa, huffa, tanderum, tanderum, tain, huffa, huffa!

Cl. Col. This was properly prated, sirs! what said a?

Court. Ab. Rutty bully, jolly rutterkin, heyda!

Cl. Col. De que pays êtes vous?
                     [*With an ironical air he makes as if to doff his hat.*

Court. Ab. Deck your hoftė and cover a louse.

Cl. Col. Say vous[1] *chanter, 'Ventre très douce'?*

Court. Ab. Oui-da, oui-da.

How sayest thou, man, am not I a jolly rutter?

Cl. Col. Give this gentleman room, sirs, stand utter!

By God, sir, what need all this waste?

What is this, a beetle, or a bateau, or a buskin laced?

Court. Ab. What, wendest thou that I know thee not,
      Cloakéd Collusion?

[1] i.e. *savez-vous.*

Cl. Col. And wendest thou that I know not thee, cankered
  Abusion?

Court. Ab. Cankered Jack Hare! look thou be not rusty,
For thou shalt well know I am neither dirty nor dusty!

Cl. Col. Dusty! nay, sir, ye be all of the lusty,
Howbeit of scape-thrift your cloak smelleth musty.
But whither art thou walking, in faith unfeignéd?

Court. Ab. Mary, with Magnificence I would be retainéd.

Cl. Col. By the mass, for the court thou art a meet man:
Thy slippers they swop it, yet thou footest it like a swan.

Court. Ab. Yea, so I can devise my gear after the courtly
  manner.

Cl. Col. So thou art personable to bear a prince's banner.

Court. Ab. By God's foot, and I dare well fight, for I will
  not start.

Cl. Col. Nay, thou art a man good enough—but for thy
  false heart.

Court. Ab. Well, an I be a coward, there is more than I.

Cl. Col. Yea, in faith a bold man and a hardy:
A bold man in a bowl of new ale in corns!

Court. Ab. Will ye see this gentleman is all in his scorns?

Cl. Col. But are ye not advised to dwell where ye spake?

Court. Ab. I am of few wordes, I love not to bark.
Bearest thou any room, [1] or canst thou do ought?
Canst thou help in favour that I might be brought?

Cl. Col. I may do somewhat, and more I thinke shall.

Stage 2. Scene 13

Enter CRAFTY CONVEYING, *pointing with his finger*

Cr. Con. Hem, Collusion!

Court. Ab. By Cock's heart, who is yonder that for thee
  doth call?

Cr. Con. Nay, come at once, for the armes of the dice!

Court. Ab. Cock's arms, he hath callèd for thee twice!

    [1] Do you hold any office?

Cl. Col. By Cock's heart, and call shall again:
To come to me, I trow, he shall be fain.

Court. Ab. What, is thy heart prickéd with such a proud pin?

Cl. Col. Tush, he that hath need, man, let him run.

Cr. Con. Nay, come away, man: thou playest the kaiser.

Cl. Col. By the mass, thou shalt bide my leisure.

Cr. Con. 'Abide, sir,' quod he! Mary, so I do.

Court. Ab. He will come, man, when he may tend to.

Cr. Con. What the devil, who sent for thee?

Cl. Col. Here he is now, man; mayest thou not see?

Cr. Con. What the devil, man, what thou meanest?
Art thou so angry as thou seemest?

Court. Ab. What the devil, can ye agree no better?

Cr. Con. What the devil, where had we this jolly jetter?

Cl. Col. What sayest thou, man? why dost thou not supplie,
And desire me thy good master to be?

Court. Ab. Speakest thou to me?

Cl. Col. Yea, so I tell thee.

Court. Ab. Cock's bones, I ne tell can
Which of you is the better man,
Or which of you can do most.

Cr. Con. In faith, I rule much of the roast.

Cl. Col. Rule the roast! thou wouldest, ye?
As scant thou had no need of me.

Cr. Con. Need! yes, Mary, I say not nay.

Court. Ab. Cock's heart, I trow thou wilt make a fray!

Cr. Con. Nay, in good faith, it is but the guise.

Cl. Col. No, for ere we strike, we will be adv/ séd twice.

Court. Ab. What the devil, use ye not to draw no swords?

Cr. Con. No, by my troth, but crake greaté words.

Court. Ab. Why, is this the guise now-a-days?

Cl. Col. Yea, for surety—oft peace is taken for frays.
But, sir, I will have this man with me.

Cr. Con. Convey yourself first, let see.

Cl. Col. Well, tarry here till I for you send.

Cr. Con. Why, shall he be of your band?

Cl. Col. Tarry here: wot ye what I say?

Court. Ab. I warrant you, I will not go away.

Cr. Con. By Saint Mary, he is a tallè man.
Cl. Col. Yea, and do right good service he can.
I know in him no defaut,
But that the whoreson is proud and haut.

[*Exeunt* CLOAKÈD COLLUSION *and* CRAFTY CONVEYANCE.

Court. Ab. Nay, purchase ye a pardon for the pose,
For pride hath plucked thee by the nose,
As well as me.   I would, an I durst—
But now I will not say the worst.

Stage 2.   Scene 14

COURTLY ABUSION *alone in the place*

Court. Ab. What now, let see,
          Who looketh on me
     Well round about,
          How gay and how stout
     That I can wear
     Courtly my gear.

     My hair brusheth
          So pleasantly,
     My robe rusheth
          So ruttingly,
          Meseem I fly,
     I am so light
     To dance delight.

     Properly dressed,
          All point-device,
     My person prest,
          Beyond all size
          Of the newè guise,
     To rush it out
     In every rout.

Beyond measúre
    My sleeve is wide,
All of pleasúre
    My hose strait tied,
    My buskin wide
Rich to behold,
Glittering in gold.

Abusíon,
    Forsooth, I hight;
Confusíon
    Shall on him light,
    By day or by night,
That useth me:
He cannot three.

A very fon,
    A very ass,
Will take upon
    To compáss
    That never was
Abuséd before;
A very pore

That so will do,
    He doth abuse
Himself too too,
    He doth misuse
    Each man, take a fee
To crake and prate:
I befool his pate.

This new fon jet
    From out of France
First I did set,
    Made purveyance
    And such ordinance
That all men it found
Throughout England.

All this nation
   I set on fire
In my fashion,
   This their desire,
   This new attire:
This ladies have,
   I it them gave.

Spare for no cost:
   And yet indeed
It is cost lost,
   Much more than need
   For to exceed
In such array:
Howbeit, I say,

A churlés son,
   Brought up of nought,
With me will won
   Whilst he hath ought:
   He will have wrought
His gown so wide
That he may hide

His dame and his sire
   Within his sleeve;
Spend all his hire
   That men him give.
   Wherefore I preve
A Tyburn check
Shall break his neck.

Enter FANCY

Fan. Stow, stow!
Court. Ab. All is out of harre, [1]
   And out of trace,
   Aye warre and warre [2]
   In every place.

[1] Out of joint, lit. unhinged.
[2] Worse and worse.

Stage 2. *Scene* 15

But what the devil art thou,
That criest 'Stow stow!'?

Fan. What, whom have we here—Jenkin Jolly?
Now welcome, by the God holy!

Court. Ab. What, Fancy, friend! how dost thou fare?

Fan. By Christ, as merry as a March hare!

Court. Ab. What the devil hast thou on thy fist—an owl?

Fan. Nay, it is a farly fowl.

Court. Ab. Methink she frowneth and looketh sour.

Fan. Turd, man, it is an hawk of the tower; [1]
She is made for the mallard fat.

Court. Ab. Methink she is well-beaked to catch a rat.
But now what tidings can you tell, let see.

Fan. Mary, I am come for thee.

Court. Ab. For me?

Fan. Yea, for thee, so I say.

Court. Ab. How so? tell me, I thee pray.

Fan. Why, heard you not of the fray
That fell among us this same day?

Court. Ab. No, mary, not yet.

Fan. What the devil, never a whit?

Court. Ab. No, by the mass; what should I swear?

Fan. In faith, Liberty is now a lusty spere.

Court. Ab. Why, under whom was he abiding?

Fan. Mary, Measure had him a while in guiding,
Till, as the devil would, they fell a-chiding
With Crafty Conveyance.

Court. Ab.   Yea, did they so?

Fan. Yea, by God's sacrament, and with other mo.

Court. Ab. What needed that, in the devil's date?

Fan. Yes, yes, he fell with me alsó at debate.

Court. Ab. With thee alsó? what, he playeth the state?

Fan. Yea, but I bade him pick out of the gate,
By God's body, so did I!

Court. Ab. By the mass, well done, and boldlý!

[1] High-flying or towering hawks.

Fan. Hold thy peace, Measure shall from us walk.
Court. Ab. Why, is he crosséd then with a chalk?
Fan. Crossed! yea, checked out of conceit.
Court. Ab. How so?
Fan.   By God, by a pretty sleight,
As hereafter thou shalt knowė more.
But I must tarry here, go thou before.
Court. Ab. With whom shall I there meet?
Fan. Crafty Conveyance standeth in the street,
Even of purpose for the same.
Court. Ab. Yea, but what shall I call my name?
Fan. Cock's heart, turn thee, let me see thine array.
Cock's bones, this is all of John de Gay!
Court. Ab. So I am 'pointed after my conceit.
Fan. Mary, thou jettest it of height!
Court. Ab. Yea, but of my name let us be wise.
Fan. Mary, Lusty Pleasure, by mine advice,
To name thyself.   Come off, it were done!
Court. Ab. Farewell, my friend.
Fan.   Adieu, till soon.

[*Exit* COURTLY ABUSION.

Stage 2.   *Scene* 16

FANCY *alone in the place*

Fan. Stow, birdė, stow, stow!
It is best I feed my hawkė now.
There is many evil favouréd, an thou be foul.
Each thing is fair when it is young.   All hail, owl!

Lo, this is
My fancy ywis:
Now Christ it blessė̇
It is, by Jesse,

H

A bird full sweet,
For me full meet:
She is furred for the heat
All to the feet;

Her browês bent,
Her eyen glent:
From Tyne to Trent,
From Stroud to Kent,

A man shall find
Many of her kind.
How standeth the wind—
Before or behind?

Barbéd like a nun,
For burning of the sun;
Her feathers dun,
Well-favoured, bonne!

Now, let me see about
In all this rout
If I can find out
So seemly a snout

Among this press:
Even a whole mess—
Peace, man, peace!
I rede we cease.

So farly fair as it looks,
And her beak so comely crooks,
Her nailês sharp as tenter-hooks!
I have not kept her yet three wooks.

And how still she doth sit!
Tewit, tewit! Where is my wit?
The devil speed wit!

That was before, I set behind:
Now too courteous, forthwith unkind,
Sometime too sober, sometime too sad,
Sometime too merry, sometime too mad;
Sometime I sit as I were solemn proud,
Sometime I laugh over-loud,
Sometime I weep for a gee-gaw,
Sometime I laugh at wagging of a straw;
With a pear my love you may win,
And ye may lose it for a pin.
I have a thing for to say,
And I may tend thereto for play;
But in faith I am so occupied
On this half and on every side,
That I wot not where I may rest.
First to tell you what were best,
Frantic Fancy service I hight;
My wits be weak, my brains are light.
For it is I that other while
Pluck down lead, and thatch with tile;
Now will I this, and now will I that,
Make a windmill of a mat;
Now I would, and I wist what.
Where is my cap?   I have lost my hat!
And within an hour after
Pluck down a house, and set up a rafter.
Hither and thither, I wot not whither:
Do and undo, both together.
Of a spindle I will make a spar:
All that I make forthwith I mar!
I blunder, I bluster, I blow, and I blother,
I make on the one day, and I mar on the other.
Busy, busy, and ever busy,
I dance up and down till I am dizzy.
I can find fantasies where none is:
I will not have it so, I will have it this.

Stage 2.   *Scene* 17

Enter FOLLY, *shaking his bauble, capering about,
and playing on an instrument*

Fol. Masters, Christ save every one!
What, Fancy, art thou here alone?
Fan. What, fonnish Folly! I befool thy face!
Fol. What, frantic Fancy in a fool's case? [1]
What is this, an owl or a glede?
By my troth, she hath a great head!
Fan. Tush, thy lips hang in thine eye!
It is a French butterfly.
Fol. By my troth, I trow well!
But she is less a great deal
Than a butterfly of our land.
Fan. What pilléd cur leadest thou in thy hand?
Fol. A pilléd cur!
Fan. Yea so, I tell thee, a pilléd cur!
Fol. Yet I sold his skin to Mackmur
In the stead of a budgè fur.
Fan. What, flayest thou his skin every year?
Fol. Yes, in faith, I thank God I may hear.
Fan. What, thou wilt cough me a daw for forty pence?
Fol. Mary, sir, Cockermouth is a good way hence.
Fan. What? of Cockermouth spake I no word.
Fol. By my faith, sir the furbisher hath my sword.
Fan. Ay, I trow ye shall cough me a fool.
Fol. In faith, truth ye say; we went together to school.
Fan. Yea, but I can somewhat more of the letter.
Fol. I will not give a halfpenny for to chose the better.
Fan. But, brother Folly, I wonder much of one thing,
That thou so high from me doth spring,
And I so little alway still.
Fol. By God, I can tell, an I will.
Thou art so feeble fantastical,
And so brainsick therewithal,

[1] A fool's habit.

And thy wit wandering here and there,
That thou canst not grow out of thy boy's gear.
And as for me, I take but one foolish way,
And therefore I grow more on one day
Than thou can in yearės seven.
Fan. In faith, truth thou sayest now, by God of heaven!
For so with fantasies my wit doth fleet,
That wisdom and I shall seldom meet.
Now, of good fellowship, let me buy thy dog.
Fol. Cock's heart, thou liest, I am no hog!
Fan. Here is no man that callėd thee hog nor swine.
Fol. In faith, man, my brain is as good as thine.
Fan. The devil's turd for thy brain!
Fol. By my sire's soul, I feel no rain.
Fan. By the mass, I hold thee mad.
Fol. Mary, I knew thee when thou wast a lad.
Fan. Cock's bones, heard ye ever such another?
Fol. Yea, a fool the one, and a fool the other.
Fan. Nay, but wottest thou what I do say?
Fol. Why, sayest thou that I was here yesterday?
Fan. Cock's arms, this is a work, I trow!
Fol. What, callest thou me a dunnish crow?
Fan. Now, in good faith, thou art a fond guest.
Fol. Yea, bear me this straw to a dawės nest.
Fan. What, wendest thou that I were so foolish and so fond?
Fol. In faith, yet is there none in all England.
Fan. Yet for my fancy's sake, I say,
Let me have thy dog, whatsoever I pay.
Fol. Thou shalt have my purse, and I will have thine.
Fan. By my troth, there is mine.
Fol. Now, by my troth, man, take, there is my purse.
And I beshrew him that hath the worse.
Fan. Turd, I say, what have I do?
Here is nothing but the buckle of a shoe,
And in my purse was twenty mark.
Fol. Ha, ha, ha! hark, sirs, hark!
For all that my name hight Follý,
By the mass, yet art thou more fool than I.

Fan. Yet give me thy dog, and I am content,
And thou shalt have my hawk to a botchment.
Fol. That ever thou thrive, God it forfend!
For God's cope thou wilt spend.
Now take thou my dog, and give me thy fowl.
Fan. Hey, chish, come hither!
Fol. Nay, turd, take him by time.
Fan. What callest thou thy dog?
Fol. Tush, his name is Grime.
Fan. Come, Grime, come, Grime. It is my pretty dogs!
Fol. In faith, there is not a better dog for hogs,
Not from Anwick unto Angey.
Fan. Yea, but trowest thou that he be not mangy?
Fol. No, by my troth, it is but the scurf and the scab.
Fan. What, he hath been hurt with a stab?
Fol. Nay, in faith, it was but a stripe
That the whoreson had for eating of a tripe.
Fan. Where the devil gat he all these hurts?
Fol. By God, for snatching of puddings and worts.
Fan. What, then, he is some good poor man's cur?
Fol. Yea, but he will in at every man door.
Fan. Now thou hast done me a pleasure great.
Fol. In faith, I would thou hadst a marmoset.
Fan. Cock's heart, I love such japes!
Fol. Yea, for all thy mind is on owls and apes.
But I have thy poultry, and thou hast my cattle.
Fan. Yea, but thrift and we have made a battle.
Fol. Rememberest thou not the japes and the toys—
Fan. What, that we used when we were boys?
Fol. Yea, by the rood, even the same.
Fan. Yes, yes, I am yet as full of game
As ever I was, and as full of trifles,
Nil, nihilum, nihil anglice, nifles.
Fol. What, cannest thou all this Latin yet,
And hath so mazed a wandering wit?
Fan. Tush, man, I keep some Latin in store.
Fol. By Cock's heart, I ween thou hast no more!
Fan. No? yes, in faith, I can versify.

Fol. Then I pray thee heartily
Make a verse of my butterfly:
It forceth not of the reason, so it keep rime.
Fan. But wilt thou make another on Grime?
Fol. Nay, in faith, first let me hear thine.
Fan. Mary, as for that thou shalt soon hear mine:
Est snavi snago with a shrewd face *vilis imago*.
Fol. Grimbaldus greedy, snatch a pudding till the roast be
    ready.
Fan. By the heart of God, well done!
Fol. Yea, so readily and so soon!

Stage 2. Scene 18

Enter CRAFTY CONVEYANCE

Cr. Con. What, Fancy! Let me see who is the other.
Fan. By God, sir, Folly, mine own sworn brother.
Cr. Con. Cock's bones, it is a farly freke:
Can he play well at the hodipeke?
Fan. Tell by thy troth what sport canst thou make.
Fol. Ah, hold thy peace: I have the tooth-ache.
Cr. Con. The tooth-ache! lo, a turd ye have!
Fol. Yea, thou hast the four quarters of a knave.
Cr. Con. Wottest thou, I say, to whom thou speaks?
Fan. Nay, by Cock's heart, he ne recks,
For he will speak to Magnificence thus.
Cr. Con. Cock's arms, a meet man for us!
Fol. What, would ye have more fools, and are so many
Fan. Nay, offer him a counter instead of a penny.
Cr. Con. Why, thinkest thou he can no better skill?
Fol. In faith, I can make ye both fools, an I will.
Cr. Con. What hast thou on thy fist—a kestril?
Fol. Nay, ywis, fool, it is a dotteril.
Cr. Con. In a coat thou can play well the diser.
Fol. Yea, but thou can play the fool without a viser.
Fan. How rode he by you? how put he you there?
Cr. Con. Mary, as thou sayest, he gave me a blur.
But where gat you that mangy cur?

Fan. Mary, it was his, and now it is mine.

Cr. Con. And was it his, and now it is thine?
Thou must have thy fancy and thy will,
But yet thou shalt hold me a fool still.

Fol. Why, wendest thou that I cannot make thee play the
        fon?

Fan. Yes, by my faith, good Sir John.

Cr. Con. For you both it were enough.

Fol. Why, wendest thou that I were as much a fool as thou?

Fan. Nay, nay, thou shalt find him another manner of man.

Fol. In faith, I can do masteries, so I can.

Cr. Con. What canst thou do but play cock wat?

Fan. Yes, yes, he will make thee eat a gnat.

Fol. Yes, yes, by my troth, I hold thee a groat
That I shall laugh thee out of thy coat.

Cr. Con. Then will I say that thou hast no peer.

Fan. Now, by the rood, and he will go near.

Fol. Hem, Fancy, *regardez, voyez.*

> [*Here* FOLLY *pretends to take a louse from*
> CRAFTY CONVEYANCE'S *shoulder.*

Fan. What hast thou found there?

Fol. By God, a louse.

Cr. Con. By Cock's heart, I trow thou liest.

Fol. By the mass, a Spanish moth with a gray list.

Fan. Ha ha ha ha ha ha!

Cr. Con. Cock's arms, it is not so, I trow.

> [*Here* CRAFTY CONVEYANCE *takes off his gown.*

Fol. Put on thy gown again, for thou hast lost now.

Fan. Lo, John of Boham,[1] where is thy brain?
Now put on, fool, thy coat again.

Fol. Give me my groat, for thou hast lost.

> [*Here* FOLLY *pretends to take money of*
> CRAFTY CONVEYANCE.

[1] One of the persons in the old metrical tale, *The Hunting of the
Hare.*

Shut thy purse, daw, and do no cost.

Fan. Now hast thou not a proud mock and a stark?

Cr. Con. With, yes, by the rood of Woodstock Park!

Fan. Nay, I tell thee, he maketh no doubts
To turn a fool out of his clouts.

Cr. Con. And for a fool a man would him take.

Fol. Nay, it is I that fools can make:
For be he kaiser or be he king,
To fellowship with Folly I can him bring.

Fan. Nay, wilt thou hear now of his schools,
And what manner of people he maketh fools?

Cr. Con. Yea, let us hear a word or twain.

Fol. Sir, of my manner I shall tell you the plain.
First I lay before them my bauble,
And teach them how they should sit idle,
To pick their fingers all the day long;
So in their ear I sing them a song
And make them so long to muse
That some of them runneth straight to the stews.
To theft and bribery I make some fall,
And pick a lock and climb a wall;
And where I spy a nisot gay,
That will sit idle all the day,
And cannot set herself to work,
I kindle in her such a lither spark
That rubbéd she must be on the gall
Between the tappet and the wall.

Cr. Con. What, whoreson, art thou such a one?

Fan. Nay, beyond all other set him alone.

Cr. Con. Hast thou any more?   Let see, proceed.

Fol. Yea, by God, sir, for a need
I have another manner of sort
That I laugh at for my disport;
And those be they that come up of nought,
As some be not far, an if it were well sought.
Such daws, whatsoever they be
That be set in authorit̀y,
Anon he waxeth so high and proud,

*H

He frowneth fiercely, brimly browed,
The knave would make it coy, an he could;
All that he doth must be allowed,
And, 'This is not well done, sir, take heed!'
And maketh himself busy where is no need:
He dances so long, hey, trolly lolly,
That every man laugheth at his folly.
Cr. Con. By the good Lord, truth he saith!
Fan. Thinkest thou not so, by thy faith?
Cr. Con. 'Think I not so!' quod he.   Else have I shame,
For I know divers that useth the same.
Fol. But now, forsooth, man, it maketh no matter,
For they that will so busily smatter,
So help me God, man, ever at the length
I make them lose much of their strength;
For with folly so do I them lead,
That wit he wanteth when he hath most need.
Fan. Forsooth, tell on: hast thou any mo?
Fol. Yes, I shall tell you, ere I go,
Of divers mo that haunteth my schools.
Cr. Con. All men beware of suchė fools!
Fol. There be two lither, rude and rank,
Simkin Titivell and Pierce Pykthank;
These lithers I learn them for to lere
What he saith and she saith to lay good ear,
And tell to his sovereign every whit,
And then he is much made of for his wit.
And, be the matter ill more or less,
He will make it mickle worse than it is:
But all that he doth, and if he reckon well,
It is but folly every deal.
Fan. Are not his words cursedly couchéd?
Cr. Con. By God, there be some that be shrewdly touchéd.
But, I say, let see an if thou have any more.
Fol. I have an whole armoury of such haberdash in store;
For there be others that folly doth use,
That follow fond fantasies and virtue refuse.
Fan. Nay, this is my part that thou speakest of now.

Fol. So is all the remnant, I make God avow;
For thou formest such fantasies in their mind
That every man almost groweth out of kind.
Cr. Con. By the mass, I am glad that I came hither,
To hear you two rutters dispute together.
Fan. Nay, but Fancy must be either first or last.
Fol. But when Folly cometh, all is past.
Fan. I wot not whether it cometh of thee or of me.
But all is folly that I can see.
Cr. Con. Mary, sir, ye may swear it on a book!
Fol. Yea, turn over the leaf, read there and look
How frantic Fancy first of all
Maketh man and woman in folly to fall.
Cr. Con. Ay, sir, ay, ay! how by that!
Fan. A perilous thing to cast a cat
Upon a naked man, an if she scrat.
Fol. Soho, I say, the hare is squat!
For, frantic Fancy, thou makest man mad;
And I, Folly, bringeth them to *qui fuit* gad,[1]
With *qui fuit*, brain-sick, I have them brought,
From *qui fuit aliquid*, to sheer shaking nought.
Cr. Con. Well argued and surely on both sides!
But for thee, Fancy, Magnificence abides.
Fan. Why, shall I not have Folly with me alsó?
Cr. Con. Yes, perdee, man, whether that ye ride or go:
Yet for his name we must find a sleight.
Fan. By the mass, he shall hight Conceit.
Cr. Con. Not a better name under the sun!
With Magnificence thou shalt won.
Fol. God have mercy, good godfather.
Cr. Con. Yet I would that he had gone rather;
For, as soon as ye come in Magnificence' sight,
All measure and good rule is gonè quite.
Fan. And shall we have liberty to do what we will?
Cr. Con. Riot at liberty rusheth it out still.
Fol. Yea, but tell me one thing.

---

[1] i e. to a state of regret.

Cr. Con.   What is that?

Fol. Who is master of the mash-vat?

Fan. Yea, for he hath a full dry soul.

Cr. Con. Cock's arms, thou shalt keep the brewhouse bowl.

Fol. But may I drink thereof whiles that I stare?

Cr. Con. When Measure is gone, what needest thou spare?
When Measure is gone, we may slay care.

Fol. Now then go we hence. 'Away the mare . . .!'

                                [Exeunt FOLLY *and* FANCY.

Stage 2.   Scene 19

CRAFTY CONVEYANCE *alone in the place*

Cr. Con. It is wonder to see the world about,
    To see what folly is used in every place;
Folly hath a room, I say, in every rout,
    To put where he list Folly hath free chace;
    Folly and Fancy all where, every man doth face and brace;
Folly footeth it properly, Fancy leadeth the dance;
And next come I after, Counterfeit Countenance.
Whoso to me giveth good ádvertence
    Shall see many things done craftily:
By me conveyéd is wanton insolence,

           .   .   .   .   .¹

    Privy 'pointments conveyéd so properly,
(For many times much kindness is deniéd
For dread that we dare not oft lest we be spiéd.)

By me is conveyéd mickle pretty ware,
    Sometime, I say, behind the door for need;
I have an hobby can make larkès to dare; ²
    I knit together many a broken thread.
    It is great almès the hungry to feed,
To clothe the naked where is lacking a smock,
Trim at her tail, ere a man can turn a sock.

           ¹ Line missing.
           ² A hawk that can terrify larks so as to catch them.

What ho, be ye merry! was it not well conveyéd?
　　As oft as ye list, so honesty be savéd.
'Alas, dear heart, look that we be not perceivéd!'
　　Without craftè nothing is well behavéd;
　　Though I shew you courtesy, say not that I cravéd,
Yet convey it craftily, and hardly spare not for me,
So that there know no man, but I and she.

Theft alsó and petty briberý
　　Without me be full oft espiéd;
My inwit dealing there can no man descry,
　　Convey it by craft, lift and lay aside.
　　Full much flattery and falsèhood I hide,
And by crafty conveyance I will, an I can,
Save a strong thief and hang a true man.

But some men wouldè convey, and can no skill,
　　As malapert taverners that check with their betters,
Their conveyance welteth the work all by will;
　　And some will take upon them to counterfeit letters,
　　And therewithal convey himself into a pair of fetters;
And some will convey by the pretence of sadnéss,
Till all their conveyance is turned into madnéss.

Crafty conveyance is no childès game:
　　By crafty conveyance many one is brought up of nought;
Crafty Conveyance can cloak himself from shame,
　　For by crafty conveyance wonderful things are wrought.
　　By conveyance crafty I have brought
Unto Magnificence a full ungracious sort,
For all hookès unhappy to me have resort.

Stage 3.　*Scene* 20.　Delusion

Enter Magnificence *with* Liberty *and* Felicity

Magn. Trust me, Liberty, it grieveth me right sore
　　To see you thus ruléd and stand in such awe.

Lib. Sir, as by my will, it shall be so no more.

  Fel. Yet Liberty without rule is not worth a straw.

  Magn. Tush, hold your peace, ye speak like a daw!
Ye shall be occupiéd, Wealth, at my will.

Cr. Con. All that ye say, sir, is reason and skill.

Magn. Master Surveyor, where have ye been so long?
  Remember ye not how my Liberty by Measure ruléd was?

Cr. Con. In good faith, sir, meseemeth he had the more
    wrong.

  Lib. Mary, sir, so did he exceed and pass,
  They drove me to learningé like a dull ass.

Fel. It is good yet that Liberty be ruléd by reason.

Magn. Tush, hold your peace, ye speak out of season!

Yourself shall be ruléd by Liberty and Largesse.

  Fel. I am content, so it in measure be.

  Lib. Must Measure, in the mare's name, you furnish and
    dress?

  Magn. Nay, nay, not so, my friend Felicitý.

  Cr. Con. Not, an your grace would be ruléd by me.

  Lib. Nay, he shall be ruléd even as I list.

  Fel. Yet it is good to beware of 'Had I wist.'

Magn. Sir, by Liberty and Largesse I will that ye shall
  Be governed and guided: wot ye what I say?
Master Surveyor, Largesse to me call.

  Cr. Con. It shall be done.

  Magn.   Yea, but bid him come away
At once, and let him not tarry all day.

                          [*Exit* CRAFTY CONVEYANCE.

Fel. Yet it is good wisdom to work wisely by wealth.

Lib. Hold thy tongue, an thou love thy health.

Magn. What, will ye waste wind, and prate thus in vain?
  Ye have eaten sauce, I trow, at the Tailors' Hall.

Lib. Be not too bold, my friend; I counsel you, bear a brain.
   Magn. And whatso we say, hold your content withal.
   Fel. Sir, yet without sapience your substance may be small;
For, where is no measure, how many worship endure?

                        [Enter FANCY.

Fan. Sir, I am here at your pleasúre.

Your Grace sent for me, I ween; what is your will?
   Magn. Come hither, Largesse, take here Felicity.
Fan. Why, ween you that I can keep him long still?
   Magn. To rule as ye list, lo here is Liberty.
   Lib. I am here ready.
Fan. What, shall we have Wealth at our guiding to rule as
        we list?
Then farewell thrift, by Him that cross kist!

Fel. I trust your Grace will be agreeable
   That I shall suffer none impeachment
By their demenance, nor loss reprovable.
   Magn. Sir, ye shall follow mine appetite and intent.
   Fel. So it be by measure I am right well content.
Fan. What, all by measure, good sir, and none excess?
Lib. Why, wealth hath made many a man brainléss.

Fel. That was by the means of too much liberty.
   Magn. What, can ye agree thus and oppose?
Fel. Sir, as I say, there was no fault in me.
   Lib. Yea, of Jack-a-Thrum's babble can ye make a gloss?
   Fan. Sore said, I tell you, and well to the purpóse:
What should a man do with you?—lock you under key.
Fel. I say, it is folly to give all wealth away.

Lib. Whether should Wealth be ruléd by Liberty,
   Or Liberty by Wealth? Let see, tell me that.
Fel. Sir, as meseemeth, ye should be ruléd by me.
   Magn. What need you with him thus prate and chat?
   Fan. Show us your mind then, how to do and what.
Magn. I say, that I will ye have him in guidíng.
Lib. Master Felicity, let be your chidíng,

And so, as ye see it will be no better,
   Take it in worth such as you find.
Fan. What the devil, man, your name shall be the greater,
   For Wealth without Largesse is all out of kind.
  Lib. And Wealth is nought worth if Liberty be behind.
Magn. Now hold ye content, for there is none other shift.
Fel. Then waste must be welcome, and farewell thrift!

Magn. Take of his substance a sure inventory,
   And get you home together; for Liberty shall bide,
And wait upon me.
Lib.   And yet for a memory,
   Make indentures how ye and I shall guide.
  Fan. I can do nothing but he standė beside.
Lib. Sir, we can do nothing the one without the other.
Magn. Well, get you hence then, and send me some other.
Fan. Whom? lusty Pleasure, or merry Conceit?
  Magn. Nay, first lusty Pleasure is my desire to have,
And let the other another time await,
   Howbeit that fond fellow is a merry knave!
   But look that ye occupy the authority that I you gave.

              [*Exeunt* FELICITY, LIBERTY, *and* FANCY.

Stage 3.   *Scene* 21

MAGNIFICENCE *alone in the place*

For now, sirs, I am like as a prince should be:
I have Wealth at will, Largesse and Liberty.

Fortune to her laws cannot abandon me,
   But I shall of Fortúne rule the rein;
I fear nothing Fortune's perplexity;
   All honour to me must needės stoop and lean;
   I sing of two partės without a mean;
I have wind and weather over all to sail,
No stormy rage against me can prevail.

Alexander, of Macedony king,
    That all the orient had in subjectíon,
Though all his conquests were brought to reckoníng,
    Might seem right well under my protectíon
    To reign, for all his martial affectíon;
For I am Prince Peerless, provéd of port,
Bathéd with bliss, embracéd with comfórt.

Cyrus, that solemn sire of Babylon,
    That Israel releaséd of their captivity,
For all his pomp, for all his royal throne,
    He may not be comparéd unto me.
    I am the diamond doubtless of dignity.
Surely it is I that all may save and spill;
No man so hardy to work against my will.

Porsena, the proud provost of Turky land,
    That rated the Romans and made them ill rest,
Nor Caesar July, that no man might withstand,
    Were never half so richly as I am drest:
    No, that I assure you: look who was the best.
I reign in my robés, I rule as me list,
I drive down these dastards with a dint of my fist.

Of Cato, the count, accounted the cane,
    Darius, the doughty chieftain of Persé,
I set not by the proudest of them a prawn,
    Ne by none other that any man can rehearsé.
    I follow in felicitý without reversé.
I dread no danger, I dancé all in delight:
My name is Magnificence, man most of might.

Hercules the hardy, with his stubborn clubbéd mace,
    That made Cerberus to couch, the cur dog of hell,
And Theseus, that proud was Pluto to face,
    It would not become them with me for to mell:
    For of all baronés bold I bear the bell,
Of all doughty, I am doughtiest duke, as I deem:
To me all princes to lowt may beseem.

Charlemagne, that maintainéd the nobles of France,
  Arthur of Albion, for all his brimmé beard,
Nor Basian [1] the bold, for all his bribance,
  Nor Alaric, that ruléd the Gothiance by sword,
  Nor no man on mould can make me afeard.
What man is so mazéd with me that dare meet,
I shall flap him as a fool to fall at my feet.

Galba, whom his gallants garde for to gasp,
  Nor Nero, that neither set by God nor man,
Nor Vespasian, that bore in his nose a wasp,
  Nor Hannibal against Rome gatés that ran
  Nor yet Scipio, that noble Carthage wan,
Nor none so hardy of them with me that durst crake,
But I shall frounce them on the foretop, and gar them to
    quake.

Stage 3.   Scene 22

Enter COURTLY ABUSION, *doing reverence
and courtesy*

Court. Ab. At your commandment, sir, with all due rever-
      ence.
Magn. Welcome, Pleasure, to our magnificence.
Court. Ab. Pleaseth it your Grace to show what I do shall?
Magn. Let us hear of your pleasure to pass the time withal.
Court. Ab. Sir, then, with the favour of your benign suffer-
      ance
To shew you my mind myself I will advance,
If it like your Grace to take it in degree.
Magn. Yes, sir, so good man in you I see,
And in your dealing so good assurance,
That we delight greatly in your dalliance.
Court. Ab. Ah, sir, your Grace me doth extol and raise,
And far beyond my merits ye me commend and praise;
Howbeit, I would be right glad, I you assure,

        [1] Antoninus Bassianus Caracalla.

Any thing to do that might be to your pleasúre.
Magn. As I be saved, with pleasure I am surpriséd
Of your language, it is so well devisèd;
Polishéd and freshè is your ornacy.
Court. Ab. I would to God that I were half so crafty,
Or in elect utterance half so eloquent,
As that I might your noble Grace content!
Magn. Trust me, with you I am highly pleaséd,
For in my favour I have you fieféd and seiséd.
He is not living your manners can amend;
Mary, your speech is as pleasant as though it were penned;
To hear your commune, it is my high comfórt;
Point-devise all pleasure is your port.
Court. Ab. Sir, I am the better of your noble report;
But, of your patíence under the support,
If it would like you to hear my poorè mind—
Magn. Speak, I beseech thee, leave nothing behind.
Court. Ab. So as ye be a prince of great might,
It is seeming your pleasure ye delight,
And to acquaint you with carnal delectatíon,
And to fall in acquaintance with every newè fashíon;
And quickly your appetitès to sharpè and address,
To fasten your fancy upon a fairè mistréss,
That quickly is envivéd with ruddies of the rose,
Inpurturéd with features after your purpóse;
The strains of her veins as azure Indy blue,
Enbudded with beauty and colour fresh of hue,
As lily-white to look upon her lerè,
Her eyen relucent as carbuncle so clearè,
Her mouth embalméd, delectable and merry,
Her lusty lippès ruddy as the cherry.
How like you? ye lack, sir, such a lusty lass.
Magn. Ah, that were a baby to 'brace and to bass!
I would I had, by Him that hell did harrow,
With me in keeping such a Philip Sparrow!
I would hawkè whilest my head did wark,[1]
So I might hobby for such a lusty lark!

[1] i.e. until my head did ache.

These wordès in mine ear they be so lustily spoken,
That on such a female my flesh would be wroken;
They touch me so thoroughly, and tickle my conceit,
That weriéd I would be on such a bait.
Ah, Cock's arms, where might such one be found?

Court. Ab. Will ye spend any money?

Magn.   Yea, a thousand pound!

Court. Ab. Nay, nay, for less I warrant you to be sped,
And brought home, and laidè in your bed.

Magn. Would money, trowest thou, make such one to the
call?

Court. Ab. Money maketh merchants, I tell you, over all.

Magn. Why, will a mistress be won for money and for gold?

Court. Ab. Why, was not for money Troy both bought and
sold?
Full many a strongè city and town hath been won
By the meanès of money without any gun.
A mistress, I tell you, is but a small thing;
A goodly ribbon, or a goldè ring,
May win with a saute the fortress of the hold.
But one thing I warn you, press forth and be bold.

Magn. Yea, but some be full coy and passing hard-hearted.

Court. Ab. But, blessed be our Lord, they will be soon converted!

Magn. Why, will they then be entreated, the most and the
least?

Court. Ab. Yea, for *omnis mulier meretrix, si celari potest.*[1]

Magn. Ah, I have spiéd ye can much brooken sorrow!

Court. Ab. I could hold you with such talk hence till to-
morrow;
But if it like your Grace, more at large
Me to permit my mindè to discharge,
I would yet shew you further of my conceit.

Magn. Let see what ye say, show it straight.

Court. Ab. Wisely let these wordès in your mind be weighéd;
By wayward wilfulness let each thing be conveyéd;
Whatsoever ye do, follow your now will;

[1] Every woman is a whore, if she can be on the sly.

Be it reason or none, it shall not greatly skill;
Be it right or wrong, by the advice of me,
Take your pleasure and use free libertý;
And if you see anything against your mind,
Then some occasion of quarrel ye must find,
And frown it and face it, as though ye would fight,
Fret yourself for anger and for despite;
Hear no man, whatsoever they say,
But do as ye list, and take your own way.
Magn. Thy words and my mind oddly well accord.
Court. Ab. What should ye do else? are not you a lord?
Let your lust and liking stand for a law;
Be wresting and writhing, and away draw.
An ye see a man that with him ye be not pleaséd,
And that your mind cannot well be easéd,
As if a man fortune to touch you on the quick,
Then feign yourself diseaséd and make yourself sick:
To stir up your stomach you must you forge,
Call for a caudle and cast up your gorge,
With 'Cock's arms, rest shall I none have
Till I be revenged on that whoreson knave!
Ah, how my stomach wambleth! I am all in a sweat!
Is there no whoreson that knave that will beat?'
Magn. By Cock's wounds, a wondrous fellow thou art!
For ofttimes such a wambling goeth over my heart;
Yet I am not heart-sick, but that me list
For mirth I have him curried, beaten, and blist.
Him that I lovéd not and made him to lowt
I am forthwith as whole as a trout—
For such abusíon I use now and then.
Court. Ab. It is none abusíon, sir, in a noble man,
It is a princely pleasure and a lordly mind;
Such lustés at large may not be left behind.

Stage 3. *Scene* 23

Enter CLOAKÉD COLLUSION *with* MEASURE

Cl. Col. (aside to MEASURE). Stand still here, and ye shall see
That for your sake I will fall on my knee.

[MEASURE *waits at the door.*

Court. Ab. Sir, Sober Sadness cometh, wherefore it be?
Magn. Stand up, sir, ye are welcome to me.
Cl. Col. Please it your Grace, at the contemplatíon
Of my poor instance and supplicatíon,
Tenderly to consider in your advertence,
Of our blessed Lord, sir, at the reverence,
Remember the good service that Measure hath you done,
And that ye will not cast him away so soon.
Magn. My friend, as touching to this your motíon,
I may say to you I have but small devotíon;
Howbeit, at your instance I will the rather
Do as much as for mine owné father.
Cl. Col. Nay, sir, that affectíon ought to be reservéd,
For of your Grace I have it nought deservéd;
But if it like you that I might round in your ear
To show you my mindé, I would have the less fear.
Magn. Stand a little aback, sir, and let him come hither.
Court. Ab. With a good will, sir, God speed you both
        together.
Cl. Col. (aside to MAGNIFICENCE). Sir, so it is: this man is
        hereby,
That for him to labour he hath prayed me heartily;
Notwithstanding to you be it said,
To trust in me he is but diceivéd;
For, so help me God, for you he is not meet:
I speak the softlier, because he should not weet.
Magn. Come hither, Pleasure, you shall hear mine intent.
Measure, ye know well, with him I cannot be content,
And surely, as I am now adv_iséd_,
I will have him rehated and despiséd.
How say ye, sirs, herein what is best?

Court. Ab. By mine advise with you, in faith, he shall not rest.
Cl. Col. Yet, sir, reservéd your better advertisement,
It were better he spake with you ere he went,
That he know not but that I have suppleed
All that I can his matter for to speed.
Magn. Now, by your troth, gave he you not a bribe?
Cl. Col. Yes, with his hand I made him to subscribe
A bill of record for an annual rent.
Court. Ab. But for all that he is like to have a glent.
Cl. Col. Yea, by my troth, I shall warrant you for me,
An he go to the devil, so that I may have my fee,
What care I?
Magn.   By the mass, well said.
Court. Ab. What force ye, so that ye be paid?
Cl. Col. But yet, lo, I would, ere that he went,
Lest that he thought that his money were evil spent,
That ye would look on him, though it were not long.
Magn. Well canst thou help a priest to sing a song!
Cl. Col. So it is all the manner nowadays,
For to use such hafting and crafty ways.
Court. Ab. He telleth you truth, sir, as I you ensure.
Magn. Well, for thy sake the better I may endure
That he come hither, and to give him a look
That he shall like the worse all this woke.[1]
Cl. Col. I care not how soon he be refuséd,
So that I may craftily be excuséd.
Court. Ab. Where is he?
Cl. Col.   Mary, I made him abide,
Whilst I came to you, a little here beside.
Magn. Well, call him, and let us hear him reason,
And we will be communing in the meané season.
Court. Ab. This is a wise man, sir, wheresoever ye had him.
Magn. An honest person, I tell you, and a sad.
Court. Ab. He can full craftily this matter bring about.
Magn. Whilst I have him, I need nothing doubt.

[CLOAKÉD COLLUSION *brings* MEASURE *forward*,
while MAGNIFICENCE *looks on him very loftily.*

[1] i.e. week.

Cl. Col. By the mass, I have done that I can,
And more than ever I did for any man:
I trow, ye heard yourself what I said.
Meas. Nay, indeed; but I saw how ye prayed,
And made instance for me by likelihood.
Cl. Col. Nay, I tell you, I am not wont to fode
Them that dare put their trust in me;
And thereof ye shall a larger proof see.
Meas. Sir, God reward you as ye have deservéd:
But think you with Magnificence I shall be reservéd?
Cl. Col. By my troth, I cannot tell you that;
But, an I were as ye, I would not set a gnat
By Magnificence, nor yet none of his,
For, go when ye shall, of you shall he miss.
Meas. Sir, as ye say.
Cl. Col.   Nay, come on with me.
Yet once again I shall fall on my knee
For your sake, whatsoever befall;
I set not a fly, and all go to all.
Meas. The Holy Ghost be with your Grace.
Cl. Col. Sir, I beseech you, let pity have some place
In your breast towards this gentleman.
Magn. I was your good lord till that ye began
So masterfully upon you for to take
With my servants, and such masteries 'gan make,
That wholly my mind with you is miscontent;
Wherefore I will that ye be resident
With me no longer.
Cl. Col.   Say somewhat now, let see,
For your self.
Meas.   Sir, if I might permitted be,
I would to you say a wordé or twain.
Magn. What, wouldest thou, lurdain, with me brawl again?
Have him hence, I say, out of my sight;
That day I see him I shall be worse all night!
Court. Ab. Hence, thou haynard, out of the doorés fast!

                    [*Exit* MEASURE *with* COURTLY ABUSION.

Stage 3. Scene 24

Magn. Alas, my stomach fareth as it would cast!

Cl. Col. Abide, sir, abide, let me hold your head.

Magn. A bowl or a basin, I say, for God's bread!
Ah, my head!   But is the whoreson gone?
God give him a mischief!   Nay, now let me alone.

Cl. Col. A good drift, sir, a pretty feat!
By the good Lord, yet your temples beat.

Magn. Nay, so God me help, it was no great vexation,
For I am pangéd ofttimes of this same fashíon.

Cl. Col. Cock's arms, how Pleasure plucked him forth!

Magn. Yea, walk he must, it was no better worth.

Cl. Col. Sir, now methink your heart is well easéd.

Magn. Now Measure is gone I am the better pleaséd.

Cl. Col. So to be ruled by Measure, it is a pain!

Magn. Mary, I ween he would not be glad to come again!

Cl. Col. So I wot not what he should do here:
Where men's bellies is measured, there is no cheer;
For I hear but fewé men that give any praise
Unto Measure, I say, nowadays.

Magn. Measure, tut! what, the devil of hell!
Scantly one with Measure that will dwell.

Cl. Col. Not among noblemen, as the world goeth.
It is no wonder therefore though ye be wroth
With Measure.   Where all nobleness is, there I have past.
They catch that catch may, keep and hold fast,
Out of all measure themselvés to enrich.
No force what though his neighbour die in a ditch.
With polling and plucking out of all measúre,
Thus must ye stuff and storé your treasúre.

Magn. Yet sometime, pardee, I must use largesse.

Cl. Col. Yea, mary, sometime in a mess of verjuice,
As in a trifle or in a thing of nought,
As giving a thing that ye never bought.
It is the guise now, I say, over all:
Largesse in words, for rewards are but small.
To make fairé promise, what are ye the worse?

Let me have the rule of your purse.
Magn. I have taken it to Largesse and Libertý.
Cl. Col. Then it is done as it should be.
But use your largesse by the advice of me,
And I shall warrant you wealth and libertý.
Magn. Say on, methink your reasons be profound.
Cl. Col. Sir, of my counsel this shall be the ground:
To choose out ii. iii. of such as you love best,
And let all your fancies upon them rest;
Spare for no cost to give them pound and penny,
Better to make three rich than for to make many;
Give them more than enough and let them not lack,
And as for all other let them truss and pack;
Pluck from an hundred, and give it to three,
Let neither patent 'scape them nor fee;
And wheresoever you will fall to a reckoning,
Those three will be ready even at your beckoning,
For them shall you have at liberty to lowt;
Let them have all, and the other go without;
Thus joy without measure you shall have.
Magn. Thou sayst truth, by the heart that God me gave!
For, as thou sayst, right so shall it be.
And here I make thee upon Libertý
To be supervisor, and on Largesse alsó,
For as thou wilt, so shall the gamé go;
For in Pleasure, and Surveyance, and also in thee
I have set my whole felicitý,
And such as you will shall lack no promotíon.
Cl. Col. Sir, sith that in me ye have such devotíon,
Committing to me and to my fellows twain
Your wealth and felicity, I trust we shall obtain
To do you service after your appetite.
Magn. In faith, and your service right well I shall acquite;
And therefore hie you hence, and take this oversight.
Cl. Col. Now, Jesu preserve you, sir, prince most of might!

         [*Exit* CLOAKÉD COLLUSION.

Stage 3.   Scene 25

Magn. Thus, I say, I am environed with soláce;
I dread no dints of fatal destiny.
Well were that lady might stand in my grace,
Me to embrace and love most specíally:
Ah, Lord, so I would halse her heartily,
So I would clip her, so I would kiss her sweet!

Enter FOLLY

Fol. Mary, Christ grant ye catch no cold on your feet!
Magn. Who is this?
Fol.   Conceit, sir, your ownė man.
Magn. What tidings with you, sir?   I befool thy brain-pan!
Fol. By our lakin, sir, I have been a hawking for the wild
      swan.
My hawk is ramage, and it happed that she ran—
Flew I should say—into an oldė barn
To reach at a rat, I could not her warn;
She pinched her pinion, by God, and catchéd harm:
It was a runner; nay, fool, I warrant her blood warm!
Magn. Ah, sir, thy gerfalcon and thou be hanged together!
Fol. And, sir, as I was coming to you hither,
I saw a fox suck on a cow's udder,
And with a lime-rod I took them both together.
I trow it be a frost, for the way is slidder:
See, for God avow, for cold as I chidder.
Magn. Thy words hang together as feathers in the wind.
Fol. Ah, sir, told I not you how I did find
A knave and a churl, and all of one kind?
I saw a weathercock wag with the wind;
Great marvel I had, and mused in my mind;
The hounds ran before, and the hare behind;
I saw a losel lead a lurdain, and they were both blind;
I saw a sowter go to supper ere ever he had dined.
Magn. By Cock's heart, thou art a fine merry knave!
Fol. I make God avow, ye will none other men have.
Magn. What sayst thou?

Fol.   Mary, I pray God your mastership to save:
I shall give you a gaud of a gosling that I gave,
The gander and the goose both grazing on one grave;
Then Rowland the reve ran, and I began to rave,
And with a bristle of a boar his beard did I shave.
Magn. If ever I heard such another, God give me shame!
Fol. Sim Saddlegoose was my sire, and Dawcock my dame:
I could, an I list, gar you laugh at a game,
How a woodcock wrestled with a lark that was lame:
The bittern said boldly that they were to blame;
The fieldfare would have fiddled, and it would not frame;
The crane and the curlew thereat 'gan to grame;
The snite snivelled in the snout and smiled at the game.
Magn. Cock's bones, heard you ever such another!
Fol. See, sir, I beseech you, Largesse my brother.

Enter FANCY

Magn. What tidings with you, sir, that you look so sad?
Fan. When ye know what I know ye will not be glad!
Fol. What, Brother Brainsick, how farest thou?
Magn. Yea, let be thy japes, and tell me how
The case requireth.
Fan.   Alas, alas, an heavy meeting!
I would tell you, an if I might for weeping.
Fol. What, is all your mirth now turnéd to sorow?
Farewell till soon, adew till to-morrow.

                                        [*Exit* FOLLY.

Magn. I pray thee, Largesse, let be thy sobbing.
Fan. Alas, sir, ye are undone with stealing and robbing!
Ye sent us a supervisor for to take heed:
Take heed of yourself, for now ye have need.
Magn. What, hath Sadness beguiléd me so?
Fan. Nay, madness hath beguiléd you and many mo;
For Liberty is gone and also Felicity.
Magn. Gone? alas, ye have undone me!
Fan. Nay, he that sent us, Cloakéd Collusíon,
And your painted Pleasure, Courtly Abusíon,

And your demeanour with Counterfeit Countenance,
And your surveyor, Crafty Conveyance,
Ere ever we were ware brought us in adversity,
And hath robbéd you quite from all felicity.
Magn. Why, is this the largesse that I have uséd?
Fan. Nay, it was your fondness that ye have uséd.
Magn. And is this the credence that I gave to the letter?
Fan. Why, could not your wit serve you no better?
Magn. Why, who would have thought in you such guile?
Fan. What? yes, by the rood, sir, it was I all this while
That you trusted, and Fancy is my name;
And Folly, my brother, that made you much game.

Enter ADVERSITY

Magn. Alas, who is yonder, that grimly lookès?
Fan. Adew, for I will not come in his clutches.

[*Exit* FANCY.

Stage 4. *Scene* 26. OVERTHROW

Magn. Lord, so my fleshè trembleth now for dread!

[*Here* MAGNIFICENCE *is beaten down, and spoiled
from all his goods and raiment.*

Adver. I am Adversity, that for thy misdeed
From God am sent to 'quite thee thy meed.
Vile vilyard, thou must now my dint withstand,
Thou must abide the dint of my hand.
Lie there, losel, for all thy pomp and pride;
Thy pleasure now with pain and trouble shall be tried.
The stroke of God, Adversity I hight;
I pluck down king, prince, lord, and knight,
I rush at them roughly, and make them lie full low,
And in their most trust I make them overthrow.
This losel was a lord, and livéd at his lust,
And now, like a lurdain, he lieth in the dust.
He knew not himself, his heart was so high;
Now is there no man that will set by him a fly;

He was wont to boast, brag, and to brace;
Now dare he not for shame look one in the face.
All wordly wealth for him too little was;
Now hath he right nought, naked as an ass.
Sometime without measure he trusted in gold,
And now without measure he shall have hunger and cold.
Lo, sirs, thus I handle them all
That follow their fancies in folly to fall.
Man or woman, of what estate they be,
I counsel them beware of Adversity.
Of sorrowful servants I have many scores:
I visit them sometimes with blains and with sores;
With botches and carbuncles in care I them knit;
With the gout I make them to groan where they sit;
Some I make lepers and lazars full hoarse;
And from that they love best some I divorce;
Some with the marmoll to halt I them make;
And some to cry out of the bone-ache;
And some I visit with burning of fire;
Of some I wring of the neck like a wire;
And some I make in a rope to totter and walter;
And some for to hang themself in a halter;
And some I visit with battle, war, and murther,
And make each man to slay other;
To drown or to slay themself with a knife;
And all is for their ungracious life.
Yet sometime I strike where is none offence,
Because I would prove men of their patience.
But, nowadays, to strike I have great cause,
Lidderns so little set by God's laws.
Fathers and mothers, that be negligent,
And suffer their children to have their intent,
To guide them virtuously that will not remember,
Them or their children oft time I dismember;
Their children because that they have no meekness;
I visit their fathers and mothers with sickness;
And if I see thereby they will not amend,
Then mischief suddenly I them send;

For there is nothing that more displeaseth God
Than from their children to spare the rod
Of correction, but let them have their will.
Some I make lame, and some I do kill;
And some I strike with a frenzý;
Of some of their children I strike out the eye;
And where the father by wisdom worship hath won,
I send oft times a fool to his son.
Wherefore of Adversity look ye beware,
For when I come cometh sorrow and care.
For I strike lordès of realmès and lands
That rule not by measure that they have in their hands,
That sadly rule not their household men;
I am God's prepositor,[1] I print them with a pen;
Because of their negligence and their wanton vaguès,
I visit them and strike them with many sore plaguès.
To take, sirs, example of that I you tell,
And beware of Adversity by my counsél,
Take heed of this caitiff that lieth here on ground;
Behold, how Fortune on him hath frowned!
For though we shew you this in game and play,
Yet it proveth earnest, ye may see, every day.
For now will I from this caitiff go,
And take mischief and vengeance of other mo
That hath deservéd it as well as he.
Ho, where art thou? come hither, Povertý,
Take this caitiff to thy lore.   [*Exit.*

Stage 4.   *Scene* 27

Enter POVERTY

Pover. Ah, my bonès ache, my limbs be sore;
Alas, I have the sciatica full evil in my hip!
Alas, where is youth that was wont for to skip?
I am lowsy, and unliking, and full of scurf,
My colour is tawny, colouréd as turf.

---

[1] A scholar that is an overseer.

I am Poverty, that all men doth hate,
I am baited with dogs at every man's gate;
I am ragged and rent, as ye may see;
Full few but they have envy at me.
Now must I this carcass lift up.
He dinéd with delight, with Poverty he must sup.
Rise up, sir, and welcome unto me.

> [*Poverty lifts up* MAGNIFICENCE, *and puts
> a coverlet over* him.

Magn. Alas, where is now my gold and fee?
Alas, I say, whereto am I brought?
Alas, alas, alas, I die for thought!
Pover. Sir, all this would have been thought on before:
He woteth not what wealth is that never was sore.
Magn. Fie, fie, that ever I should be brought in this snare!
I weenéd once never to have knowen care.
Pover. Lo, such is this world! I find it writ,
In wealth to beware, and that is wit.
Magn. In wealth to beware, if I had had grace,
Never had I been brought in this case.
Pover. Now, sith it will no other be,
All that God sendeth, take it in gre;
For, though you were sometime of noble estate,
Now must you learn to beg at every man's gate.
Magn. Alas, that ever I should be so shaméd!
Alas, that ever I Magnificence was naméd!
Alas, that ever I was so hard happed,
In misery and wretchedness thus to be lapped!
Alas, that I could not myself no better guide!
Alas, in my cradle that I had not died!
Pover. Yea, sir, yea, leave all this rage,
And pray to God your sorrows to assuage.
It is folly to grudge against his visitation.
With heart contrite make your supplication
Unto your Maker, that made both you and me,
And, when it pleaseth God, better may be.

Magn. Alas, I wot not what I should pray!

Pover. Remember you better, sir, beware what ye say,
For dread ye displease the high Deitý.
Put your will in his will, for surely it is he
That may restore you again to felicity,
And bring you again out of adversity.
Therefore poverty look patiently ye take,
And remember he suffered much more for your sake,
Howbeit of all sin he was innocent,
And ye have deservéd this punishment.

Magn. Alas, with cold my limbs shall be marred!

Pover. Yea, sir, now must ye learn to lie hard,
That was wont to lie on feather-beds of down;
Now must your feet lie higher than your crown.
Where you were wont to have caudles for your head,
Now must you munch mammocks and lumps of bread;
And where you had changes of rich array,
Now lap you in a coverlet full fain that ye may;
And where that ye were pomped with what ye wold,
Now must ye suffer both hunger and cold.
With courtly silks ye were wont to be draw,
Now must ye learn to lie on the straw;
Your skin that was wrapped in shirtès of Rennes,
Now must ye be storm-ybeaten with showers and rains;
Your head that was wont to be happed most droopy and
      drowsy,
Now shall ye be scabbéd, scurvy, and lousy.

Magn. Fie on this world, full of treachery,
That ever nobleness should lie thus wretchedly!

Pover. Sir, remember the turn of Fortune's wheel,
That wantonly can wink, and winch with her heel.
Now she will laugh, forthwith she will frown;
Suddenly set up, and suddenly plucked down.
She danceth variance with mutability;
Now all in wealth, forthwith in poverty;
In her promíse there is no sickerness;
All her delight is set in doubleness.

Magn. Alas, of Fortune I may well complain!

I

Pover. Yea, sir, yesterday will not be calléd again.
But yet, sir, now in this case,
Take it meekly, and thank God of his grace;
For now go I will beg for you some meat;
It is folly against God for to plete;
I will walké now with my beggar's bags,
And wrap you the whiles with these homely rags.

　　　　　　　　　[Going away, he says these words:

Ah, how my limbs be lither and lame!
Better it is to beg than to be hangéd with shame;
Yet many had liefer hangéd be,
Than for to beg their meat for charity:
They think it no shame to rob and steal,
Yet were they better to beg a great deal;
For by robbing they run *in manus tuas* quick,[1]
But begging is better medicine for the neck;
Yea, mary, is it, yea, so may I go.
Ah, Lord God, how the gout wringeth me by the toe!

　　　　　　　　　　　　　　　　　　[Exit.

Stage 4.　　Scene 28

Here MAGNIFICENCE *dolorously makes his moan*

Magn. O feeble fortune, O doleful destiny!
　　O hateful hap, O careful cruelty!
O sighing sorrow, O thoughtful misery!
　　O redeless ruth, O painful poverty!
　　O dolorous heart, O hard adversity!
O odious distress, O deadly pain and woe!
For worldy shame I wax both wan and blo.

Where is now my wealth and my noble estate?
　　Where is now my treasure, my lands, and my rent?
Where is now all my servants that I had here of late?

[1] i.e. get themselves quickly hanged, and say, 'Into thy hands, [O Lord, I commend my spirit].'

Where is now my gold upon them that I spent?
Where is now all my rich habiliment?
Where is now my kin, my friends, and my noble blood?
Where is now all my pleasure and my wordly good?

Alas, my folly! alas, my wanton will!
I may no moré speak, till I have wept my fill.

Stage 4. *Scene* 29

Enter LIBERTY

Lib. With, yea mary, sirs, thus should it be:
I kissed her sweet, and she kisséd me;
I dancéd the darling on my knee;
I garred her gasp, I garred her gle,
With 'Dance on the lea, the lea!'
I bussed that baby with heart so free;
She is the bote of all my bale.
Ah so! that sigh was far-fet!
To love that lovesome I will not let;
My heart is wholly on her set:
I plucked her by the partlet;
At my devise I with her met;
My fancy fairly on her I set;
So merrily singeth the nightingale!
In lust and liking my name is Liberty:
I am desiréd with highest and lowest degree;
I live as me list, I leap out at large;
Of earthly thing I have no care nor charge;
I am president of princes, I prick them with pride.
What is he living that Liberty would lack?
A thousand pound with Liberty may hold no tack;
At liberty a man may be bold for to break;
Wealth without liberty goeth all to wrack.
But yet, sirs, hardely one thing learn of me:
I warn you beware of too much liberty,

For *totum in toto* is not worth an haw;
Too hardy, or too much, too free of the daw; [1]
Too sober, too sad, too subtil, too wise;
Too merry, too mad, too gigling, too nice;
Too full of fancies, too lordly, too proud;
Too homely, too holy, too lewd, and too loud;
Too flattering, too smattering, too too out of harre;
Too clattering, too chattering, too short, and too far;
Too jetting, too jagging, and too full of japes;
Too mocking, too mowing, too like a jackanapes:
Thus *totum in toto* groweth up, as ye may see,
By means of madness, and too much liberty;
For I am a virtue, if I be well uséd,
And I am a vice where I am abuséd.

Magn. Ah, woe worth thee, Liberty, now thou sayst full
true!
That I uséd thee too much, sore may I rue.

Lib. What, a very vengeance, I say, who is that?
What brothel, I say, is yonder bound in a mat?

Magn. I am Magnificence, that sometime thy master was.

Lib. What, is the worldé thus come to pass?
Cock's arms, sirs, will ye not see
How he is undone by the means of me?
For if Measure had ruled Liberty as he began,
This lurdain that here lieth had been a nobleman.
But he abuséd so his free liberty,
That now he hath lost all his felicity,
Not thorough largesse of liberal expense,
But by the way of fancy insolence;
For liberality is most convenient
A prince to use with all his whole intent,
Largely rewarding them that have deservéd,
And so shall a nobleman nobly be servéd.
But nowadays as hucksters they huck and they stick,
And pinch at the payment of a pudding-prick; [2]

---

[1] i.e. too much fooling.
[2] Skewer that fastens the pudding-bag.

A laudable largesse, I tell you, for a lord,
To prate for the patching of a potsherd!
Spare for the 'spence of a noble,[1] that his honour might save,
And spend a hundred shillings for the pleasure of a knave!
But so long they reckon with their reasons amiss
That they lose their liberty and all that there is.
Magn. Alas, that ever I occupiéd such abusíon!
Lib. Yea, for now it hath brought thee to confusíon:
For, where I am occupiéd and uséd wilfully,
It cannot continue long prosperously;
As evidently in reckless youth you may see,
How many come to mischief for too much liberty;
And some in the worldè their brain is so idle
That they set their children to run on the bridle,
In youth to be wanton and let them have their will;
An they never thrive in their age, it shall not greatly skill.
Some fall to folly themself for to spill,
And some fall preaching at the Tower Hill;
Some hath so much liberty of one thing and other
That neither they set by father nor mother;
Some have so much liberty that they fear no sin,
Till, as ye see many times, they shame all their kin.
I am so lusty to look on, so fresh, and so free,
That nuns will leave their holiness, and run after me;
Friars with folly I make them so fain,
They cast up their obedience to catch me again,
At liberty to wander and walkè over all,
That lustily they leap sometime their cloister wall.

> [*Here someone blows a horn behind the audience.*

Yonder is a whoreson for me doth rechate:
Adew, sirs, for I think lest that I come too late.

> [*Here* LIBERTY *goes out.*

Magn. O good Lord, how long shall I endure
This misery, this careful wretchedness?
Of worldly wealth, alas, who can be sure?
In Fortune's friendship there is no steadfastness:

[1] A gold coin.

She hath deceivéd me with her doubleness.
For to be wise all men may learn of me,
In wealth to beware of hard adversity.

[*Enter* CRAFTY CONVEYANCE *and* CLOAKÉD
COLLUSION.

Cr. Con. Ha, ha, ha! for laughter I am like to brast.
C. Col. Ha, ha, ha! for sport I am like to spew and cast.
Cr. Con. What hath thou gotten, in faith, to thy share?
Cl. Col. In faith, of his coffers the bottoms are bare.
Cr. Con. As for his plate of silver, and suché trash,
I warrant you, I have given it a lash.
Cl. Col. What, then he may drink out of a stone cruse?
Cr. Con. With, yea, sir, by Jesu that slain was with Jews!
He may rinse a pitcher, for his plate is to wed.[1]
Cl. Col. In faith, and he may dream on a dagswane for any
feather-bed.
Cr. Con. By my troth, we have rifled him meetly well!
Cl. Col. Yea, but thank me thereof every deal.
Cr. Con. Thank thee thereof, in the devil's date!
Cl. Col. Leave thy prating, or else I shall lay thee on the pate.
Cr. Con. Nay, to wrangle, I warrant thee, it is but a stone-
cast.
Cl. Col. By the mass, I shall cleave thy head to the waist.
Cr. Con. Yea, wilt thou cleanly cleave me in the clifte with
thy nose?
Cl. Col. I shall thrust in thee my dagger—
Cr. Con.   Thorough the leg into the hose.
Cl. Col. Nay, whoreson, here is my glove; take it up, an thou
dare.
Cr. Con. Turd, thou art good to be a man of war!
Cl. Col. I shall skelp thee on the scalp; lo, seest thou that?
Cr. Con. What, wilt thou skelp me? thou dare not look on a
gnat.
Cl. Col. By Cock's bones, I shall bliss thee, an thou be too bold.
Cr. Con. Nay, then thou wilt ding the devil, an thou be not
hold.

[1] Pawned.

Cl. Col. But wottest thou, whoreson? I rede thee to be wise.

Cr. Con. Now I rede thee beware, I have warnéd thee twice.

Cl. Col. Why, wendest thou that I forbear thee for thine own sake?

Cr. Con. Peace, or I shall wring thy be in a brake!

Cl. Col. Hold thy hand, daw, off thy dagger, and stint of thy din,

Or I shall fawchin thy flesh, and scrape thee on the skin.

Cr. Con. Yea, wilt thou, hangman? I say, thou cavel!

Cl. Col. Nay, thou rude ravener, rain-beated javel!

Cr. Con. What, thou Colin Coward, knowen and tried!

Cl. Col. Nay, thou false-hearted dastard, thou dare not abide!

Cr. Con. An if there were none to displease but thou and I,

Thou should not 'scape, whoreson, but thou should die.

Cl. Col. Nay, I shall wring thee, whoreson, on the wrist.

Cr. Con. Mary, I defy thy best and thy worst.

[*Enter* COUNTERFEIT COUNTENANCE.

C. Count. What, a very vengeance, need all these words?

Go together by the heads, and give me your swords.

Cl. Col. So he is the worsté brawler that ever was born.

Cr. Con. In faith, so to suffer thee, it is but a scorn.

C. Count. Now let us be all one, and let us live in rest,

For we be, sirs, but a few of the best.

Cl. Col. By the mass, man, thou shalt find me reasonable.

Cr. Con. In faith, and I will be to reason agreeable.

C. Count. Then I trust to God and the holy rood,

Here shall be no great shedding of blood.

Cl. Col. By our lakin, sir, not by my will.

Cr. Con. By the faith that I owe to God, and I will sit still.

C. Count. Well said. But, in faith, what was your quarrel?

Cl. Col. Mary, sir, this gentleman called me a javel.

Cr. Con. Nay, by Saint Mary, it was ye called me knave.

Cl. Col. Mary, so ungodly language you me gave.

C. Count. Ah, shall we have more of these matters yet?

Methink ye are not greatly encumberéd with wit.

Cr. Con. God's foot, I warrant you I am a gentleman born,

And thus to be facéd I think it great scorn.

C. Count. I cannot well tell of your dispositíons;

An ye be a gentleman, ye have knavish conditíons.

Cl. Col. By God, I tell you I will not be out-facéd!

Cr. Con. By the mass, I warrant thee, I will not be bracéd.

C. Count. Tush, tush, it is a great defaut:

The one of you is too proud, the other is too haut.

Tell me briefly whereupon ye began.

Cl. Col. Mary, sir, he said that he was the prettier man

Than I was, in opening of locks;

And, I tell you, I disdain much of his mocks.

Cr. Con. Thou saw never yet but I did my part,

The lock of a casket to make to start.

C. Count. Nay, I know well enough ye are both well-handed

To grope a gardevians, though it be well banded.

Cl. Col. I am the better yet in a budget.

Cr. Con.   And I the better in a male.

C. Count. Tush, these matters that ye move are but sops in ale:

Your trimming and tramming by me must be tangéd,

For, had I not been, ye both had been hangéd,

When we with Magnificence goods made chevisaunce.

Magn. And therefore our Lord send you a very vengeance!

C. Count. What begger art thou that thus doth ban and

warry?

Magn. Ye be the thieves, I say, away my goods did carry.

Cl. Col. Cock's bones, thou beggar, what is thy name?

Magn. Magnificence I was, whom ye have brought to shame.

C. Count. Yea, but trow you, sirs, that this is he?

Cr. Con. Go we near, and let us see.

Cl. Col. By Cock's bones, it is the same.

Magn. Alas, alas, sirs, ye are to blame!

I was your master, though ye think it scorn,

And now on me ye gaure and sporn.

C. Count. Lie still, lie still now, with ill-hail!

Cr. Con. Yea, for thy language cannot thee avail.

Cl. Col. Abide, sir, abide, I shall make him to piss.

Magn. Now give me somewhat, for God's sake I crave!

Cr. Con. In faith, I give thee four quarters of a knave.

C. Count. In faith, and I bequeath him the tooth-ache.

Cl. Col. And I bequeath him the bone-ache.

Cr. Con. And I bequeath him the gout and the gin.

Cl. Col. And I bequeath him sorrow for his sin.

C. Count. And I give him Christès curse,
With never a penny in his purse.

Cr. Con. And I give him the cough, the mur, and the pose.

Cl. Col. Yea, for *requiem aeternam* groweth forth of his nose.
But now let us make merry and good cheer!

C. Count. And to the tavern let us draw near.

Cr. Con. And from thence to the halfè street,[1]
To get us there some freshè meat.

Cl. Col. Why, is there any store of rawè mutton?

C. Count. Yea, in faith, or else thou art too great a glutton!

Cr. Con. But they say it is a queasy meat;
It will strike a man mischievously in a heat.

Cl. Col. In fay, man, some ribs of the mutton be so rank
That they will fire one ungraciously in the flank.

C. Count. Yea, and when ye come out of the shop,
Ye shall be clappéd with a collop,
That will make you to halt and to hop.

Cr. Con. Some be rested there that they think on it forty
days,
For there be whorès there at all assays.

Cl. Col. For the passíon of God, let us go thither!

[And they go hurriedly out of the place.

Magn. Alas, mine own servants to shew me such reproach,
    Thus to rebuke me, and have me in despite!
So shamefully to me, their master, to approach,
    That sometime was a noble prince of might!
    Alas, to live longer I have no delight!
For to live in misery it is harder than death.
I am weary of the world, for unkindness me slèeth.

---

[1] Bankside, Southwark, where the brothels were.

*I

Stage 4.   Scene 31

Enter DESPAIR

Des. Despair is my name, that Adversity doth follow.
    In time of distress I am ready at hand;
I make heavy heartés with eyen full hollow;
    Of fervent charity I quench out the brand;
    Faith and Goodhope I make aside to stand;
In God's mercy, I tell them, is but folly to trust;
All grace and pity I lay in the dust.

What, liest thou there lingering, lewdly and loathsome?
    It is too late now thy sins to repent;
Thou hast been so wayward, so wrangling, and so wrothsome,
    And so far thou art behind of thy rent,
    And so ungraciously thy days thou hast spent,
That thou art not worthy to look God in the face.
Magn. Nay, nay, man, I look never to have part of his grace;

For I have so ungraciously my life misuséd,
Though I ask mercy, I must needs be refuséd.

Des. No, no, for thy sins be so exceeding far,
    So innumerable and so full of despite,
And against thy Maker thou hast made such war,
    That thou canst not have never mercy in his sight.
    Magn. Alas, my wickedness, that may I wite!
But now I see well there is no better rede,
But sigh and sorrow, and wish myself dead.

Des. Yea, rid thyself, rather than this life for to lead;
The world waxeth weary of thee, thou livest too long.

Enter MISCHIEF

Mis. And I, Mischief, am comen at need,
Out of thy life thee for to lead.
And look that it be not long
Ere that thyself thou go hong
With this halter good and strong;
Or else with this knife cut out a tongue

Of thy throat-bowl, and rid thee out of pain.
Thou art not the first himself hath slain.
Lo, here is thy knife and a halter! and, ere we go further,
Spare not thyself, but boldly thee murther.
Des. Yea, have done at once without delay.
Magn. Shall I myself hang with an halter? nay;
Nay, rather will I chose to rid me of this life
In sticking myself with this fairè knife.

[MAGNIFICENCE *prepares to stab himself.*

Mis. Alarum, alarum! too long we abide!
Des. Out, harrow, hell burneth! where shall I me hide?

Stage 5. Scene 32. RESTORATION

Enter GOODHOPE *and exit* DESPAIR *and* MISCHIEF.
GOODHOPE *snatches away the knife, and says:*

Good. Alas, dear son, sore cumbered is thy mind,
Thyself that thou would slay against nature and kind!
Magn. Ah, blessed may ye be, sir! what shall I you call?
Good. Goodhope, sir, my name is; remedy principal
Against all sautès of your ghostly foe.
Who knoweth me, himself may never slo.
Magn. Alas, sir, so I am lappéd in adversitie,
That Despair wellnigh had mischieved me!
For, had ye not the sooner been my refúge,
Of damnatíon I had been drawn in the luge.
Good. Undoudted ye had lost yourself eternally.
There is no man may sin more mortally
Than of wanhope through the unhappy ways,
By mischief to breviate and shorten his days.
But, my good son, learn from Despair to flee,
Wind you from wanhope, and acquaint you with me.
A great misadventure, thy Maker to displease,
Thyself mischíeving to thine endless disease!
There was never so hard a storm of misery
But through Goodhope there may come remedy.

Magn. Your words be more sweeter than any precious nard,
They mollify so easily my heart that was so hard;
There is no balm, ne gum of Araby
More delectable than your language to me.
Good. Sir, your physician is the grace of God,
That you hath punishéd with his sharp rod.
Goodhope, your pothecary assignéd am I.
That Goddés grace hath vexéd you sharplý,
And pained you with a purgation of odious povertý,
Mixed with bitter aloes of hard adversity;
Now must I make you an electuary soft,
I to minister it, you to receive it oft,
With rhubarb of repentance in you for to rest;
With drammés of devotíon your diet must be drest;
With gummés ghostly of glad heart and mind,
To thank God of his sond, and comfórt ye shall find.
Put from you presumption and admit humility,
And heartily thank God of your adversity;
And love that Lordé that for your love was dead,
Wounded from the foot to the crowné of the head.
For who loveth God can ail nothing but good;
He may help you, He may mendé your mood.
Prosperity by Him is given solaciously to man,
Adversity by Him therewith now and then;
Health of body his business to achieve,
Disease and sickness his conscíence to discrive,
Affliction and trouble to prove his patíence,
Contradictíon to prove his sapience,
Grace of assistance his measure to declare,
Sometime to fall, another time to beware.
And now ye have had, sir, a wonderous fall,
To learn you hereafter for to beware withal.
How say you, sir? can ye these wordés grope?
Magn. Yea, sir, now am I arméd with Goodhope,
And sore I repent me of my wilfulness;
I askè God mercy of my negligence,
Under Goodhope enduring ever still,
Me humbly committing unto Goddés will.

Good. Then shall you be soon delivered from distress,
For now I see coming to youward Redress.

Enter REDRESS

Red. Christ be among you, and the Holy Ghost!
Good. He be your conduct, the Lord of mightès most!
Red. Sir, is your patient anything amended?
Good. Yea, sir, he is sorry for that he hath offended.
Red. How feel you yourself, my friend? how is your mind?
Magn. A wretched man, sir, to my Maker unkind.
Red. Yea, but have ye repented with heart contrite?
Magn. Sir, the repentance I have no man can write.
Red. And have ye banishéd from you all despair?
Magn. Yea, wholly to Goodhope I have made my repair.
Good. Questionless he doth me assure
In goodhope alway for to endure.
Red. Then stand up, sir, in Goddès name!
And I trust to ratify and amend your fame.
Goodhope, I pray you with hearty affection
To send over to me Sad Circumspectíon.
Good. Sir, your requestè shall not be delayed.

[Exit GOODHOPE.

Red. Now surely, Magnificence, I am right well apayed
Of that I see you now in the state of grace;
Now shall ye be renewéd with soláce:
Take now upon you this habiliment,
And to that I say give good advertisement.

*[*MAGNIFICENCE *takes the garment.*

Magn. To your request I shall be comfortable.
Red. First, I say, with mindè firm and stable
Determine to amendè all your wanton excess,
And be ruléd by me, whichè am called Redress.
Redress my name is, that little am I used
As the world requireth, but rather I am refused.

Redress should be at the reckoning in every account,
And specially to redress that were out of joint.
Full many thingès there be that lacketh redress,
The which were too longè nowè to express;
But redress is redeless,[1] and may do no correction.
Now welcome, forsooth, Sad Circumspection.

Stage 5.   *Scene* 34

Enter Sad Circumspection

Sad Cir. Sir, after your message I hiéd me hither straight,
   For to understand your pleasure and alsó your mind.
Red. Sir, to acquaint you the continue of my conceit,
   Is from adversity Magnificence to unbind.
   Sad Cir. How fortuned you, Magnificence, so far to fall
      behind?
Magn. Sir, the long absence of you, Sad Circumspection,
Caused me of Adversity to fall in subjection.

Red. All that he saith, of truthè doth proceed;
   For where Sad Circumspection is long out of the way,
Of Adversity it is to stand in dread.
   Sad Cir. Without failè, sir, that is no nay;
   Circumspection inhateth all running astray.
But, sir, by me to rule first ye began.
Magn. My wilfulnessè, sir, excuse I ne can.

Sad. Cir. Then of folly in timès past you repent?
   Magn. Soothely, to repent me I have great cause.
Howbeit, from you I receivéd a letter sent,
   Which containéd in it a specíal clause
   That I shouldè use largesse.
   Sad Cir.   Nay, sir, there a pause.
Red. Yet let us see this matter thoroughly engrossed.
Magn. Sir, this letter ye sent to me, at Pontoise was enclosed.

[1] Powerless to act alone.

Sad Cir. Who brought you that letter, wote ye what he
hight?

Magn. Largesse, sir, by his credence was his name.

Sad Cir. This letter ye speak of, never did I write.

Red. To give so hasty credence ye were much to blame.

Magn. Truth it is, sir; for after he wrought me much
shame,

And caus**é**d me als**ó** to use too much Liberty,

And made also Measure to be put from me.

Red. Then Wealth with you might in no wise abide.

Sad Cir. Ah ha! Fancy and Folly met with you, I trow.

Red. It would be found so, if it were well tried.

Magn. Surely my wealth with them was overthrow.

Sad Cir. Remember you, therefore, how late ye were low.

Red. Yea, and beware of unhappy Abus**í**on.

Sad Cir. And keep you from counterfeiting of Cloak**é**d
Collus**í**on.

Magn. Sir, in Goodhope I am to amend**è**.

Red. Use not then your countenance for to counterfeit.

Sad Cir. And from crafters and hafters I you forfend**è**.

Stage 5.   Scene 35

Enter PERSEVERANCE

Magn. Well, sir, after your counsel my mind I will set.

Red. What, brother Pers**é**verance! surely well met.

Sad Cir. Ye come hither as well as can be thought.

Per. I heard say that Adversity with Magnificence had
fought.

Magn. Yea, sir, with Adversity I have been vex**é**d.

But Goodhope and Redress hath mended mine estate,

And Sad Circumspection to me they have annex**é**d.

Red. What this man hath said, perceive ye his conceit?

Magn. Yea, sir, from him my corage shall never flit.

Sad Cir. According to truth they be well devis**é**d.

Magn. Sirs, I am agreed to abide your ordinance,
Faithful assurance with good peradvertance.
Per. If you be so minded, we be right glad.
Red. And ye shall have more worship than ever ye had.

Magn. Well, I perceive in you there is much sadness,
    Gravity of counsel, providence, and wit;
Your comfortable advice and wit exceedeth all gladness.
    But friendly I will refrain you further, ere we flit,
    Whereto were most meetly my corage to knit:
Your mindės I beseech you herein to express,
Commencing this procéss at Master Redress.

Red. Sith unto me foremost this procéss is erected,
    Herein I will aforce me to shewė you my mind.
First, from your magnificence, sin must be abjected,
    In all workės more grace shall ye find;
    Be gentle then of corage and learn to be kind,
For of nobleness the chief point is to be liberal.
So that your largesse be not too prodigal.

Sad Cir. Libertý to a lordė belongeth of right,
    But wilful waywardness must walk out of the way;
Measure of your lustės must have the oversight,
    And not all the niggard nor the chinchard to play;
    Let never niggardship your nobleness affray;
In your rewardės use such moderatíon
That nothing be given without consideratíon.

Per. To the increase of your honour then arm you with
      right,
    And fumously address you with magnanimity;
And ever let the dread of God be in your sight;
    And know yourself mortal, for all your dignity;
      .   .   .   .   .[1]
Set not all your affiance in Fortune full of guile;
Remember this life lasteth but a while.

               [1] Line missing.

Magn. Redress, in my remembrance your lesson shall rest,
  And Sad Circumspectíon I markè in my mind:
But, Perséverance, meseemeth your problem was best;
  I shall it never forget, nor leave it behind,
  But wholly to Perséverance myself I will bind,
Of that I have misdonè to make a redress,
And with Sad Circumspectíon correct my wantonness.

Red. Unto this procéss briefly compiléd,
  Comprehending the world casual and transitory,
Who list to consider shall never be beguiléd,
  If it be registeréd well in memory;
  A plain example of worldly vain-glory,
How in this world there is no sickerness,
But fallible flattery enmixed with bitterness.

Sad Cir. A mirror encircléd is this interlude,
  This life inconstant for to behold and see;
Suddenly advancéd, and suddenly subdued,
  Suddenly riches, and suddenly poverty,
  Suddenly comfort, and suddenly adversity;
Suddenly thus Fortune can both smile and frown,
Suddenly set up, and suddenly cast down.

Suddenly promoted, and suddenly put back,
  Suddenly cherishéd, and suddenly cast aside,
Suddenly commended, and suddenly find a lack,
  Suddenly granted, and suddenly deniéd,
  Suddenly hid, and suddenly espiéd;
Suddenly thus Fortune can both smile and frown,
Suddenly set up, and suddenly cast down.

Per. This treatise, deviséd to make you disport,
  Sheweth nowadays how the world cumberéd is,
To the pith of the matter who list to resort;
  To-day it is well, to-morrow it is all amiss,
  To-day in delight, to-morrow bare of bliss,
To-day a lord, to-morrow lie in the dust:
Thus in the world there is no earthly trust.

To-day fair weather, to-morrow a stormy rage,
 To-day hot, to-morrow outragéous cold,
To-day a yeoman, to-morrow made a page,
 To-day in surety, to-morrow bought and sold,
 To-day masterfist, to-morrow he hath no hold,
To-day a man, to-morrow he lieth in the dust:
Thus in this world there is no earthly trust.

Magn. This matter we have movéd, you mirthful to make,
 Pressly purposéd under pretence of play,
Showeth wisdom to them that wisdom can take,
 How suddenly worldly wealth doth decay,
 How wisdom through wantonness vanishes away,
How none estate living of himself can be sure,
For the wealth of this worldé cannot endure;

Of the terrestre richery we fall in the flood,
 Beaten with stormés of many a froward blast,
Ensorbéd with the wavés savage and wood,
 Without our ship be sure, it is likely to brast,
 Yet of magnificence oft made is the mast;
Thus none estate living of him can be sure,
For the wealth of this worldé cannot endure.

Red. Now seemeth us fitting that ye then resort
 Home to your palace with joy and royalty.
Sad Cir. Where everything is ordainéd after your noble port.
 Per. There to endure with all felicity.
 Magn. I am content, my friendés, that it so be.
Red. And ye that have heardé this disport and game,
Jesus preserve you from endless woe and shame!

         Amen.

AGAINST VENOMOUS TONGUES

Enpoisoned with Slander and False Detractions

Quid detur tibi, aut quid apponatur tibi ad linguam dolosam?
(Ps. cxx. 3).
*Deus destruet te in finem; evellet te, et emigrabit te de taber-
nacula tuo, et radicem tuam de terra viventium.*(Ps. lii.5).

All matters well ponderéd and well to be regarded,
How should a false lying tongue then be rewarded?
Such tongues should be torn out by the hardé roots,
Hoyning like hoggés that groynés and roots.

Dilexisti omnia verba praecipitationis, lingua dolosa.[1]

For, as I have read in volumés old,
A false lying tongue is hard to withhold;
A slanderous tongue, a tongue of a scold,
Worketh more mischief than can be told;
That, if I wist not to be controlled,
Yet somewhat to say I dare well be bold,
How some delight for to lie thick and threefold.

Ad sannam hominem redigit comice et graphice.[2]

For ye said that he said that I said—wot ye what?
I made, he said, a windmill of an old mat:
If there be none other matter but that
Then ye may commend me to gentle Cock-wat.

*Hic notat purpuraria arte intextas literas Romanas in amictibus
post ambulonum ante et retro.*[3]

[1] 'Thou lovest all devouring words, O thou deceitful tongue'
(Ps. lii. 4).
[2] He brings a man to mockery, derisively and cunningly.
[3] Here he is referring to Roman letters woven in bright colours,
front and back, on the liveries of followers.

For before on your breast, and behind on your back,
In Roman letters I never found lack:
In your cross row nor Christ cross you speed,
Your Paternoster, your Ave, nor your Creed.
Whosoever that tale unto you told,
He saith untruly, to say that I wold
Control the cognizance of noble men
Either by language or with my pen.

*Paedagogium meum de sublimiori Minerva constat esse: ergo,
etc.*

My school is more solemn and somewhat more haut
Than to be found in any such fault.

*Paedagogium meum male sanos maledicos sibilis complosisque
manibus explodit, etc.*

My schools are not for unthrifts untaught,
For frantic faitors half mad and half straught; [1]
But my learning is of another degree
To taunt them like lithrons, lewd as they be.

Laxent ergo antennam elationis suae inflatem vento vanitatis.

For though some be lither, and list for to rail,
Yet to lie upon me they cannot prevail.
Then let them vale a bonet [2] of their proud sail,
And of their taunting toys rest with ill-hail.

Nobilitati ignobilis cedat vilitas, etc.

There is no nobleman will judge in me
Any such folly to rest or to be.
I care much the less whatever they say,
For tongues untied be running astray;

[1] Half in their senses.
[2] Lower one of the smaller sails.

But yet I may say safely, so many well-lettered,
Embroidered, enlacéd together, and fettered,
And so little learning, so lewdly allowed,
What fault find ye herein but may be avowed?
But ye are so full of vertibility,[1]
And of frantic folability,[2]
And of melancholy mutability,
That ye would coerce and enforcé me
Nothing to write, but hey the guy of three,[3]
And I to suffer you lewdly to lie
Of me with your language full of villany!

Sicut novacula acuta fecisti dolum.[4] *Ubi s.*

Malicious tongues, though they have no bones,
Are sharper than swords, sturdier than stones.

Lege Philostratum de vita Tyanaei Apollonii.[5]

Sharper than razors that shave and cut throatės.
More stinging than scorpions that stung Pharaotis.[6]

Venenum aspidum sub labiis eorum.[7]

More venomous and much more virulent
Than any poisoned toad or any serpént.

Quid peregrinis egemus exemplis?—ad domestica recurramus,
etc.[8] *li. ille.*

Such tongués unhappy hath made great division
In realms, in cities, by such false abusion;
Of false fickle tongues such cloakéd collusion
Hath brought noble princes to extreme confusion.

[1] Variableness.   [2] Folly.   [3] i.e. ballads.
[4] Ps. lii. 2 (Vulg.).
[5] Read Philostratus concerning the life of Apollonius of Tyana.
[6] Pharaoh (?).
[7] 'Adders' poison is under their lips' (Ps. cxl. 3).
[8] Why do we need foreign examples?—let us revert to our own
country.

Quicquid loquantur, ut effeminantur, ita effantur, etc.[1]

> Sometime women were put in great blame,
> Men said they could not their tongués atame;
> But men take upon them now all the shame,
> With scolding and slandering make their tongues lame.

*Novarum rerum cupidissimi, captatores, delatores, adulatores,
invigilatores, deliratores, etc.,*[2] *id genus li. ille.*

> For men be now tratlers and tellers of tales:
> What tidings at Totnam, what newés in Wales,
> What shippés are sailing to Scalis Malis?
> And all is not worth a couple of nut-shellés:
> But leering and lurking here and there like spies—
> The devil tear their tongues and pick out their eyes!
> Then run they with lesings and blow them about,
> With 'He wrote such a bill withouten doubt!'
> With 'I can tell you what such a man said—
> An you knew all, ye would be ill-apayéd.'

De more vulpino, gannientes ad aurem, fictas fabellas fabricant,[3]
li. ille.

*Inauspicatum, male ominatum, infortunatum se fateatur
habuisse horoscopum, quicunque maledixerit vati Pierio,
Skeltonidi Laureato, etc.*[4]

> But if that I knew what his name hight,
> For clattering of me I would him soon 'quite;
> For his false lying, of that I spake never,
> I could make him shortly repent him for ever:
> Although he made it never so tough,
> He might be sure to have shame enough.

[1] Whatever they say, they chatter like women.

[2] Greedy of novelty, legacy-hunters, informers, flatterers, spies,
madmen.

[3] Wolfishly, snarling in the ear, they frame their false fables.

[4] Whoever shall have spoken ill of the Pierian poet, Skelton
Laureate, let him confess that he has an inauspicious, ill-omened
horoscope.

Cerberus horrendo barathri latrando sub antro
Te rodatque voret, lingua dolosa, precor.[1]

A false double tongue is more fierce and fell
Than Cerberus the cur couching in the kennel of hell;
Whereof hereafter I think for to write,
Of false double tongues in the despite.

Recipit se scripturum opus sanctum, laudabile, acceptabile,
memorabileque, et nimis honorificandum.[2]

Disperdat Dominus universa labia dolosa et linguam magni-
loquam![3]

[1] I pray that Cerberus, with horrid barking beneath the cave of
the abyss, may bite you and devour you, deceitful tongue.

[2] He undertakes to write a book holy, laudable, acceptable, memorable and altogether honourable.

[3] May God destroy all deceitful lips and boasting tongues!

COLIN CLOUT

Quis consurget mecum adversus malignantes? Aut quis stabit mecum adversus operantes iniquitatem? Nemo, Domine! [1]

WHAT can it avail
To drive forth a snail,
Or to make a sail
Of an herring's tail?
To rhyme or to rail,
To write or to indict,
Either for delight
Or else for despite?
Or bookès to compile
Of divers manner style,
Vice to revile
And sin to exile?
To teach or to preach,
As reason will reach?
Say this, and say that,
His head is so fat,
He wotteth never what
Nor whereof he speaketh;
He crieth and he creaketh,
He prieth and he peeketh,
He chides and he chatters,
He prates and he patters,
He clitters and he clatters,
He meddles and he smatters,
He gloses and he flatters;
Or if he speak plain,
Then he lacketh brain,
He is but a fool;

[1] 'Who will rise up with me against evil-doers? or who will stand up with me against the workers of iniquity? No one, O Lord!' (Ps. xciv.).

Let him go to school,
On a three-footed stool
That he may down sit,
For he lacketh wit!
And if that he hit
The nail on the head,
It standeth in no stead.
The Devil, they say, is dead
The Devil is dead!

It may well so be,
Or else they would see
Otherwise, and flee
From worldly vanity,
And foul covetousness,
And other wretchedness,
Fickle falseness,
Variableness,
With unstableness.

And if ye stand in doubt
Who brought this rhyme about,
My name is Colin Clout.
I purpose to shake out
All my conning bag,
Like a clerkly hag.
For though my rhyme be ragged,
Tattered and jaggéd,
Rudely rain-beaten,
Rusty and moth-eaten,
If ye take well therewith,
It hath in it some pith.
For, as far as I can see,
It is wrong with each degree:
For the temporality
Accuseth the spirituality;
The spiritual again
Doth grudge and complain
Upon the temporal men:

Thus each of other blother
The one against the other.
Alas, they make me shudder!
For in hugger-mugger
The Church is put in fault;
The prelates ben so haut,
They say, and look so high,
As though they woulde fly
Above the starry sky.

Laymen say, indeed,
How they take no heed
Their silly sheep to feed,
But pluck away and pull
The fleeces of their wool,—
Unneth they leave a lock
Of wool among their flock!
And as for their conning,
A glumming and a mumming,
And make thereof a jape!
They gasp and they gape
All to have promotion,—
There is their whole devotion:
With money, if it will hap,
To catch the forkéd cap.[1]
Forsooth they are too lewd
To say so, all beshrewed!

What trow ye they say more
Of the bishops' lore?
How in matters they be raw,
They lumber forth the law,
To hearken Jack and Gill,
When they put up a bill,
And judge it as they will,
For other mennès skill,

[1] i.e. the mitre.

Expounding out their clauses,
And leave their ownė causes.
In their provincial cure
They make but little sure,
And meddle very light
In the Church's right;
But *ire* and *venire*,
And sol-fa so a-la-mi-re,
That the praemunire
Is like to be set afire
In their jurisdictions
Through temporal afflictions.
Men say they have prescriptions
Against spiritual contradictions,
Accounting them as fictions!

And while the heads do this,
The remnant is amiss
Of the clergy all,
Both great and small.
I wot never how they wark,
But thus the people bark,
And surely thus they say:
Bishops, if they may,
Small houses wouldė keep,
Not slumber forth and sleep,[1]
And essay to creep
Within the noble walls
Of the kingės halls,
To fat their bodies full,
Their soulės lean and dull,
And have full little care
How evil their sheep fare!

The temporality say plain,
How bishoppės disdain

[1] Sleep around.

Sermons for to make,
Or suchè labour to take.
And, for to say troth,
A great part is for sloth,
But the greatest part
Is they have little art
And right slender conning
Within their headès wonning.
But this reason they take:
How they are able to make
With their gold and treasure
Clerkès out of measure,—
And yet that is a pleasure!
Howbeit some there be
(Almost two or three)
Of that dignity,
Full worshipful clerkès,
As appeareth by their workès
Like Aaron and Ure,
The wolf from the door
To werrin and to keep
From their ghostly sheep,
And their spiritual lambs
Sequesteréd from rams
And from the bearded goats
With their hairy coats;
Set nought by gold ne groats,—
Their names if I durst tell!

But they are loth to mell,
And loth to hang the bell
About the cattès neck,[1]
For dread to have a check;
They are fain to play deuz deck![2]

[1] Loth to fix the blame.
[2] A card game.

They are made for the beck![1]
Howbeit they are good men,
Much hearted like an hen!
Their lessons forgotten they have
That Becket them gave.
Thomas *manum mittit ad fortia,*
Spernit damna, spernit opprobria,
Nulla Thomam frangit injuria![2]
But now every spiritual father,
Men say, they had rather
Spend much of their share
Than be 'cumbered with care.
Spend! nay, nay, but spare!
For let see who that dare
Shoe the mockish mare;[3]
They make her winch and kick,
But it is not worth a leek.
Boldness is to seek
The Church for to defend.

   Take me as I intend,
For loth I am to offend
In this that I have penned:
I tell you as men say.
Amend when ye may,
For, *usque ad montem Seir,*[4]
Men say ye cannot apeir![5]
For some say ye hunt in parkès,
And hawk on hobby larkès,[6]
And other wanton warkès,
When the night darkès.

---

[1] They are yes-men.

[2] . . . puts his hand to braver things, spurns loss, spurns dishonour, nothing daunts Thomas.

[3] Catch the offender.

[4] 'Even as far as Mount Seir' (Joshua xv. 10).

[5] Be worse.

[6] Wolsey lived with a mistress called Miss Lark.

What hath laymen to do
The gray goose for to shoe? [1]
Like houndès of hell,
They cry and they yell,
How that ye sell
The grace of the Holy Ghost.
Thus they make their boast
Throughout every coast,
How some of you do eat
In Lenten season flesh meat,
Pheasants, partridge, and cranes;
Men call you, therefore, profanes.
Ye pick no shrimpès nor pranes,
Salt-fish, stock-fish, nor herring,
It is not for your wearing;
Nor in holy Lenten season
Ye will neither beans ne peason.
But ye look to be let loose
To a pig or to a goose;
Your gorgè not endewéd
Without a capon stewéd,
Or a stewéd cock,
To know what is o'clock
Under her surfléd smock,
And her wanton woodècock!

And how when ye give orders
In your provincial borders,
As at *Sitientes*, [2]
Some are *insufficientes*,
Some *parum sapientes*,
Some *nihil intelligentes*,
Some *valde negligentes*,
Some *nullum sensum habentes*,
But bestial and untaught.
But when they have once caught

[1] i.e. meddle in everything.
[2] i.e. at mass—particularly on Passion Sunday.

Dominus vobiscum by the head [1]
Then run they in every stead,
God wot, with drunken nolls!
Yet take they cure of souls,
And wotteth never what they read,
Paternoster, Ave, nor Creed;
Construe not worth a whistle
Neither Gospel nor Epistle;
Their matins madly said,
Nothing devoutly prayed;
Their learning is so small,
Their primes and hourés [2] fall
And leap out of their lippés
Like sawdust or dry chippés!
I speak not now of all,
But the most part in general.
Of such vagabundus
Speaketh *totus mundus*;
How some sing *Laetabundus*
At every alé stake,
With, 'Welcome, hake and make!'
By the bread that God brake,
I am sorry for your sake.
I speak not of the good wife,
But of their apostles' life. [3]
Cum ipsis vel illis
Qui manent in villis
Est uxor vel ancilla [4]—
Welcome Jack and Jilla!
My pretty Petronilla,
An you will be stilla,
You shall have your willa!

---

[1] When they have once become priests.
[2] i.e. devotions and prayers.
[3] i.e. of the lives of the priests' women.
[4] With those very fellows [i.e. prelates] who stay in villas is a wife or a maid.

Of such Paternoster pekes
All the worldè speaks.

    In you the fault is supposéd,
For that they are not apposéd
By just examinatíon
In conning and conversatíon;
They have none instructíon
To make a true constructíon.
A priest without a letter,[1]
Without his virtue be greater,
Doubtless were much better
Upon him for to take
A mattock or a rake.
Alas, for very shame!
Some cannot decline their name,
Some can scantly read,
And yet he will not dread
For to keep a cure,
And in nothing is sure.
This *Dominus vobiscum,*
As wise as Tom-a-Thrum,
A chaplain of trust
Layeth all in the dust!

    Thus I, Colin Clout,
As I go about,
And wandering as I walk
I hear the people talk.
Men say, for silver and gold
Mitres are bought and sold;
There shall no clergy apposè
A mitre nor a crosè,[2]
But a full purse:
A straw for God's curse!
What are they the worse?

---

[1] Ignorant, unlettered.
[2] i.e. learning won't get you a bishopric or an abbey.

For a simoniac
Is but a hermoniac;
And no more ye make
Of simony, men say,
But a child's play.

Over this, the foresaid lay,
Reportè how the Pope may
An holy anchor [1] call
Out of the stonè wall,
And him a bishop make,
If he on him can take
To keep so hard a rule
To ride upon a mule [2]
With goldè all betrappéd,
In purple and pall belappéd;
Some hatted and some cappéd,
Richly and warm bewrappéd,
(God wot to their great pains!)
In rochets of fine Rennes,
White as morrow's milk;
Their tabards of finè silk,
Their stirrups of mixt gold begared:
There may no cost be spared.
Their mulès gold doth eat,
Their neighbours die for meat.

What care they though Gill sweat,
Or Jack of the Noke?
The poorè people they yoke
With summons and citatíons
And excommunicatíons,
About churches and market.
The bishop on his carpet
At home full soft doth sit.
This is a farly fit,

---

[1] Anchorite.   [2] i.e. like Wolsey.

K

To hear the people jangle,
How warlike they wrangle.
Alas, why do ye not handle
And them all to-mangle?
Full falsely on you they lie,
And shamefully you ascry,
And say as untruély
That a butterfly
(A man might say in mock)
Were the weathercock
Of the steeple of Poulès.[1]
And thus they hurt their soulès
In slandering you for truth.
Alas, it is great ruth!
Some say ye sit in thronès,
Like princes *aquilonis*,[2]
And shrine your rotten bones
With pearls and precious stones
But how the commons groans,
And the people moans
For prestès [3] and for loans
Lent and never paid,[4]
But from day to day delayed,
The commonwealth decayed,
Men say ye are tongue-tied,
And thereof speak nothing
But dissimuling and glosing.
Wherefore men be supposing
That ye give shrewd counsél
Against the common well,
By polling and pillage
In cities and village.
By taxing and tollage,
Ye make monks to have the culerage
For [5] covering of an old cottáge,

---

[1] Paul's.   [2] Lucifers.   [3] i.e. forced advances.
[4] i.e. paid back.   [5] i.e. for want of.

That committed is a college
In the charter of dotage,
Tenure par service de sottage,
And not *par service de socage*,[1]
After oldė seigneurs,
And the learning of Littleton's *Tenures*.
Ye have so overthwarted,
That good lawės are subverted,
And good reason perverted.

Religious men are fain
For to turn again
In secula seculorum,
And to forsake their quorum
And *vagabundare per forum*,[2]
And take a fine *meritorum,*
Contra regulam morum,
Aut black *monachorum,*
Aut canonicorum,
Aut Bernardinorum,
Aut crucifixorum,[3]
And to sing from place to place,
Like apostates.

And the selfsame game
Begun is now with shame
Among the silly nuns.
My lady now she runs,
Dame Sibyl our abbėss,
Dame Dorothy and Lady Bess,
Dame Sarah our prioress,
Out of their cloister and choir
With an heavy cheer,

[1] i.e. held for being dolts and not as payment for labours done.
[2] To wander through the market-place.
[3] To beg, or work for money, contrary to the rule of the order, either of the Dominicans, or of the Augustinian Canons, or of the Benedictines, or of the Cistercians.

Must cast up their black veils
And set up their fuck-sails,[1]
To catch wind with their ventales —
What, Colin, there thou shales!
Yet thus with ill-hails [2]
The laity rails.

And all the fault they lay
On your precept, and say
Ye do them wrong and no right
To put them thus to flight;
No matins at midnight,
Book and chalice gonè quite;
And pluck away the leads
Even over their heads,
And sell away their bells,
And all that they have else!
Thus the people tells,
Rails like rebèls,
Redes shrewdly and spells,
And with foundations mells,
And talks like titivels,
How ye brake the deadès wills,
Turn monasteries into water-mills;[3]
Of an abbey ye make a grange
(Your works, they say, are strange)
So that their founders' souls
Have lost their beadèrolls,
The money for their masses
Spent among wanton lasses;
The *Diriges* are forgotten;
Their founders lie there rotten,
But where their soulès dwell,
Therewith I will not mell.

[1] Foresails—fashionable head-dresses. The implication is that they are forced to become prostitutes.

[2] Unhealthily.

[3] Bromhall, suppressed 5 Dec. 1521.

What could the Turk do more
With all his falsè lore,
Turk, Saracen, or Jew?
I report me to you,
O merciful Jesu,
Your support and rescue,
My style for to direct,
It may take some effect!
For I abhor to write
How the laity despite
You prelates, that of right
Should be lanterns of light.
Ye live, they say, in delight,
Drownéd *in deliciis*,
In gloria et divitiis,
In admirabili honore,
In gloria et splendore
Fulgurantis hastae,
Viventes parum caste.[1]
Yet sweet meat hath sour sauce:
For after *gloria, laus*,
Christ by crueltý
Was nailéd upon a tree;
He paid a bitter pension
For man's redemption;
He drank eisel and gall
To redeem us withal;
But sweet hippocras ye drink,
With, 'Let the cat wink!'
Ich wot what each other think.
Howbeit, *per assimile*,
Some men think that ye
Shall have penalty
For your iniquity.
Nota what I say,
And bear it well away.

[1] . . . in luxury, in glory and riches, in amazing state, in pomp
and magnificence with splendid possessions, living unchastely.

If it please not theologues,
It is good for astrologues:
For Ptolemy told me
The sun sometime to be
In Ariete [1]
Ascendant a degree,
When Scorpion descending
Was so then portending
A fatal fall of one [2]
That should sit on a throne,
And rule all things alone.
Your teeth whet on this bone
Amongst you every one,
And let Colin Clout have none
Manner of cause to moan.
Lay salve to your owné sore,
For else, as I said before,
After *gloria, laus,*
May come a souré sauce.
Sorry therefore am I,
But truth can never lie.

With language thus polluted
Holy Church is bruted
And shamefully confuted.
My pen now will I sharp,
And wrest up my harp
With sharp twinking trebles,
Against all suché rebels
That labour to confound
And bring the Church to the ground;
As ye may daily see
How the laity
Of one affinity

[1] Aries, the Ram.
[2] Wolsey.

Consent and agree
Against the Church to be,
And the dignity
Of the bishops' see.

And either ye be too bad,
Or else they are mad
Of this to report.
But, under your support,
Till my dying day
I shall both write and say,
And ye shall do the same,
How they are to blame
You thus to defame.
For it maketh me sad
How that the people are glad
The Church to deprave;
And some there are that rave,
Presuming on their wit,
When there is never a whit
To maintain arguments
Against the sacraments.

Some make epilogatíon
Of high predestinatíon;
And of recidivatíon
They make interpretatíon
Of an awkward fashíon;
And of the prescience
Of divine essence;
And what hypostasis
Of Christ's manhood is.
Such logic men will chop,
And in their fury hop,
When the good ale sop
Doth dance in their foretop!
Both women and men,
Such ye may well know and ken.

That against priesthood
Their malice spread abroad,
Railing heinously
And disdainously
Of priestly dignities,
With their malignities.

    And some have a smack
Of Luther's sack,
And a burning spark
Of Luther's wark,
And are somewhat suspect
In Luther's sect;
And some of them bark,
Clatter and carp
Of that heresiarch
Called Wicliffista,
The devilish dogmatista;
And some be Hussians,
And some be Arians,
And some be Pelagians,
And make much variance
Between the clergy
And the temporalty,
How the Church hath too mickle,
And they have too little,
And bring in materialities
And qualified qualities
Of pluralities,
Of trialities,[1]
And of tot quots [2]
They commune like sots,
As cometh to their lots;
Of prebendaries and deans,
How some of them gleans
And gathereth up the store
For to catch more and more;

[1] Triple Benefices.   [2] Dispensations.

Of parsons and vicaries
They make many outcries—
They cannot keep their wives
From them for their lives!
And thus the losels strives,
And lewdly says, by Christ,
Against the silly priest.
Alas, and wellaway,
What ails them thus to say?
They might be better adviséd
Than to be so disguiséd! [1]
But they have enterprised,
And shamefully surmiséd,
How prelacy is sold and bought,
And come up of nought;
And where the prelates be
Come of low degree,
And set in majesty
And spiritual dignity,
Farewell benignity,
Farewell simplicity,
Farewell humility,
Farewell good charity!

Ye are so puffed with pride,[2]
That no man may abide
Your high and lordly looks:
Ye cast up then your books,
And virtue is forgotten;
For then ye will be wroken
Of every light quarrél,
And call a lord a javel,
A knight a knave ye make;
Ye boast, ye face, ye crake,
And upon you ye take
To rule both king and kaiser;
An if ye may have leisure,

[1] Behave so badly.   [2] Wolsey.

Ye will bring all to nought,
And that is all your thought!
For the lordės temporal,
Their rule is very small,
Almost nothing at all.
Men say how ye appal
The noble blood royall.
In earnest and in game,
Ye are the less to blame,
For lords of noble blood,
If they well understood
How conning might them advance,
They would pipe you another dance.
But noblemen born
To learn they have scorn,
But hunt and blow an horn,
Leap over lakės and dykes,
Set nothing by politics.
Therefore ye keep them base,
And mock them to their face.
This is a piteous case!
To you that be on the wheel [1]
Great lords must crouch and kneel
And break their hose at the knee,
As daily men may see,
And to remembrance call.
Fortune so turneth the ball
And ruleth so over all,
That honour hath a great fall.

Shall I tell you more? yea, shall.
I am loth to tell all;
But the commonalty you call [2]
Idols of Babylon,
De Terra Zabulon,
De Terra Neptalim;

[1] i.e. atop of Fortune's wheel.
[2] Call you.

For ye love to go trim,
Brought up of poor estate,
With pride inordinate,
Suddenly upstart
From the dung-cart,
The mattock and the shule,
To reign and to rule;
And have no grace to think
How ye were wont to drink
Of a leather bottle
With a knavish stopple,
When mammocks was your meat,
With mouldy bread to eat;
Ye could none other get
To chew and to gnaw,
To fill therewith your maw;
Lodging in fairė straw,
Couching your drowsy heads
Sometime in lousy beds.
Alas, this is out of mind!
Ye grow now out of kind.
Many one ye have untwined,
And made the commons blind.
But *qui se existimat stare*,[1]
Let him well bewarė
Lest that his foot slip,
And have such a trip,
And fall in such decay,
That all the world may say,
'Come down, in the devil way!'

Yet, over all that,
Of bishops they chat,
That though ye round your hair
An inch above your ear,
And have *aures patentes* [2]

[1] 'Who thinketh he standeth   .' (1 Cor. x. 12).
[2] Open ears.

And *parum intendentes*,[1]
And your tonsures be croppéd,
Your ears they be stoppéd!
For Master *Adulator*,[2]
And Doctor *Assentator*,[3]
And *Blandior blandiris*,[4]
With *Mentior mentiris*,[5]
They follow your desirės,
And so they blear your eye,[6]
That ye cannot espy
How the male doth wry.[7]

Alas, for God's will,
Why sit ye, prelates, still
And suffer all this ill?
Ye bishops of estates [8]
Should open the broad gates
Of your spiritual charge,
And come forth at large,
Like lanterns of light,
In the people's sight,
In pulpits authentic,
For the weal public
Of priesthood in this case;
And always to chase
Such manner of schismatics
And half heretics,
That would intoxicate,
That would coinquinate,
That would contaminate,
And that would violate,
And that would derogate,
And that would abrogate
The Church's high estates,[9]

---

[1] Too little hearing.   [2] Sycophant.   [3] Yes-man.
[4] I flatter, you flatter.   [5] I lie, you lie.   [6] Do you in the eye.
[7] How everything goes awry.   [8] Of high rank.
[9] Dignitaries.

After this manner rates,—
The which should be
Both frank and free,
And have their liberty,
As of antiquity
It was ratified,
And also gratified
By holy synodals
And bulls papals,
As it is *res certa*
Contained in *Magna Charta*.

But Master Damyan,
Or some other man,
That clerkly is and can
Well scripture expound
And his textès ground,
His benefice worth ten pound,
Or scant worth twenty mark,
And yet a noble clerk,
He must do this wark;
As I know a part,
Some masters of art,
Some doctors of law,
Some learned in other saw,
As in divinity,
That hath no dignity
But the poor degree
Of the university;
Or else friar Frederic,
Or else friar Dominic,
Or friar Hugulinus,
Or friar Augustinus,
Or friar Carmelus,
That ghostly can heal us;
Or else if we may
Get a friar gray,
Or else of the order

Upon Greenwich border,
Calléd Observance,
Or a friar of France;
Or else the poor Scot,
It must come to his lot
To shoot forth his shot;
Or of Babwell beside Bury,
To postel [1] upon a *Kyrie*,
That would it should be noted
How scripture should be quoted,
And so clerkly promoted;
And yet the friar doted.

But men say your authority,
And your noble see,
And your dignity,
Should be imprinted better
Than all the friars' letter;
For if ye would take pain
To preach a word or twain,
Though it were never so plain,
With clauses two or three,
So as they might be
Compendiously conveyed,
These words should be more weighed,
And better perceivéd,
And thankfullerly receivéd,
And better should remain
Among the people plain,
That would your words retain
And rehearse them again,
Than a thousand thousand other
That blabber, bark, and blother,
And make a Welshman's hose [2]
Of the text and of the glose.

[1] Annotate.
[2] i.e. turn it anyway to suit their purpose.

For protestation made,
That I will not wade
Farther in this brook,
Nor farther for to look
In devising of this book,
But answer that I may
For myself alway,
Either *analogice*
Or else *categorice*,
So that in divinity
Doctors that learnéd be,
Nor bachelors of that faculty
That hath taken degree
In the university,
Shall not be object at by me.

But Doctor Bullatus,
Parum litteratus,
Dominus doctoratus
At the Broadgatus,[1]
Doctor Dawpatus,
And bachelor *bacheleratus*,
Drunken as a mouse,
At the ale house,
Taketh his pillion and his cap
At the good ale tap,
For lack of good wine;
As wise as Robin swine,
Under a notary's sign
Was made a divine;
As wise as Waltham's calf,[2]
Must preach, a God's half,
In the pulpit solemnly—
More meet in the pillory!
For, by Saint Hilary,

[1] Broadgates Hall, Oxford, now Pembroke College.
[2] That ran nine miles to suck a bull.

He can nothing smatter
Of logic nor school matter,
Neither *syllogisare*,[1]
Nor *enthymemare*,[2]
Nor knoweth his elenchès,[3]
Nor his predicamentès; [4]
And yet he will mell
To amend the Gospél,
And will preach and tell
What they do in hell;
And he dare not well neven [5]
What they do in heaven,
Nor how far Temple Bar is
From the Seven Starrès.

Now will I go
And tell of other mo,
Semper protestando
De non impugnando [6]
The four orders of friars,
Though some of them be liars;
As limiters [7] at large
Will charge and discharge;
As many a friar, God wote,
Preaches for his groat,
Flattering for a new coat
And for to have his fees;
Some to gather cheese;
Loth they are to lese
Either corn or malt;
Sometime meal and salt,
Sometime a bacon flick,
That is three fingers thick

---

[1] Syllogize. [2] Construct an enthymeme.
[3] Elenchis—in logic. [4] In logic. [5] Name.
[6] Always protesting about not attacking.
[7] Friars licensed to beg within certain districts.

Of lardé and of grease,
Their convent to increase.

I put you out of doubt,
This cannot be brought about
But they their tongués file,
And make a pleasant style
To Margery and to Maud,
How they have no fraud;
And sometime they provoke
Both Gill and Jack at Noke
Their duties to withdraw,
That they ought by law
Their curates to content
In open time [1] and Lent.
God wot, they take great pain
To flatter and to feign;
But it is an old-said saw,
That need hath no law.
Some walk about in melottes, [2]
In gray russet and hairy coats;
Some will neither gold nor groats;
Some pluck a partridge in remotes,
And by the bars of her tail
Will know a raven from a rail,
A quail, the rail, and the old ravén!
Sed libera nos a malo!   Amen.
And by *Dudum*, their Clementine, [3]
Against curates they repine;
And say properly they are *sacerdotes*,
To shrive, assoil, and release
Dame Margery's soul out of hell.
But when the friar fell in the well,

[1] When no fasts were imposed.

[2] Skin or hair garments, reaching from neck to loins, worn by monks during manual labour.

[3] A bull of Clement V beginning with the word *Dudum* (see *Clement.*, lib. III, tit. vii, cap. 2).

He could not sing himself thereout
But by the help of Christian Clout.[1]
Another Clementine alsó,
How friar Fabian, with other mo,
Exivit de Paradiso;
When they again thither shall come,
De hoc petimus consilium:
And through all the world they go
With *Dirige* and *Placebo*.

But now my mind ye understand,
For they must take in hand
To preach, and to withstand
All manner of objections;
For bishops have protections,
They say, to do corrections,
But they have no affections
To take the said directions.
In such manner of cases,
Men say, they bear no faces
To occupy such places,
To sow the seed of graces:
Their heartès are so fainted,
And they be so attainted
With covetise and ambition,
And other superstition,
That they be deaf and dumb,
And play silence and glum,
Can say nothing but 'Mum!'

They occupy them so
With singing *Placebo*,
They will no farther go:
They had liefer to please,
And take their worldly ease,

[1] Refers to the ballad *The Friar Well-fitted* (see *Ballads*, British Museum, 643 m).

Than to take on hand
Worshipfully to withstand
Such temporal war and bate
As now is made of late
Against Holy Church estate,
Or to maintain good quarrels.
The lay men call them barrels
Full of gluttony
And of hypocrisy,
That counterfeits and paints
As they were very saints.
In matters that them like
They shew them politic,
Pretending gravity
And signiority,
With all solemnity,
For their indemnity!
For they will have no loss
Of a penny nor of a cross [1]
Of their predial lands,
That cometh to their hands,
And as far as they dare set,
All is fish that cometh to net.
Building royally [2]
Their mansions curiously,
With turrets and with towers,
With hallès and with bowers,
Stretching to the stars,
With glass windows and bars;
Hanging about the wallès
Cloths of gold and pallès,
Arras of rich array,
Fresh as flowers in May;
With dame Diana naked;
How lusty Venus quakéd,
And how Cupid shakéd

[1] Coin so marked.
[2] Refers especially to Wolsey's building of Hampton Court.

His dart, and bent his bow
For to shoot a crow
At her tirly tirlow;
And how Paris of Troy
Dancéd a lege de moy,
Made lusty sport and joy
With dame Helen the queen;
With such stories bydene
With Triumphs of Cæsar,[1]
And of Pompeius' war,
Of renown and of fame,
By them to get a name.
Now all the worldè stares,
How they ride in goodly chairs
Conveyéd by elephants,
With laureate garlants,
And by unicornès
With their seemly hornès;
Upon these beastès riding,
Naked boyès striding,
With wanton wenches winking.
Now truly, to my thinking,
That is a speculatíon
And a meet meditatíon
For prelates of estate,
Their corage to abate
From worldly wantonness,
Their chambers thus to dress
With such parfitness
And all such holiness!
Howbeit they let down fall
Their churches cathedrall.

Squire, knight, and lord,
Thus the Church remord;

[1] This, and the following, is a description of a definite set of
tapestries at Hampton Court known as 'Petrarch's Triumphs.'

With all temporal people
They run against the steeple,
Thus talking and telling
How some of you are melling,
Yet soft and fair for swelling—
Beware of a quean's yelling.[1]
It is a busy thing
For one man to rule a king
Alone and make reckoning,
To govern over all
And rule a realm royall
By one man's very wit.
Fortune may chance to flit,
And when he weneth to sit,
Yet may he miss the cushion.
For I rede a preposition—
Cum regibus amicare,
Et omnibus dominari,
Et supra te pravare.[2]
Wherefore he hath good ure
That can himself assure
How fortune will endure.
Then let reason you support,
For the commonalty doth report
That they have great wonder
That ye keep them so under;
Yet they marvel so much less,
For ye play so at the chess,
As they suppose and guess,
That some of you but late
Hath playéd so checkmate
With lords of great estate,
After such a rate,
That they shall mell nor make,

[1] i.e. a woman's chatter.
[2] To be friendly with kings, and all things to rule, and to overleap thyself.

Nor upon them take,
For king's nor kaiser's sake,
But at the pleasure of one
That ruleth the roast alone.

Helas, I say, helas!
How may this come to pass,
That a man shall hear a mass,
And not so hardy on his head
To look on God in form of bread,
But that the parish clerk
Thereupon must hark,
And grant him at his asking
For to see the sacring?

And how may this accord,
No man to our sovereign lord
So hardy to make suit,
Nor yet to execute
His commandment,
Without the assent
Of our president,
Nor to express to his person,
Without your consentation
Grant him his licence
To press to his presence,
Nor to speak to him secretly,
Openly nor privily,
Without this president be by,
Or else his substitute
Whom he will depute?
Neither earl ne duke
Permitted?   By saint Luke,
And by sweet saint Mark,
This is a wondrous wark!
That the people talkë this,
Somewhat there is amiss.

The Devil cannot stop their mouths,
But they will talk of such uncouths,
All that ever they ken
Against all spiritual men!

Whether it be wrong or right,
Or else for despite,
Or however it hap,
Their tongues thus do clap,
And through such detraction
They put you to your action;
And whether they say truly
As they may abide thereby.
Or else that they do lie,
Ye know better than I!
But now *debetis scire*,
And groundly *audire*,
In your *convenire*,
Of this praemunire,
Or else in the mirè
They say they will you cast.
Therefore stand sure and fast!

Stand sure, and take good footing,
And let be all your mooting,
Your gasping and your tooting,
And your partíal promoting
Of those that stand in your grace.
But oldè servants ye chase,
And put them out of their place.
Make ye no murmuration,
Though I write after this fashion;
Though I, Colin Clout,
Among the wholè rout
Of you that clerkès be,
Take now upon me
Thus copiously to write,
I do it for no despite.

Wherefore take no disdain
At my style rude and plain;
For I rebuke no man
That virtuous is: why then
Wreak ye your anger on me?
For those that virtuous be
Have no cause to say
That I speak out of the way.

Of no good bishop speak I,
Nor good priest I ascry,
Good friar, nor good chanon,
Good nunnė, nor good canon
Good monkė, nor good clerk,
Nor yet of no good work.
But my recounting is
Of them that do amiss,
In speaking and rebelling,
In hindering and disavailing [1]
Holy Church, our mother,
One against another.
To use such despiting
Is all my wholė writing;
To hinder no man,
As near as I can,
For no man have I naméd:
Wherefore should I be blaméd?
Ye ought to be ashaméd,
Against me to be graméd,
And can tell no cause why,
But that I write truly!

Then if any there be
Of high or low degree
Of the spirituality,
Or of the temporality,

[1] Acting to the detriment of.

That doth think or ween
That his conscience be not clean,
And feeleth himself sick,
Or touchéd on the quick,
Such grace God them send
Themselfé to amend,—
For I will not pretend
Any man to offend.

Wherefore, as thinketh me,
Great idiots they be,
And little grace they have,
This treatise to deprave;
Nor will hear no preaching,
Nor no virtuous teaching,
Nor will have no resting
Of any virtuous writing;
Will know none intelligence
To reform their negligence,
But live still out of fashíon,
To their own damnatíon.
To do shame they have no shame,
But they would no man should them blame!
They have an evil name,
But yet they will occupy the same!

With them the word of God
Is counted for no rod;
They count it for a railing,
That nothing is availing.
The preachers with evil hailing:
'Shall they daunt us prelates,
That be their primates?
Not so hardy on their pates!
Hark, how the losel prates,
With a wide wesaunt!
Avaunt, sir Guy of Gaunt!
Avaunt, lewd priest, avaunt!

Avaunt, sir doctor Devias!
Prate of thy matins and thy mass,
And let our matters pass!
How darest thou, dawcock, mell?
How darest thou, losél,
Allegate the Gospel
Against us of the council?
Avaunt to the devil of hell!
Take him, Warden of the Fleet,[1]
Set him fast by the feet!
I say, Lieutenant of the Tower,
Make this lurdain for to lour;
Lodge him in Little Ease,[2]
Feed him with beans and peas!
The King's Bench or Marshalsea,
Have him thither by and by!
The villain preacheth openly,
And declareth our villany;
And of our free simpleness,
He says that we are reckeless,
And full of wilfulness,
Shameless and merciless,
Incorrigible and insatiate;
And after this rate
Against us doth prate!

'At Paulés Cross or elsewhere,
Openly at Westminstere,
And Saint Mary Spittle,
They set not by us a whistle!
At the Austin Friars
They count us for liars!
And at Saint Thomas of Akers
They clack of us like crakers,
How we will rule all at will
Without good reason or skill;

[1] i.e. Fleet Prison.
[2] Concerning this famous cell, see Ainsworth's *Tower of London*.

And say how that we be
Full of partialitý;
And how at a prong
We turn right into wrong,
Delay causes so long
That right no man can fong;
They say many matters be born
By the right of a ramés horn![1]
Is not this a shameful scorn,
To be tearéd thus and torn?

'How may we this endure?
Wherefore we make you sure,
Ye preachers shall be yawed;
And some shall be sawed,
As noble Isaias,
The holy prophet, was;
And some of you shall die,
Like holy Jeremy;
Some hangéd, some slain,
Some beaten to the brain;
And we will rule and reign,
And our matters maintain,
Who dare say there again,[2]
Or who dare disdain,
At our pleasure and will.
For, be it good or be it ill,
As it is, it shall be still,—
For all master doctor of Civil,
Or of Dominic, or doctor Drivel,
Let him cough, rough, or snivel!
Run God, run Devil,
Run who may run best,
And let take all the rest!
We set not a nutshell
The way to heaven or hell!'

[1] By justice as crooked as a ram's horns.
[2] Whoever dare say anything against it.

Lo, this is the guise nowadays!
It is to dread, men says,
Lest they be Sadducees,
As they be said sain,[1]
Which determinéd plain
We should not rise again
At dreadful doomésday.
And so it seemeth they play,
Which hate to be corrected
When they be infected,
Nor will suffer this book
By hook ne by crook
Printed for to be,
For that no man should see
Nor read in any scrolls
Of their drunken nolls,
Nor of their nodipolls,
Nor of their silly souls,
Nor of some witless pates
Of divers great estates,
As well as other men.

Now to withdraw my pen,
And now a while to rest,
Meseemeth it for the best.

The forecastle of my ship
Shall glide, and smoothly slip
Out of the wavés wood
Of the stormy flood;
Shoot anchor, and lie at road,
And sail not far abroad,
Till the coast be clear,
And the lode-star appear.
My ship now will I steer
Toward the port salu
Of our Saviour Jesu,

[1] Called commonly.

Such grace that He us send,
To rectify and amend
Things that are amiss,
When that His pleasure is.
        Amen!

In opere imperfecto,
In opere semper perfeito,
Et in opere plusquam perfecto! [1]

Colinus Cloutus, quanquam mea carmina multis
Sordescunt stultus, sed puevinate sunt rare cultis,
Pue vinatis altisem divino flamine flatis.
Unde mea refert tanto minus, invida quamvis
Lingua nocere parat, quia, quanquam rustica canto,
Undique cantabor tamen et celebrabor ubique,
Inclita dum maneat gens Anglica.   Laurus honoris,
Quondam regnorum regina et gloria regum,
Heu, modo marcescit, tabescit, languida torpet!
Ah pudet, ah miseret! vetor hic ego pandere plura
Pro genitu et lacrimis: praestet peto praemia paena. [2]

[1] In an imperfect work, in a work always perfect, and in a work more than perfect.

[2] [First three lines unintelligible.]   Whence it concerns me so much the less, although the envious tongue prepares to hurt, because, although I sing of rustic things, yet I shall be sung about on all sides, and everywhere shall be celebrated, so long as the glorious English race remains.   The laurel of honour, once the queen of possessions and the glory of kings, alas! now decays and rots and grows languid and torpid!   Ah, the shame! ah, the pity!   Here I am forbidden, for groaning and tears, to speak more.   I pray the rewards may exceed the punishment.

SPEAK, PARROT

My name is Parrot, a bird of Paradise,
  By nature devisèd of a wonderous kind,
Daintily dieted with divers delicate spice
  Till Euphrates, that flood, driveth me into Ind;
  Where men of that countrý by fortune me find
And send me to greatè ladyès of estate:
Then Parrot must have an almond or a date.

A cage curiously carven, with a silver pin,
  Properly painted, to be my coverture;
A mirror of glassè, that I may toot therein:
  These, maidens full meekly with many a divers flower,
  Freshly they dress, and makè sweet my bower,
With 'Speak, Parrot, I pray you!' full curtesly they say,
'Parrot is a goodly bird, a pretty popinjay!'

With my bekè bent, my little wanton eye,
  My feathers fresh as is the emerald green,
About my neck a circulet like the rich rubý,
  My little leggès, my feet both feat and clean,
  I am a minion to wait upon a queen
'My proper Parrot, my little pretty fool!'
With ladies I learn, and go with them to school.

'Ha! Ha! Ha! Parrot, ye can laugh prettily!'
  Parrot hath not dinèd all this long day.
Like your puss-cat, Parrot can mew and cry
  In Latin, Hebrew, Araby and Chaldy;
  In Greekè tongue Parrot can both speak and say,
As Persius, that poet, doth report of me,
'*Quis expedivit psittaco suum chaire?*' [1]

[1] Who taught Parrot to say 'Hallo!' ($\chi a \hat{\iota} \rho \epsilon$)?
288

Doucè French of Paris Parrot can learne,
   Pronouncing my purpose after my propertý,
With 'Parlez bien, Parrot, ou parlez rien!'
   With Dutch, with Spanish, my tongue can agree,
   In English to God Parrot can supply: [1]
'Christ save King Henry the Eighth, our royal king,
The red rose in honour to flourish and spring!

With Katherine incomparable, our royal queen alsó,
   That peerless pomegranate, Christ save her noble grace!'
Parrot *sabe hablar Castiliano*,[2]
   With *fidarsi di se stesso* [3] in Turkey and in Thrace;
   Vis consilii expers, as teacheth me Horáce,
Mole ruit sua,[4] whose dictates are pregnánt,
Soventez foys, Parrot, *en souvenante*.[5]

My lady mistress, Dame Philology,
   Gave me a giftè, in my nest when I lay,
To learn all language, and it to speak aptlý.
   Now *pandez mory*, wax frantic, some men say,
   Phronesis for Phrenesis may not hold her way.[6]
An almond now for Parrot, delicately drest:
In *Salve festa dies*, *toto* there doth best.[7]

Moderata juvant,[8] but *toto* doth exceed:
   Discretion is mother of noble virtues all.
Myden agan [9] in Greekè tongue we read.
   But reason and wit wanteth their provincial
   When wilfulness is vicar general.
Haec res acu tangitur,[10] Parrot, *par ma foy*:
Taisez-vous, Parrot, *tenez-vous coy!* [11]

[1] Pray.   [2] Can speak Castillian.   [3] To trust in oneself.
[4] Strength without wisdom falls by its own weight.
[5] Many times within memory.
[6] Understanding (or Prudence) may not avail against Frenzy.
[7] On holiday it is best to go the whole hog.
[8] Moderation delights us.
[9] i.e. Μηδὲν ἄγαν—Nothing in excess.
[10] i.e. this hits the nail on the head.
[11] 'Shut up, Parrot, be quiet!'

Busy, busy, busy, and business again!
　　Que pensez-vous, Parrot? what meaneth this business?
Vitulus [1] in Horeb troubléd Aaron's brain,
　　Melchizadek merciful made Moloch merciless:
　　Too wise is no virtue, too meddling, too restléss.
In measure is treasure, *cum sensu maturato*,[2]
Ne tropo sanno, ne tropo mato.[3]

Aaron was fíréd with Chaldee's fire called Ur,
　　Jobab [4] was brought up in the land of Hus,
The lineage of Lot took support of Assúr,
　　Jereboseth is Hebrew, who list the cause discuss—
　　'Peace, Parrot, ye prate as ye were *ebrius*: [5]
Hist thee, *lieber Got von Himmelsreich, ich seg!*' [6]
In Popering grew pears when Parrot was an egg.

What is this to purpose?　'Over in a whinny Meg!' [7]
　　Hob Lobin of Lowdeon [8] would hae a bit a' bread;
The gibbet of Baldock was made for Jack Leg;
　　An arrow unfeatheréd and without an head,
　　A bagpipe without blowing standeth in no stead:
Some run too far before, some run too far behind,
Some be too churlish, and some be too kind.

Ich dien serveth for the ostrich feather,
　　Ich dien is the language of the land of Beme; [9]
In Afric tongue *byrsa* is a thong of leather;
　　In Palestina there is Jerusaleme.
　　Colostrum [10] now for Parrot, white bread and sweet cream!
Our Thomasen she doth trip, our jennet she doth shale:
Parrot hath a blacké beard and a fair green tail.

'Morish mine own shelf!' the costermonger saith,
　　'*Fate, fate, fate!*' [11] ye Irish waterlag;

　　　　[1] The calf.　　　　　　[2] With a mature perception.
　　[3] Not too sane, and not too mad.　　　[4] Job.　　　[5] Drunk.
　　[6] i.e. *sage*.　　　[7] The beginning of a ballad.　　　[8] Lothian.
　　[9] Bohemia.　　　[10] Milk beestings.　　　[11] Water, water, water!

In flattering fables men find but little faith,
  But *moveatur terra*, let the world wag;
  Let Sir Wrig-wrag wrestle with Sir Dalyrag;
Every man after his manner of ways,
Paub yn ei arver,[1] so the Welchman says.

Such shreddès of sentence, strewéd in the shop
  Of ancíent Aristippus and such other mo,
I gader together and close in my crop,
  Of my wanton conceit, *unde depromo*
  Dilemmata docta in paedagogio
Sacro vatem,[2] whereof to you I break.
I pray you, let Parrot have liberty to speak!

But 'Ware the cat, Parrot, ware the falsé cat!'
  With 'Who is there—a maid? Nay, nay, I trow!'
'Ware riot, Parrot! Ware riot, ware that!'
  'Meat, meat for Parrot, meat I say, ho!'
  Thus diverse of language by learning I grow,
With 'Buss me, sweet Parrot, buss me, sweet sweet!'
To dwell among ladyès Parrot is meet.

'Parrot, Parrot, Parrot, pretty popinjay!'
  With my beak I can pick my little pretty toe;
My delight is solace, pleasure, disport, and play.
  Like a wanton, when I will, I reel to and fro.
  Parrot can say *Caesar, ave!* alsó.
But Parrot hath no favour to Esebon.[3]
Above all other birdès, set Parrot alone.

Ulula, Esebon, for Jeremy doth weep!
  Zion is in sadness, Rachel ruely doth look;
Madionita Jethro, our Moses keepeth his sheep;
  Gideon is gone, that Zalmane undertook,
  Horeb *et* Zeb, of *Judicum* read the book.

[1] Every one in his manner.

[2] Whence I produce learned arguments in the poet's sacred school.

[3] i.e. Heshbon, capital of Sihon, King of the Amorites—that is, London.

L

Now Zebul, Ammon, and Abimalech—'Hark, hark!
Parrot pretendeth to be a Bible clerk!'

O Esebon, Esebon! to thee is come again
   Sihon, the regent *Amorraeorum*,
And Og,[1] that fat hog of Bashan, doth retain
   The crafty *coistronus Cananaeorum*;
    And *asylum*, whilom *refugium miserorum*,
Non fanum, sed profanum, standeth in little stead.[2]
Ulula, Esebon, for Jephthah is stark dead!

Esebon, Marylebone, Whetstone next Barnet;
   A trim-tram for an horse-mill it were a nice thing!
Dainties for damoiselles, chaffer far-fet: [3]
   Bo-ho doth bark well, but Hough-ho he ruleth the ring;
   From Scarpary to Tartary renown therein doth spring,
With 'He said,' and 'We said,' ich wot now what ich wot [4]—
Quod magnus est dominus Judas Iscariot.[5]

Ptolemy and Haly were cunning and wise
   In the volvel,[6] in the quadrant, and in the astroloby,
To prognosticate truly the chance of Fortune's dice;
   Some treat of their tirykis, some of astrology,
   Some *pseudo-propheta* with chiromancy.
If Fortune be friendly, and grace be the guide,
Honour with renown will run on that side.

> *Monon calon agaton,*[7]
> Quod Parrato
> *In Graeco.*

[1] Wolsey. Josephus (*Ant.* IV. v. 3) represents Og as Sihon's friend and ally.

[2] Wolsey and Veysey were chiefly instrumental in abolishing the right of sanctuary.

[3] Far-fetched merchandise.

[4] I know now what I know.

[5] But mighty is lord Judas Iscariot (Wolsey).

[6] A kind of astronomical clock.

[7] i.e. Μόνον καλὸν ἀγαθόν—the only beauty is goodness.

Let Parrot, I pray you, have liberty to prate,
   For *aurea lingua Graeca* ought to be magnifiéd,
If it were conned perfitely, and after the rate,
   As *lingua Latina*, in school matter occupiéd.
    But our Greekės their Greek so well have appliéd
That they cannot say in Greek, riding by the way,
'Ho, hostler, fetch my horse a bottle of hay!'

Neither frame a syllogism in *phrisesomorum*,
   Formaliter et Graece, cum medio termino.
Our Greekės wallow in the wash-bowl *Argolicorum*;
   For though ye can tell in Greek what is *phormio*,[1]
Yet ye seek out your Greek *in Capricornio*;
For they scrape out good scripture, and set in a gall,
Ye go about to amendė, and ye mar all.

Some argue *secundum quid ad simpliciter*,
   And yet he would be reckonéd *pro Areopagita*;[2]
And some make distinctions *multiplicita*,
   Whether *ita* were before *non*, or *non* before *ita*,
   Neither wise nor well-learnéd, but like *hermaphrodita*.
Set *sophia* aside, for every Jack Raker
And every mad meddler must now be a maker.

In Academia Parrot dare no problem keep,
   For *Graece fari* so occupieth the chair
That *Latinum fari* may fall to rest and sleep,
   And *syllogisari* was drownéd at Stourbridge Fair;
   Trivials and quatrivials so sore now they impair[3]
That Parrot the popinjay hath pity to behold
How the rest of good learning is roufled up and trold.[4]

Albertus de modo significandi,[5]
   And *Donatus*[6] be driven out of school;

[1] A straw mat.   [2] As one of the senators or judges.
[3] Are impaired.   [4] Trundled away.
[5] Albertus's *Margarita Poetica*, a classical anthology (1472).
[6] A Latin grammar by Aelius Donatus.

Priseian's head broken now handy-dandy,
    And *Inter didascolos* is reckoned for a fool;
    Alexander,[1] a gander of Maeander's pool,
With *De Conciles* [2] is cast out of the gate,
And *De Rationales* [3] dare not shew his pate.

Plautus in his comedies a child shall now rehearse,
    And meddle with Quintilian in his *Declamations*,
That Petty Cato [4] can scantly construe a verse,
    With *Áveto in Graeco*,[5] and such solemn salutatíons,
    Can scantly the tenses of his conjugatíons;
Setting their minds so much on eloquence
That of their school matters lost is the whole senténce.

Now a nutmeg, a nutmeg, *cum garyophyllo*,[6]
    For Parrot to pick upon, his brain for to stable,
Sweet cinnamon-stickès and *pleris cum musco*!
    In Paradise, that place of pleasure perduráble,
    The progeny of Parrots were fair and favouráble;
Now *in valle* Hebron Parrot is fain to feed:
Christ-Cross and Saint Nicholas, Parrot, be your good speed!

The mirror that I toot in, *quasi diaphanum*,[7]
    Vel quasi speculum, in aenigmate,[8]
Elencticum, or else *enthymematicum*,[9]
    For logicians to look on, somewhat *sophistice*:
    Rhetoricians and orators in freshè humanity,[10]
Support Parrot, I pray you, with your suffrage ornate,
Of *confuse tantum* [11] avoiding the checkmate.

[1] A medieval grammarian.   [2] The canon law (?).   [3] i.e. logic.
[4] *Cato Parvus* (a sort of supplement to *Cato Magnus*, i.e. *Dionysii Catonis Disticha de Moribus*) was written by Daniel Church, or Ecclesiensis, a domestic in the court of Henry II.
[5] Good-morning in Greek.   [6] With a clove.
[7] As though transparent.
[8] Or like a looking-glass, in a riddle.
[9] An elenchus [in logic] . . . an enthymeme.
[10] Elegant literature.   [11] So much confusion.

But of this supposition that calléd is art,
   Confuse distributive,[1] as Parrot hath devised,
Let every man after his merit take his part,
   For in this process Parrot nothing hath surmiséd,
   No matter pretended, nor nothing enterprised,
But that *metaphora, allegoria* with all,
Shall be his protectíon, his paves, and his wall.

For Parrot is no churlish chough, nor no flecked pie,
   Parrot is no pendugum, that men call a carling,
Parrot is no woodcock, nor no butterfly,
   Parrot is no stammering stare, that men call a starling.
   But Parrot is my own dear heart and my dear darling.
Melpomene, that fair maid, she burnishéd his beak:
I pray you, let Parrot have liberty to speak!

Parrot is a fair bird for a ladý:
   God of His goodness him framéd and wrought;
When Parrot is dead, she doth not putrefy.[2]
   Yea, all things mortal shall turn unto nought,
   Except man's soul, that Christ so dearè bought;
That never may die, nor never die shall—
Make much of Parrot, the popinjay royall.

For that peerless Prince that Parrot did create,
   He made you of nothing by His Majesty.
Point well this problem that Parrot doth prate,
   And remember among how Parrot and ye
   Shall leap from this lifè, as merry as we be:
Pomp, pride, honour, riches, and worldly lust,
Parrot saith plainly, shall turn all to dust.

       Thus Parrot doth pray you,
         With heart most tender,
      To reckon with this recueil [3] now,
         And it to remember.

[1] Methodical confusion.
[2] 'I can confirm this observation' (Robert Graves).
[3] Compilation.

Psittacus, ecce, cano; nec sunt mea carmina Phoebo
Digna scio; tamen est plena camena deo.[1]

Secundum Skeltonida famigeratum,
In Piereorum catalogo numeratum.

Itaque consolamini invicem in verbis istis.[2]

Candidi lectores, callide callete vestrum fovete Psittacum.[3]

GALATHEA

Speak, Parrot, I pray you, for Mary's sake,
What moan he made when Pamphilus lost his make.

PARROT

My proper Bess,
My pretty Bess,
 Turn once again to me!
For sleepest thou, Bess,
Or wakest thou, Bess,
 Mine heart it is with thee.

My daisy delectable,
My primrose commendable,
My violet amiable,
My joy inexplicable,
 Now turn again to me.

I will be firm and stable,
And to you serviceable,
And also profitable,
If ye be agreeable
 To turn again to me,
  My proper Bess.

[1] Behold Parrot, I sing; I know my songs are not worthy of Phoebus; yet the inspiration comes from the god.

[2] 'Wherefore comfort one another with these words' (1 Thess. iv. 18).

[3] Fair readers, shrewdly cherish your Parrot.

Alas, I am disdainéd,
And as a man half maiméd,
My heart is so sore painéd!
I pray thee, Bess, unfeignéd,
    Yet come again to me!
By love I am constrainéd
To be with you retainéd,
It will not be refrainéd:
I pray you, be reclaiméd,
    And turn again to me,
        My proper Bess.
        Quoth Parrot, the popinjay royal.

Martialis cecinit carmen, fit mihi scutum:—
    Est mihi lasciva pagina, vita proba.[1]

GALATHEA

Now kus me, Parrot, kus me, kus, kus, kus!
God's blessing light on thy sweet little mus!

        Vita et anima,
        Zoe kai psyche.[2]

Concumbunt Graece.   Non est hic sermo pudicus.[3]

    Ergo Attica dictamina
        Sunt plumbi lamina,[4]
        Vel spuria vitulamina:[5]
        Avertat haec Urania!
        Amen, Amen,
            And set too a D,
        And then it is Amend
            Our new found A.B.C.

        Cum caeteris paribus.[6]

[1] cf. Martial, Ep. i. 5.
[2] Life and soul (Ζωὴ καὶ ψυχή).
[3] They will lie together in Greek (Juvenal *Sat.* vi. 191).   This
is not obscene talk.
[4] Greek is my shield.
[5] *Spuria vitulamina non dabunt radices altas* (Vulg., *Sap.* iv. 3).
[6] With the other like things.

LENVOY PRIMERE

Go, little quaire,[1] naméd the Popinjay,
    Home to resort Jeroboseth persuade;
For the cliffs of Scalop they roar wellaway,
    And the sands of Cefas begin to waste and fade,
      For replication restless that he of late there made.
Now Neptune and Aeolus are agreed of likelihood,
For Titus at Dover abideth in the road;

Lucina she wadeth among the watery floods,
    And the cocks begin to crow against the day;
Le toison de Jason [2] is lodgéd among the shrowds,
    Of Argus revengéd, recover when he may;
      Lycaon [3] of Libyk and Lydy hath caught his prey: [4]
Go, little quaire, pray them that you behold
In their remembrance ye may be enrolled.

Yet some fools say that ye are furnishéd with knacks,
    That hang together as feathers in the wind;
But lewdly are they letteréd that your learning lacks,
    Barking and whining, like churlish curs of kind:
      For who looketh wisely in your workès may find
Much fruitful matter. But now, for your defence
Against all remordès, arm you with patiénce.

[1] Book.

[2] Jason's golden fleece. A reference, perhaps, to the 400,000 crowns with which the French commissioners came to purchase Tournai, captured in 1513.

[3] Who, for his impiety to Jupiter, was changed into a wolf. This probably refers to Wolsey. See later 'His wolf's head, wan, blo as lead, gapeth over the crown.'

[4] The bishopric of Tournai (?).

MONOSTICHON

Ipse sagax aequi ceu verax nuntius ito.[1]
Morda puros mal desires.[2]   *Portugues.*
Penultimo die Octobris, 33°

SECUNDE LENVOY

Pass forth, Parrot, towards some passenger,
  Require him to convey you over the salté foam;
Addressing yourself, like a saddé messenger,
  To our sullen seignor Sadok, desire him to come home,
  Making his pilgrimage by *Nostre Dame de Crome.*
For Jerico and Jersey shall meet together as soon
As he to exploit the man out of the moon.

With porpoise and grampus he may feed him fat,
  Though he pamper not his paunché with the Great Seal.
We have longéd and lookéd long time for that,
  Which causeth poor suitors have many a hungry meal:
  As president and regent he ruleth every deal.[3]
Now pass forth, good Parrot, our Lordé be your steed,
In this your journey to prosper and speed!

And though some disdain you, and say how ye prate,
  And how your poemés are barren of polishéd eloquence,
There is none that your name will abrogate
  Than nodipolls and gramatolls of smallé intelligence;
  Too rude is their reason to reach to your senténce.
Such melancholy mastiffs and mangy cur dogs
Are meet for a swineherdé to hunt after hogs.

MONOSTICHON

Psittace perge volans, fatuorum tela retundas.[4]
Morda puros mal desires.   Portugues.
In diebus Novembris,

34.

[1] Himself fair-minded, let him go like a truthful messenger.
[2] Dyce translates: 'To bite the pure is an evil desire.'
[3] This should refer to Wolsey. Yet Wolsey had the Great Seal in 1515.
[4] Parrot, go on flying, turn back the shafts of fatuity.

*L

LE DEREYN LENVOY

Prepare you, Parrot, bravely your passage to take,
  Of Mercury under the trinál aspect,
And sadly salute our sullen sire Sydrake,[1]
  And show him that all the world dothé conject
  How the matters he mells in come to small effect;
For he wanteth of his wits that all would rule alone:
It is no little burden to bear a great mill-stone.

To bring all the sea into a cherrystone pit,
  To number all the starrés in the firmament,
To rule ix. realms by one man's wit,
  To such things impossible reason cannot consent.
  Much money, men say, there madly he hath spent—
Parrot, ye may prate this under protestation,
Was never such a senator since Christés incarnation!

Wherefore he may now come again as he went,
  Non sine postica sanna,[2] as I trow,
From Calais to Dover, to Canterbury in Kent,
  To make reckoning in the resset how Robin lost his bow,
  To sow corn in the sea-sand, there will no crop grow.
Though he be taunted, Parrot, with tongués attainted,
Yet your problems are pregnant, and with loyalty acquainted.

MONOSTICHON

I, properans Parrote, malas sic corripe linguas.[3]
  Morda puros mal desires.   Portugues.
    15 *Kalendis Decembris,*
        34.

DISTICHON MISERABILE

Altior, heu, cedro, crudelior, heu, leopardo!
Heu, vitulus bubali fit dominus Priami! [4]

[1] Wolsey. (Cf. *The Historie of King Boccus and Sydracke,*
1510.)
  [2] Not without a grimace behind his back.
  [3] Go in haste, Parrot, and thus reprove the evil tongues.
  [4] Higher, alas, than the cedar, more cruel, alas, than the leopard!
Alas, the calf of the wild ox becomes the lord of Priam!

TETRASTICHON

Unde species Priami est digna imperio.[1]

Non annis licet et Priamus sed honore voceris:
  Dum foveas vitulum, rex, regeris, Britonum;
Rex, regeris, non ipse regis: rex inclyte, calle;
  Subde tibi vitulum, ne fatuet nimium.[2]

> God amend all,
>   That all amend may!
> Amen, quoth Parrot,
>   The royal popinjay.

Kalendis Decembris,
34.

LENVOY ROYAL

Go, proper Parrot, my popinjay,
  That lordès and ladies this pamphlet may behold,
With notable clerkès: supply to them, I pray,
  Your rudeness to pardon, and also that they wold
  Vouchsafe to defend you against the brawling scold
Callèd Detraction, encankeréd with envý,
Whose tongue is attainted with slanderous obloquy.

For truth in parable ye wantonly pronounce,
  Languages divers, yet under that doth rest
Matter more precious than the rich jacounce,[3]
  Diamondè, or ruby, or balas [4] of the best,
  Or Indy sapphire with orient pearlès drest:
Wherefore your remorders are mad, or else stark blind,
You to remord erst ere they know your mind.

[1] Whence the race of Priam is worthy to rule.

[2] . . . While you cherish the calf, king of Britain, you are ruled: king, you are ruled, you do not yourself rule: illustrious king, be wise, subdue the calf, lest he become too foolish.

[3] Jacinth.

[4] Another kind of ruby.

DISTICHON

I, volitans, Parrote, tuam moderare Minervam:
Vix tua percipient, qui tua teque legent.[1]

HYPERBATON

Psittacus hic notus seu Persius est puto notus,
Nec reor est nec erit licet est erit.

Maledite soit bouche malheureuse!
34.

LECTURE DE PARROT

O my Parrot, *O unice dilecte, votorum meorum omnis lapis,*
lapis pretiosus operimentum tuum! [2]

PARROT

Sicut Aaron populumque, sic bubali vitulus, sic bubali vitulus,
sic bubali vitulus.[3]

> Thus much Parrot hath openly expressed:
> Let see who dare make up the rest.

Le Popinjay s'en va complaindre:

Helas! I lament the dull abuséd brain,
   The infatuate fantasies, the witless wilfulness
Of one and other at me that have disdain.
   Some say, they cannot my parables express,
   Some say, I rail at riot reckeless,
Some say but little, and think more in their thought,
How this process I prate of it is not all for nought.

[1] Go, flying Parrot, moderate your wit: scarce will they understand you who read you and your writings.
[2] O only loved one, the whole jewel of my prayers, a precious stone is thy covering.   (Cf. Ezek. xxviii. 13.)
[3] As Aaron and the people, so the calf of the wild ox, etc.

O causeless cowards, O heartless hardiness!
  O manless manhood, enfainted all with fear!
O conning clergy, where is your readiness
  To practise or postil this process [1] here and there?
  For dread ye dare not meddle with such gere,
Or else ye pinch courtesy, truly as I trow,
Which of you first dare boldly pluck the crow.

The sky is cloudy, the coast is nothing clear;
  Titan hath trust up his tresses of fine gold;
Jupiter for Saturn dare make no royal cheer;
  Lycaon laugheth thereat, and beareth him more bold;
  Rachel, ruely ragged, she is like to catchè cold;
Moloch, that mawmet, there dare no man withstay—
The rest of suchè reckoning may make a foul fray.

> *Dixit*, quod Parrot, the royal popinjay.

> > *C'est chose malheureuse,*
> > *Que male bouche.*

PARROT

> *Jupiter ut nitido deus est veneratus Olympo,*
>   *Hic coliturque deus.*
> *Sunt data thura Jovi, rutilo solio residenti;*
>   *Cum Jove thura capit.*
> *Jupiter astrorum rector dominusque polorum,*
>   *Anglica sceptra regit.* [2]

GALATHEA

I compass the conveyance unto the capitall
  Of our clerk Cleros, whither, thither, and why not hither?
For pass a pace apace [3] is gone to catch a moll,

[1] Annotate this matter.
[2] As Jove is venerated in shining Olympus, he is worshipped here as a god. Incense is given to Jove, sitting on his red-gold throne; with Jove he takes the incense. Jove, ruler of the stars and lord of the poles, rules the English kingdom.
[3] An allusion to Secretary Pace (?).

Over Scrapary *mala vi*, Monsire cry and slither:
What sequel shall follow when pendugums meet together?
Speak, Parrot, my sweet bird, and ye shall have a date,
Of franticness and foolishness which is the great state?

PARROT

Difficile it is to answer this demand:
Yet, after the sagacity of a popinjay,—
Franticness doth rule and all thing command;
Wilfulness and brainless now rule all the ray;
Against frantic frenzy there dare no man say nay,
For franticness and wilfulness, and brainless ensemble,
The neb of a lion they make to trete and tremble;

To jumble, to stumble, to tumble down like foolès,
To lour, to droop, to kneel, to stoop, and to play couch
quail,
To fish afore the net and to draw poolès;
He maketh them to bear baubles, and to bear a low sail;
He carrieth a king in his sleeve, if all the world fail;
He faceth out at a flush with 'Shew, take all!'
Of Pope Julius' cards he is chief cardinall.

He triumpheth, he trumpeth, he turned all up and down,
With 'Skirgalliard, proud palliard, vauntperler, ye prate!'
His wolf's head, wan, blo as lead, gapeth over the crown.
It is to fear lest he would wear the garland on his pate,
Paregal with all princes far passing his estate.
For of our regent the regiment he hath, *ex qua vi*,
Patet per versus, quod *ex vi bolte harvi*.

Now, Galathea, let Parrot, I pray you, have his date;
Yet dates now are dainty, and wax very scant,
For grocers were grudgéd at and groinéd at but late;
Great raisins with reasons be now reprobitant,
For raisins are no reasons, but reasons currant.
Run God, run Devil! yet the date of our Lord
And the date of the Devil doth shrewdly accord

Dixit, quod Parrot, the popinjay royal.

GALATHEA

Now, Parrot, my sweet bird, speak out yet once again,
Set aside all sophims, and speak now true and plain.

PARROT

So many moral matters, and so little uséd;
   So much new making, and so mad time spent;
So much translatíon into English confuséd;
   So much noble preaching, and so little amendment;
   So much consultation, almost to none intent;
So much provisíon, and so little wit at need—
Since Deucalion's flood there can no clerkès rede.

So little discretion, and so much reasoníng;
   So much hardy dardy, and so little manliness;
So prodigal expense, and so shameful reckoníng;
   So gorgeous garments, and so much wretchedness;
   So much portly pride, with purses penniless;
So much spent before, and so much unpaid behind—
Since Deucalion's flood there can no clerkès find.

So much forecasting, and so far an after deal;
   So much politic prating, and so little standeth in stead;
So little secretness, and so much great counsel;
   So many bold barons, their hearts as dull as lead;
   So many noble bodies under a daw's head;
So royal a king as reigneth upon us all—
Since Deucalion's flood was never seen nor shall.

So many complaintès, and so smallè redress;
   So much calling on, and so small taking heed;
So much loss of merchandise, and so remediless;
   So little care for the common weal, and so much need;
   So much doubtful danger, and so little drede;
So much pride of prelates, so cruel and so keen—
Since Deucalion's flood, I trow, was never seen.

So many thieves hangéd, and thievés never the less;
  So much 'prisonment for matters not worth an haw;
So much papers wering for right a small excess;
  So much pillory-pageants under colour of good law;
  So much turning on the cuck-stool for every gee-gaw;
So much mockish making of statutes of array—
Since Deucalion's flood was never, I dare say.

So brainless calves' heads, so many sheepés tails;
  So bold a bragging butcher,[1] and flesh sold so dear;
So many plucked partridges, and so fatté quails;
  So mangy a mastiff cur, the great greyhound's [2] peer;
  So big a bulk of brow-antlers cabbagéd [3] that year;
So many swannés dead, and so small revél—
Since Deucalion's flood, I trow, no man can tell.

So many truces taken, and so little perfite truth;
  So much belly-joy, and so wasteful banquetíng;
So pinching and sparing, and so little profit groweth;
  So many hugy houses building, and so small householdíng;
  Such statutes upon diets, such pilling and pollíng;
So is all thing wrought wilfully withouté reason and skill—
Since Deucalion's flood the world was never so ill.

So many vagabonds, so many beggars bold;
  So much decay of monasteries and of religious places;
So hot hatred against the Church, and charity so cold;
  So much of 'my Lord's Grace,' [4] and in him no graces;
  So many hollow hearts, and so double faces;
So much sanctuary-breaking, and privilege barréd—
Since Deucalion's flood was never seen nor lyerd.

[1] Wolsey was reported to be the son of a butcher.

[2] Henry VIII, in allusion to the royal arms.

[3] Cuckold's horns growing to a head.

[4] At this time 'His Grace' was the royal style, so that it was an impertinence for Wolsey to adopt it.

So much ragged right of a rammès horn;
　　So rigorous ruling in a prelate specially;
So bold and so bragging, and was so basely born;
　　So lordly in his looks and so disdainously;
　　So fat a maggot, bred of a fleshè-fly;
Was never such a filthy Gorgon, nor such an epicure,
Since Deucalion's flood, I make thee fast and sure.

So much privy watching in cold winters' nights;
　　So much searching of losels, and is himself so lewd;
So much conjurations for elfish mid-day sprites;
　　So many bulls of pardon publishèd and shewed;
　　So much crossing and blessing, and him all beshrewed;
Such pole-axes and pillars,[1] such mules trapt with gold—
Since Deucalion's flood in no chronicle is told.

Dixit, quod Parrot.

Crescet in immensum me vivo Psittacus iste;
Hinc mea dicetur Skeltonidis inclita fama.[2]

Quod Skelton Laureat,
Orator Regius.
34.

[1] A reference to the two silver pillars and four gilt pole-axes
that Wolsey had carried before him in his train as he rode on his
mule through the streets. (*See* Cavendish, *Life of Wolsey.*)
[2] This Parrot will grow immensely in my lifetime; hence my
glorious Skeltonian fame will be celebrated.

WHY COME YE NOT TO COURT?

*The relucent mirror for all Prelates and Presidents, as well
spiritual as temporal, sadly to look upon,
deviséd in English*

ALL noblemen of this take heed,
And believe it as your Creed.

Too hasty of sentence,
Too fierce for none offence,
Too scarce of your expense,
Too large in negligence,
Too slack in recompense,
Too haut in excellence,
Too light intelligence,
And too light of credénce;
Where these keep residence
Reason is banishéd thence,
And also Dame Prudence,
With sober Sapience.

All noblemen of this take heed,
And believe it as your Creed.

Then, without collusion,
Mark well this conclusion,
Thorough such abusion,
And by such illusion,
Unto great confusion
A nobleman may fall,
And his honour appal;
And if ye think this shall
Not rub you on the gall
Then the devil take all!

All noblemen of this take heed,
And believe it as your Creed.

Haec vates ille,
De quo loquuntur mille.[1]

WHY COME YE NOT TO COURT?

For age is a page
For the court full unmeet,
For age cannot rage,
Nor buss her sweet sweet.
    But when age seeth that rage
Doth assuage and refrain,
Then will age have a corage
To come to court again.
        But
Helas, sage over-age
So madly decays
That age for dotage
Is reckoned nowadays.
    Thus age (a *grand dommage*)
Is nothing set by,
And rage in over-age
Doth run lamentably.
        So
That rage must make pilláge
To catch that catch may,
And with such foráge
Hunt the boscage,
That harts will run away!
Both hartès and hindès
With all good mindès.
Farewell, then, have good-day!

[1] The poet every one will be talking about.

Then, have good-day, adew!
For default of rescue
Some men may haply rue,
And some their headès mew;
The time doth fast ensue
That bales begin to brew.
I drede, by sweet Jesu,
This tale will be too true—
'In faith, deacon, thou crew,
In faith, deacon, thou crew!'

'Deacon, thou crew!' doubtless!
For, truly to express,
There hath been much excess,
With banqueting brainless,
With rioting reckeless,
With gambolling thriftless,
With spend and waste witless,
Treating of truce restless,
Prating of peace peaceless.
The countering at Calais [1]
Wrung us on the males. [2]
Chief Counsellor was careless,
Groaning, grudging, graceless;
And, to none intent,
Our tallwood all is brent,
Our faggots are all spent.
We may blow at the coal.
Our mare hath lost her foal,
And 'Mock hath lost her shoe:
What may she do thereto?'

---

[1] Probably refers to Wolsey's expedition to Calais, July–November, 1521, as mediator between Francis and Charles.   It has been formerly supposed that this passage referred to the Field of the Cloth of Gold (1520).   It may refer to both expeditions.

[2] Purses.   Cost us something.

An end of an oldė song.
Do right and do no wrong!
As right as a rammės horn!
For thrift is threadbare worn,
Our sheep are shrewdly shorn,
And truth is all to-torn;
Wisdom is laughed to scorn,
Favel is false forsworn,
Javel is nobly born,
Havel and Harvy Hafter,
Jack Travel and Cole Crafter—
We shall hear more hereafter.
With polling and shaving,
With borrowing and craving,
With reaving and raving,
With swearing and staring,
There 'vaileth no reasoning,
For Will doth rule all thing,
Will, Will, Will, Will, Will!
He ruleth alway still.
Good reason and good skill,
They may garlic pill,
Carry sacks to the mill,
Or peascods they may shill,
Or else go roast a stone!
There is no man but one
That hath the strokes alone.
Be it black or white,
All that he doth is right—
As right as a cammock crooked.
This bill well over-lookéd,
Clearly perceive we may
There went the hare away,
The hare, the fox, the gray,
The hart, the hind, the buck:[1]

---

[1] A reference, probably, to the Duke of Buckingham, who was believed to have been impeached and brought to the block by Wolsey in 1521.

God send us better luck,
God send us better luck!

Twit, Andrew, twit, Scot,
Ge hame, ge scour the pot:
For we have spent our shot.
We shall have a *tot quot* [1]
From the Pope of Rome,
To weave all in one loom
A web of linsey-woolsey,
Opus male dulce:
The devil kiss his cule!
For, whilès he doth rule
All is warse and warse,
The devil kiss his arse!
For whether he bless or curse
It cannot be much worse.
From Bamborough to Botham Bar
We have cast up our war,
And made a worthy truce
With 'Gup, level suse!'
Our money madly lent,
And more madly spent:
From Croydon to Kent
Wot ye whither they went?
From Winchelsea to Rye,
And all not worth a fly!
From Wentbridge to Hull
Our army waxeth dull,
With 'Turn all home again!'
And never a Scot slain.
Yet the good Earl of Surréy [2]
The Frenchmen he doth fray,
And vexeth them day by day
With all the power he may;
The Frenchmen he hath fainted,
And made their hearts attainted:

[1] A dispensation.   [2] Surrey's expedition, July 1522.

Of chivalry he is the floure,
Our Lord be his succóur!
The Frenchmen he hath so mated [1]
And their courage abated
That they 're but halfé men.
Like foxes in their den,
Like cankered cowards all,
Like urchins in a stonè wall,
They keep them in their holdès,
Like hen-hearted cuckoldés.

But yet they over-shoot us
With crownès and with scutus; [2]
With scutès and crownès of gold
I drede we are bought and sold.
It is a wondrous wark!
They shoot all at one mark,—
At the Cardinal's hat,
They shoot all at that.
Out of their strongè towns
They shoot at him with crowns:
With crowns of gold emblazéd
They make him so amazéd
And his eyen so dazéd
That he ne see can
To know God nor man!
He is set so high
In his hierarchy
Of frantic frenesy
And foolish fantasy,
That in the Chamber of Stars [3]
All matters there he mars.
Clapping his rod on the board,
No man dare speak a word,
For he hath all the saying
Without any renaying.

[1] i.e. checkmated. [2] French coins. [3] Star-Chamber.

He rolleth in his recordès,
He saith 'How say ye, my lordès?
Is not my reason good?'
(Good even, good Robin Hood! [1])
Some say 'Yes!' and some
Sit still as they were dumb!
Thus thwarting over them
He ruleth all the roast
With bragging and with boast.
Borne up on every side
With pompè and with pride,
With 'Trump up, Alleluia!'
For dame Philargeria [2]
Hath so his heart in hold
He loveth nothing but gold;
And Asmodeus of hell
Maketh his members swell
With Dalida [3] to mell,
That wanton damosel.
Adew, Philosophia!
Adew, Theologia!
Welcome, dame Simonia, [4]
With dame Gastrimargia, [5]
To drink and for to eat
Sweet hippocras and sweet meat!
To keep his flesh chaste,
In Lent, for a repast
He eateth capons stewéd,
Pheasant and partridge mewéd,
Hens, chickens, and pigs:
He froyns and he frigs,
Spareth neither maid ne wife:
This is a 'postle's life!

Helas! my heart is sorry
To tell of vain glory.

[1] A proverbial expression for civility extorted by fear.
[2] Cupidity.   [3] Delilah.   [4] Simony.   [5] Gluttony.

But now upon this story
I will no further rime
Till another time,
Till another time.

What newės, what newės?
Small newės that true is,
That be worth two cuės.
But at the naked stewės,
I understand how that
The Sign of the Cardinal's Hat,[1]
That inn is now shut up,
With 'Gup, whore, gup, now, gup!
Gup, Guilliam Trevelyan!'
With 'Jaist you, I say, Julian!
Will ye bear no coals?'[2]
A meiny of marė-foals,
That occupy[3] their holes,
Full of poxy moles.

What hear ye of Lancashire?
They were not paid their hire;
They are fell as any fire.

What hear ye of Cheshire?
They have laid all in the mire;
They grudgéd, and said
Their wages were not paid;
Some said they were afraid
Of the Scottish host,—
For all their crake and boast,
Wild fire and thunder;

[1] A Southwark brothel mentioned in Stow's *Survey*.
[2] Will ye not brook this insult? (being driven out).
[3] i.e. use (a reference to their profession).

For all this worldly wonder,
A hundred mile assunder
They were when they were next—
That is a true text.

What hear ye of the Scots?
They make us all sots,
Popping foolish daws!
They make us to pil straws!
They play their oldé pranks,
After Huntly-banks:
At the stream of Bannockburn
They did us a shrewd turn,
When Edward of Carnarvon
Lost all that his father won.

What hear ye of the Lord Dacres? [1]
He maketh us Jack Rakers;
He says we are but crakers;
He calleth us England men
Strong-hearted like an hen!
For the Scottés and he
Too well they do agree,
With 'Do thou for me,
And I shall do for thee!'
Whiles the Red Hat doth endure
He maketh himself cocksure;
The Red Hat with his lure
Bringeth all things under cure.

But, as the world now goes,
What hear ye of the Lord Rose? [2]
Nothing to purpóse,
Not worth a cockly fose:
Their hearts be in their hose!

[1] The Warden of the West Marches.
[2] i.e. Lord Roos, Warden of the East Marches.

The Earl of Northumberland
Dare take nothing on hand!
Our barons be so bold
Into a mousehole they wold
Run away and creep,
Like a meiny of sheep:
Dare not look out at door
For dread of the mastiff cur,[1]
For dread of the butcher's dog
Would worry them like an hog.

    For an this cur do gnar,
They must stand all afar,
To hold up their hand at the Bar.
For all their noble blood
He plucks them by the hood,
And shakes them by the ear,
And brings them in such fear;
He baiteth them like a bear,
Like an oxe or a bull.
Their wits, he saith, are dull;
He saith they have no brain
Their estate to maintain;
And maketh them to bow their knee
Before his majesty.
Judges of the kinges laws,
He counts them fools and daws;
Sergeants of the Coife eke,
He saith they are to seek
In pleading of their case.
At the Common Place,[2]
Or at the Kinges Bench;
He wringeth them such a wrench
That all our learned men
Dare not set their pen

---

[1] i.e. Wolsey; so in next line.
[2] i.e. Pleas.

To plead a true triall
Within Westminster Hall.
In the Chancery, where he sits,
But such as he admits,
None so hardy to speak;
He sayth, 'Thou hoddipeke,
Thy learning is too lewd,
Thy tongue is not well-thewed
To seek before our Grace!'
And openly in that place
He rages and he raves,
And calls them 'cankered knaves.'
Thus royally he doth deal
Under the king's broad seal;
And in the 'Chequer he them checks;
In the Star Chamber he nods and becks,
And beareth him there so stout
That no man dare rowt,
Duke, earl, baron, nor lord,
But to his sentence must accord;
Whether he be knight or squire,
All men must follow his desire.

What say ye of the Scottish king?
That is another thing.
He is but a youngling,
A stalworthy sripling!
There is a whispering and a whipling
He should be hither brought;
But, an it were well sought,
I trow all will be nought,
Not worth a shuttle-cock,
Not worth a sour calstock!
There goeth many a lie
Of the Duke of Albaný,
That off should go his head,
And brought in quick or dead,

And all Scotland ours
The mountenance of two hours.
But, as some men sayn,
I dread of some false train
Subtily wrought shall be
Under a feignéd treaty.
But, within moneths three,
Men may haply see
The treachery and the pranks
Of the Scottish banks!

*What hear ye of Burgonions,
And the Spaniards' onions?*
They have slain our Englishmen,
Above threescore and ten.
For all your amitý
No better they agree!

God save my Lord Admiral!

What hear ye of Mutrell? [1]
Therewith I dare not mell!

*Yet what hear ye tell
Of our Grand Council?*
I could say somewhat . . .
But speak ye no more of that,
For dread the Red Hat
Take pepper in the nose,—
For then thine head off goes,
Off by the hard arse.
But there is some travarse [2]
Between some and some
That maketh our sire to glum.
It is somewhat wrong
That his beard is so long.

[1] Montreuil.   Refers to the suspicion during the autumn of 1522
that a French fleet was gathering there to invade England.
[2] Conference.

He mourneth in black clothíng.
I pray God save the king!
Wherever he go or ride
I pray God be his guide!
Thus will I conclude my style,
And fall to rest a while,
And so to rest a while.

Once yet again
Of you I would frain,
Why come ye not to court?
To which court?
To the kings court,
Or to Hampton Court?
Nay, to the kingés court.
The kingés court
Should have the excellence,
But Hampton Court
Hath the preéminence,
And Yorkés Place,[1]
With my lordés Grace!
To whose magnificence
Is all the confluence,
Suits and supplicatíons,
Embassades of all natíons.
Straw for Law Canon,
Or for the Law Common,
Or for Law Civil!
It shall be as he will.
Stop at Law Tancrete,[2]
An abstract or a concrete,
Be it sour, be it sweet,
His wisdom is so discreet
That, in a fume or an heat—
'Warden of the Fleet,

[1] Wolsey's palace as Archbishop of York in Whitehall.
[2] Transcript, or copy.

Set him fast by the feet!'
And of his royal power,
When him list to lower,
Then, 'Have him to the Tower,
Sannz aulter remedy!
Have him forth, by and by,
To the Marshalsea,
Or to the Kingès Bench!'
He diggeth so in the trench
Of the court royall
That he ruleth them all.
So he doth undermind,
And suchè sleights doth find,
That the kingès mind
By him is subverted,
And so straitly coarcted
In credencing his talès
That all is but nut-shellès
That any other saith—
He hath in him such faith.

Now, yet all this might be
Suffered and taken in gre
If that that he wrought
To any good end were brought.
But all he bringeth to nought,
By God, that me dear bought!
He beareth the king on hand [1]
That he must pill [2] his land
To make his coffers rich;
But he layeth all in the ditch.
And useth such abusíon
That in the conclusíon
All cometh to confusíon.

Perceive the cause why?
To tell the truth plainly,

[1] Persuades the king.　　[2] Tax.

He is so ambitíous,
So shameless, and so vicíous,
And so superstitíous,
And so much oblivious
From whence that he came
That he falleth into a *caeciam*,—
Which, truly to express,
Is a forgetfulness,
Or wilful blindness,
Wherewith the Sodomites
Lost their inward sights,
The Gomorrhians alsó
Were brought to deadly woe,
As Scripture recordès:
A caecitate cordis,
(In the Latin sing we)
Libera nos, Domine! [1]

But this mad Amaleck,
Like to a Mamelek,
He regardeth lordès
No more than potsherdès!
He is in such elatíon
Of his exaltatíon,
And the supportatíon
Of our sovereign lordè,
That, God to recordè,
He ruleth all at will
Without reason or skill.
Howbeit, the primordial
Of his wretched original,
And his base progeny,
And his greasy genealogy,
He came of the sang royall
That was cast out of a butcher's stall.

[1] From blindness of heart, deliver us, O Lord!

But however he was born,
Men would have the lessé scorn
If he couldé consider
His birth and roomé [1] together,
And call to his minde
How noble and how kindé
To him he hath found
Our sovereign lord, chief ground
Of all this prelacy,
That set him noblý
In great authority
Out from a low degree,
Which he cannot see.
For he was, pardee,
No doctor of divinity,
Nor doctor of the law,
Nor of none other saw;
But a pooré master of art,
God wot, had little part
Of the quatrivials,
Nor yet of trivials,[2]
Nor of philosophy,
Nor of philology,
Nor of good policy,
Nor of astronomy,
Nor acquainted worth a fly
With honourable Halý,
Nor with royal Ptolemy,
Nor with Albumazar,
To treat of any star
Fixed or else mobile.
His Latin tongue doth hobble,
He doth but clout and cobble

[1] Place, office.
[2] The two school courses of the time: (1) higher, (2) lower, i.e.
(1) astrology, astronomy, geometry, arithmetic, music; (2) grammar,
rhetoric, logic.

M

In Tully's faculty
Calléd humanity.
Yet proudly he dare pretend
How no man can him amend.
But have ye not heard this,—
How a one-eyed man is
Well-sighted when
He is among blind men?

Then, our process for to stable,
This man was full unable
To reach to such degree
Had not our Princé be
Royal Henry the Eight,
Take him in such conceit
That he set him on height,
In exemplifying
Great Alexander the king,
In writing as we find
Which (of his royal mind,
And of his noble pleasure,
Transcending out of measure)
Thought to do a thing
That pertaineth to a king—
To make up one of nought,
And made to him be brought
A wretched pooré man,
Which his living wan
With plantíng of leeks
By the days and by the weeks;
And of this pooré vassal
He made a king royall,
And gave him a realm to rule
That occupiéd a shule,
A mattock, and a spade,
Before that he was made
A king, as I have told,
And ruléd as he wold.

Such is a kingės power,—
To make within an hour,
And work such a miracle
That shall be a spectacle
Of renown and worldly fame.
In likewise now the same
Cardinal is promoted,
Yet with lewd conditions coated,
As hereafter ben noted,—
Presumption and vainglory,
Envy, wrath, and lechery,
Couvetise and gluttony,
Slothful to do good,
Now frantic, now starkė wood.

Should this man of suchė mood
Rule the sword of might
How can he do right?
For he will as soon smite
His friendė as his foe—
A proverb long ago.
Set up a wretch on high
In a throne triumphantly,
Make him a great estate,
And he will play checkmate
With royal majestý,
Count himself as good as he;
A prelate potentíal
To rule under Belial,
As fierce and as cruel
As the Fiend of hell.
His servants menial
He doth revile, and brawl
Like Mahound in a play;
No man dare him withsay.
He hath despite and scorn
At them that be well-born;
He rebukės them and rails:

'Ye whoresons! Ye vassails!
Ye knaves! Ye churls' sonnés!
Ye ribalds, not worth two plummés!
Ye rain-beaten beggars rejagged!
Ye recrayéd ruffians, all ragged!
With 'Stoop, thou havel!
Run, thou javel!
Thou peevish pie peckéd!
Thou losel long-neckéd!'
Thus, daily, they be deckéd,
Taunted and checkéd,
That they are so woe,
They wot not whither to go.

No man dare come to the speech
Of this gentle Jack-breech,
Of what estate he be
Of spiritual dignity;
Nor duke of high degree,
Nor marquis, earl nor lord;
Which shrewdly doth accord,
Thus he bornè so base
All noblemen should out-face,
His countenance like a kaiser.
'My Lord is not at leisure!
Sir, we must tarry a stound,
Till better leisure be found!
And, sir, ye must dance attendance,
And take patient sufferance,
For my lordès Grace
Hath now no time nor space
To speak with you as yet.'
And thus they shall sit.
Chose them sit or flit,
Stand, walk, or ride,
And at his leisure abide,
Perchance, half a year,
And yet never the near.

This dangerous dousépeer,[1]
Like a kingès peer!
And within this xvi. year
He would have been right fain
To have been a chaplain,
And have taken right great pain
With a poorè knight,
Whatsoever he hight.[2]
The chief of his own council,
They cannot well tell
When they with him should mell,
He is so fierce and fell!
He rails and he rates,
He calleth them doddipates;
He grins and he gapes,
As it were jack'napes!
Such a mad bedleme
For to rule this reame!
It is a wondrous case
That the kingès grace
Is toward him so minded
And so far blinded
That he cannot perceive
How he doth him deceive.
I doubt lest by sorcery,
Or such other loselry,
As witchècraft, or charmíng,
For he is the kingès darlíng,
And his sweet heart-root,
And is governed by this mad coot!
For what is a man the better
For the kingès letter?

[1] Noble—actually, one of the *douze pairs*, the twelve equals, or peers, of Charlemagne.

[2] Sir Richard Nanfan, Deputy of Calais, whose chaplain Wolsey was, and who promised him his position as chaplain to King Henry VII.

For he will tear it asunder.
Whereat much I wonder
How such a hoddipole
So boldly dare control,
And so malapertly withstand
The king's own hand,
And set not by it a mite.
He saith the king doth write
And writeth he wotteth not what.
And yet, for all that,
The king his clemency
Dispenseth with his demency.

But what His Grace doth think
I have no pen nor ink
That therewith can mell;
But well I can tell
How Francis Petrarch,
That much noble clerk,
Writeth how Charlemagne
Could not himself refrain,
But was ravished with a rage
Of a like dotáge.
But how that came about
Read ye the story out,
And ye shall find surelý
It was by necromancy,
By carects [1] and conjuration
Under a certain constellation,
And a certain fumigation
Under a stone on a goldé ring,
Wrought to Charlemagne the king,
Which constrained him forcibly
For to love a certain body
Above all other inordinately.
This is no fable nor no lie;

[1] Magical characters.

At Acon[1] it was brought to pass,
As by mine author tried it was.[2]
But let my masters mathematical
Tell you the rest!   For me, they shall;
They have the full intelligence,
And dare use the experience,
In their absolute conscíence
To practise such obsolete science;
For I abhor to smatter
Of one so devilish a matter.

But I will make further relation
Of this isagogical collation,
How Master Gaguin, the chronicler
Of the featés of war
That were done in France,
Maketh remembránce
How King Lewis, of late,
Made up a great estate[3]
Of a pooré wretched man,
Whereof much care began.
Johannes Balue was his name,
Mine author writeth the same.
Promoted was he
To a cardinal's dignity,
By Lewis the king aforesaid,
With him so well apayéd
That he made him his chancellor
To make all or to mar,
And to rule as him list,
Till he checked at the fist,[4]
And, against all reason,
Committed open treason
Against his lord soveréign:

[1] Aix-la-Chapelle.
[2] *See* Petrarch, *Fam. Epist.*, lib. i, ep. iii.
[2] A person of great estate.
[4] i.e. turned on the hand that fed him.

Wherefore he suffered pain,
Was 'headed, drawen, and quartered,
And died stinkingly martyred.[1]
Lo, yet for all that
He wore a cardinal's hat,
In him was small faith,
As mine author saith—
Not for that I mean
Such a casualty should be seen,
Or such chance should fall
Unto our cardinal!

Almighty God, I trust,
Hath for him discust
That of force he must
Be faithful, true, and just
To our most royal king,
Chief root of his making.
Yet it is a wily mouse
That can build his dwelling house
Within the cattès ear,
Withouten dread or fear.
It is a nice reckoning
To put all the governing,
All the rule of this land
Into one mannès hand.
One wise mannès head
May stand somewhat in stead:
But the wits of many wise
Much better can devise,
By their circumspection,
And their sad direction,
To cause the common weal
Long to endure in heal.

[1] As a matter of fact Cardinal Balue was confined by order of
Louis XI in an iron cage at the castle of Loches for eleven years.
The rest of his life he spent prosperously in Italy.

Christ keep King Henry the Eight
From treachery and deceit,
And grant him grace to know
The falcon from the crow,
The wolfè from the lamb,
From whence that mastiff came!
Let him never confound
The gentle greyhound.
Of this matter the ground
Is easy to expound,
And soon may be perceivéd,
How the worldè is conveyéd.

*But hark, my friend, one word
In earnest or in bord!
Tell me now, in this stead,
Is Master Meautis dead,
The king's French secretary,
And his untrue adversary?
For he sent in writing
To Francis, the French king,
Of our master's counsel in everything.
That was a perilous reckoning!*
Nay, nay, he is not dead,
But he was so painéd in the head
That he shall never eat more bread.
Now he is gone to another stead
With a bull under lead,[1]
By way of commissíon,
To a strange jurisdictíon
Calléd Domingos Dale,
Farrè beyond Portingale,
And hath his passport to pass
Ultra Sauromatas,
To the devil, Sir Satanas,
To Pluto, and Sir Belial,

---

[1] i.e. a seal

*M

The Devil's vicar general,
And to his college conventual,
As well calodemonial,[1]
As to cacodemonial,[2]
To purvey for our cardinal
A palace pontificial,
To keep his court provincial,
Upon articles judicial,
To contend and to strive
For his prerogative,
Within that consistory
To make summons peremptory
Before some protonotary
Imperial or papal.
Upon this matter mystical
I have told you part, but not all.
Hereafter perchance I shall
Make a larger memorial,
And a further rehearsal,
And more paper I think to blot,
To the court why I came not;
Desiring you above all thing
To keep you from laughing
When ye fall to reading
Of this wanton scrollé,
And pray for Meautis' soulé,
For he is well past and gone;
That would God every one
Of his affinity
Were gone as well as he!
Amen, amen, say ye,
Of your inward charity;
    Amen,
Of your inward charity!

---

[1] Consisting of good angels.
[2] Consisting of bad angels.

It were great ruth,
For writing of truth,
Any man should be
In perplexitý
Of displeasúre;
For I make you sure,
Where truth is abhored
It is a plainė recórd
That there wanteth grace;
In whose place
Doth occupy,
Full ungraciously,
False Flattery,
False Treachery,
False Bribery,
Subtle Sim Sly,
With mad Follý;
For who can best lie
He is best set by.
Then farewell to thee,
Wealthful Felicity!
For Prosperity
Away then will flee.
Then must we agree
With Poverty;
For Misery
With Penury
Miserably
And wretchedly
Hath made ascry
And outcry,
Following the chase
To drive away grace.
Yet sayest thou percace,
We can lackė no grace,
For my lordės grace,
And my lady's grace,
With trey, deuce, ace,

And ace in the face,
Some haut and some base,
Some dance the trace
Ever in one case.
Mark me that chase [1]
In the tennis play,
For cinque quater trey
Is a tall man.
He rode, but we ran!
Hey the gye and the gan! [2]
The grey goose is no swan;
The waters wax wan,
And beggars they ban,
And they cursed Datan,
De tribu Dan,
That this work began,
Palam et clam,
With Balak and Balam,
The golden ram
Of Fleming dam,
Shem, Japhet, or Ham.

But how come to pass
Your cupboard that was
Is turnéd to glass,
From silver to brass,
From goldé to pewter,
Or else to a neuter,
To copper, to tin,
To lead, or alcumin? [3]
A goldsmith your mayor; [4]

[1] i.e. mark well that point.

[2] The goose and the gander—a play on the words, referring to the dance hey-de-guise.

[3] 'Alchemy gold, a composition, mainly of brass, imitating gold' (*O.E.D.*).

[4] i.e. Sir John Mundy, a member of the Goldsmiths' Company, who became Lord Mayor of London on 28th October (the old Lord Mayor's Day), 1522

But the chief of your fair
Might stand now by potters,
And such as sell trotters,
Pitchers, potshordès.
This shrewdly accordès
To be a cupboard for lordès!

My lord now, and sir knight,
Good even and good night!
For now, Sir Tristram
You must wear buckram,
Or canvas of Caen,
For silkès are wane.[1]
Our royals [2] that shone,
Our nobles [2] are gone
Among the Burgunians,
And Spaniards' onions,
And the Flanderkins.
Gill sweats and Kate spins,
They are happy that wins;
But England may well say,
'Fie on this winning alway!'
Now nothing but pay, pay!
With, 'Laugh and lay down,'[3]
Borough, city, and town.

Good Spring of Levenham [4]
Must count what became
Of his cloth-making:
He is at such taking,
Though his purse wax dull
He must tax for his wool [5]
By nature of a new writ.
My lord's Grace nameth it

[1] Decreased.
[2] The coins so called.
[3] A punning allusion to the game of cards so called.
[4] A wealthy wool merchant who endowed Lavenham church.
[5] i.e. pay tax.

A *quia non satisfacit.*
In the spite of his teeth
He must pay again
A thousand or twain
Of his goldé in store;
And yet he paid before
An hundred pound and more,
Which pincheth him sore.
My lordés Grace will bring
Down this high spring,
And bring it so low
It shall not ever flow.

Such a prelate, I trow,
Were worthy to row
Through the straits of Marock [1]
To the gibbet of Baldock!
He would dry up the streams
Of nine kings' reams,
All rivers and wells,
All waters that swells;
For with us he so mells,
That within England dwells,
I would he were somewhere else;
For else by and by
He will drink us so dry,
And suck us so nigh,
That men shall scantly
Have penny or halfpenny.
God save his noble Grace,
And grant him a place
Endless to dwell
With the Devil of hell!
For, an he were there,
We need never fear
Of the fiendés blake:

[1] Morocco.

For I undertake
He would so brag and crake
That he would then make
The devils to quake,
To shudder and to shake,
Like a fire-drake,
And with a coal-rake
Bruise them on the brake,[1]
And bind them to a stake,
And set hell on fire
At his owné desire.
He is such a grim sire,
He is such a potestolate,[2]
And such a potestate,[3]
That he would break the brains
Of Lucifer in his chains,
And rule them each one
In Lucifer's throne.
I would he were gone;
For among us is none
That ruleth but he alone,
Without all good reason,
And all out of season.
For Fulham peason [4]
With him be not geson;
They grow very rank
Upon every bank
Of his herbers green,
With my lady bright and sheen;
On their game it is seen
They play not all clean,
An it be as I ween.

But as touching discretíon,
With sober directíon,

---

[1] An engine of torture.   [2] Legate.   [3] Chief magistrate.
[4] Loaded dice.   Fulham was once a haunt of gamesters.

He keepeth them in subjectíon.
They can have no protectíon
To rule nor to guide;
But all must be tried,
And abide the correctíon
Of his wilful affectíon.
For as for wit,
The Devil speed whit!
But brainsick and brainless,
Witless and reckless,
Careless and shameless,
Thriftless aud graceless,
Together are banded,
And so condescended,
That the commonwealth
Shall never have good health,
But tattered and tuggéd,
Ragged and ruggéd,
Shaven and shorn,
And all threadbare worn.
Such greediness,
Such neediness,
Miserableness,
With wretchedness,
Hath brought in distress
And much heaviness
And great dolour
England, the floure
Of relucent honóur,
In old commemoration
Most royal English nation.
Now all is out of fashion,
Almost in desolation.
I speak by protestation.
God of his miseration
Send better reformation!

Lo, for to do shamefully
He judgeth it no folly!
But to write of his shame
He saith we are to blame.
What a frenzy is this—
No shame to do amiss,
And yet he is ashaméd
To be shamefully naméd!
And oft preachers be blaméd
Because they have proclaiméd
His madness by writing,
His simpleness reciting,
Remording and biting,
With chiding and with flyting,
Shewing him Goddés laws.
He calleth the preachers daws,
And of holy scripture's saws
He counteth them for gee-gaws,
And putteth them to silence
With wordés of violence,
Like Pharaoh, void of grace,
Did Moses sore menáce,
And Aaron sore he threat,
The word of God to let.
This maumet in like wise
Against the Church doth rise.
The preacher he doth dispise,
With craking in such wise,
So bragging all with boast,
That no preacher almost
Dare speakè for his life
Of my lord's Grace, nor his wife;
For he hath such a bull
He may take whom he wull,
And as many as him likes;
May eat pigs in Lent for pikes,
After the sects of heretics,
For in Lent he will eat

All manner of flesh meat
That he can anywhere get;
With other abusíons great,
Whereof for to treat
It would make the Devil to sweat.
For all privileged places
He breaks and defaces,
All places of religíon
He hath them in derisíon,
And maketh such provisíon
To drive them at divisíon,
And finally in conclusíon
To bring them to confusíon:
Saint Albans, to record,
Whereof this ungracíous lord
Hath made himself abbot,
Against their wills, God wot!
All this he dothė deal
Under strength of the Great Seal,
And by his legacy: [1]
Which madly he doth apply
Unto an extravagancy
Pickéd out of all good law,
With reasons that ben raw.

Yet, when he took first his hat,
He said he knew what was what;
All justice he pretended,
All things should be amended,
All wrongs he would redress,
All injuries he would repress,
All perjuries he would oppress;
And yet this graceless elf,
He is perjuréd himself,
As plainly it doth appear
Who list to inquire

[1] Legative power.

In the registery
Of my Lord of Canterbury,
To whom he was professéd
In three pointès expresséd:
The first, to do him reverence:
The second, to owe obedience:
The third, with whole affection
To be under his subjection.
But now he maketh objection,
Under the protection
Of the king's Great Seal,
That he setteth never a deal
By his former oath,
Whether God be pleased or wroth.
He maketh so proud pretence,
That in his equipollence
He judgeth him equivalent
To God omnipotent.
But yet beware the rod
And the stroke of God

The apostle Peter
Had a poorè mitre
And a poorè cope
When he was create Pope,
First in Antioche.
He did never approach
Of Romè to the See
With suchè dignitie.

Saint Dunstan, what was he?
Nothing, he saith, like to me.
There is a diversity
Between him and me;
We pass him in degree,
As *legatus a latere.*

Ecce, sacerdos magnus,[1]
That will 'head us and hang us,
And straightly strangle us
An he may fang us!
Decree and decretal,
Constitution provincial,
Nor no law canonical,
Shall let the priest pontifical
To sit *in causa sanguinis.*
Now God amend that is amiss!
For I suppose that he is
Of Jeremy the whisking rod,
The flail, the scourge of Almighty God.

This Naaman Sirus,[2]
So fell and so irous,
So full of melancholy,
With a flap afore his eye,
Men ween that he is poxy,[3]
Or else his surgeons they lie,
For, as far as they can spy
By the craft of surgery
It is *manus Domini.*
And yet this proud Antiochus,
He is so ambitious,
So elate, and so vicious,
And so cruel-hearted,
That he will not be converted;
For he setteth God apart,
He is now so overthwart,
And so painéd with pangès,
That all his trust hangès
In Balthasar,[4] which healéd

[1] Behold the great priest.　　　　[2] i.e. the Syrian.
[3] This was one of the charges afterwards brought against Wolsey
in Parliament.
[4] Balthasar de Guercis, surgeon to Katherine of Aragon.

Domingo's nose that was wealéd;
That Lombard's nose mean I
That standeth yet awry;
It was not healéd alderbest,[1]
It standeth somewhat on the west;
I mean Domingo Lomelin
That was wont to win
Much money of the king
At the cards and hazarding.
Balthasar, that healed Domingo's nose
From the pustuled poxy pose,
Now with his gummés of Arabý
Hath promised to heal our cardinal's eye.
Yet some surgéons put a doubt
Lest he will put it clean out,
And make him lame of his nether limbès.
God send him sorrow for his sinnès!

Some men might ask a question,
By whose suggestíon
I took on hand this wark,
Thus boldly for to bark?
An men list to hark,
And my wordès mark,
I will answer like a clerk:—
For, truly and unfeignéd,
I am forcibly constrainéd
At Juvenal's request
To write of this geste
Of this vainglorious beast,
His fame to be increased
At every solemn feast;
Quia difficile est
Satiram non scribere![2]

---

[1] Thoroughly.
[2] 'Because it is difficult not to write satire' (Juvenal, *Sat.* i. 30).

Now, master doctor, how say ye?
Whatsoever your name be.
What though ye be nameless,
Ye shall not escape blameless,
Nor yet shall 'scape shameless.
Master doctor, in your degree,
Yourself madly ye oversee!
Blame Juvenal, and blame not me.
Master doctor Diricum,
Omne animi vitium, etc.[1]—
As Juvenal doth record,
A small default in a great lord,
A little crime in a great estate,
Is much more inordinate,
And more horrible to behold,
Than any other a thousandfold.
Ye put to blame ye wot ne'er whom!
Ye may wear a cockès-comb!
Your fond head in your furréd hood!
Hold ye your tongue, ye can no good!
And at more convenient time
I may fortune for to rime
Somewhat of your madness;
For small is your sadness
To put any man in lack,
And say ill behind his back.
     And my wordès mark trulý,
That ye cannot bide thereby,
For *smegma non est cinnamonum*,
But *de absentibus nil nisi bonum*.
Complain, or do what ye will,
Of your complaint it shall not skill:
This is the tenor of my bill,
     A dawcock ye be, and so shall be still.

---

[1] 'Every vice of the soul . . .' (Juvenal, *Sat.* viii. 140).

Sequitur Epitoma
De morbilloso Thoma,
Necnon obscoeno
De Polyphemo,[1] *etc.*

Porro perbelle dissimulatum
Illum Pandulphum,[2] *tantum legatum,*
Tam formidatum nuper praelatum,
Ceu Naman Syrum nunc elongatum,
In solitudine jam commoratum,
Neapolitano morbo gravatum,
Malagmate, cataplasmate stratum,
Pharmacopolae ferro foratum,
Nihilo magis alleviatum,
Nihilo melius aut medicatum,
Relictis famulis ad famulatum,
Quo tollatur infamia,
Sed major patet insania;
A modo ergo ganea
Abhorreat ille ganeus,
Dominus male creticus,
Aptius dictus tetricus,
Fanaticus, phreneticus,
Graphicus sicut metricus
        Autumat.
Hoc genus dictaminis
Non eget examinis
In centiloquio
Nec centimetro
Honorati
Grammatici
Mauri.[3]

[1] An allusion to what Skelton said before—that the cardinal had the use of only one eye.

[2] Wolsey—i.e. Pandulph was legate from the pope in the time of King John.

[3] Maurus Servius Honoratus, author of a popular text-book.

CALLIOPE [1]

Why wear ye Calliope embroidered with letters of gold?

Skelton Laureate, Orato. Reg., maketh this Answer

CALLIOPE,
As ye may see,
Regent is she
Of poets all,
Which gave to me
The high degree
Laureate to be
Of fame royall;
Whose name enrolled
With silk and gold
I dare be bold
Thus for to wear.
Of her I hold
And her househóld;
Though I wax old
And somedele sere,
Yet is she fain,
Void of disdain,
Me to retain
Her serviteur,
With her certáin
I will remain,
As my sovereígn
Most of pleasúre,
Maulgre touz malheureux.

[1] See Latin *amplificatio*, p. 439.

346

A Right Delectable Treatise upon a Goodly

GARLAND OR CHAPLET OF LAUREL

By Master Skelton, Poet Laureate, studiously Devised at Sheriff-Hutton Castle, in the Forest of Galtres, wherein are comprised many and divers solacious and right pregnant electuaries of singular pleasure, as more at large it doth appear in the process following.

> *Eterno mansura die dum sidera fulgent,*
> *Aequora dumque tument, haec laurea nostra virebit:*
> *Hinc nostrum celebre et nomen referetur ad astra,*
> *Undique Skeltonis memorabitur alter Adonis.*[1]

Arecting my sight toward the zodiac,
　　The signès xii. for to behold afar,
When Mars retrogradant reversèd his back,
　　Lord of the year in his orbicular,
　　Put up his swordè, for he could make no war,
And when Lucina plenarly did shine,
Scorpionè ascending degrees twice nine;

In place alone then musing in my thought
　　How all thing passeth as doth the summer flower,
On every half my reasons forth I sought,
　　How often fortune varieth in an hour,
　　Now clear weather, forthwith a stormy shower;
All thing compassèd, no perpetuity,
But now in wealth, now in adversity.

So deeply drownèd I was in this dumpè,
　　Encrampishèd so sore was my conceit,

[1] While the stars shine with eternal day, and while the seas swell, these our laurels shall be green; our illustrious name shall be translated to the sky, and everywhere shall Skelton be renowned as another Adonis.

347

That, me to rest, I leant me to a stumpė
   Of an oak, that sometimė grew full straight,
   A mighty tree and of a noble height,
Whose beauty blasted was with the boystors wind,
His leavės lost, the sap was from the rind.

Thus stood I in the frithy forest of Galtress,
   Ensoakėd with silt of the miry wose,
Where hartės bellowing, embosėd with distress,
   Ran on the range so long, that I suppose
   Few men can tell now where the hind-calf goes;
Fair fall that forster that so well can bate his hound!
But of my purpose now turn we to the ground.

Whiles I stood musing in this meditatíon,
   In slumbering I fell and halfė in a sleep;
And whether it were of imaginatíon,
   Or of humours superflue, that often will creep
   Into the brain by drinking over-deep,
Or it proceeded of fatal persuasíon,
I cannot well tell you what was the occasíon.

But suddenly at once, as I me advisėd,
   As one in a trance or in an ecstasy,
I saw a pavilion wondrously disguisėd,
   Garnishėd fresh after my fantasy,
   Entachėd with pearl and stonės preciously,
The ground engrosėd and bet with bournė gold,
That passing goodly it was to behold.

Within it, a princess excellent of port;
   But to recount her rich habiliment,
And what estatės to her did resort,
   Thereto am I full insufficíent;
   A goddess immortal she did represent;
As I heard say, dame Pallas was her name;
To whom supplied the royal Queen of Fame.

The Queen of Fame *to* Dame Pallas

Princess most puissant, of high pre-eminence,
　　Renownéd lady abové the starry heaven,
All other transcending, of every congruence
　　Madam regent of the sciences seven,
　　To whose estate all nobleness must leanen,
My supplicatíon to you I arect,
Whereof I beseech you to tender the effect.

Not unrememberéd it is unto your grace
　　How you gave me a royal commandèment
That in my courté Skelton should have a place,
　　Because that his time he studiously hath spent
　　In your servíce; and, to the accomplishment
Of your requests, registeréd is his name
With laureate triumph in the court of Fame.

But, good madam, the accustom and uságe
　　Of ancient poets, ye wot full well, hath been
Themself to embusy with all their whole corage,
　　So that their workés might famously be seen,
　　In figure whereof they wear the laurel green;
But how it is, Skelton is wondrous slack,
And, as we dare, we find in him great lack.

For, ne were only he hath your promotíon,
　　Out of my bookés full soon I should him rase;
But sith he hath tasted of the sugared potíon
　　Of Heliconés well, refreshéd with your grace,
　　And will not endeavour himself to purcháse
The favóur of ladies with wordés elect,
It is fittingé that ye must him correct.

Dame Pallas *to the* Queen of Fame

The sum of your purpose, as we are adv_ised,
　　Is that our servant is somewhat too dull;

Wherein this answer for him we have compriséd,
　How rivers run not till the spring be full;
　Better a dumb mouthé than a brainless skull;
For if he gloriously polish his matter,
Then men will say how he doth but flatter;

And if so him fortune to write true and plain,
　As sometime he must vices remordé,
Then some will say he hath but little brain,
　And how his wordés with reason will not accordé;
　Beware, for writing remaineth of recordé;
Displease not an hundred for one mannés pleasure;
Who writeth wisely hath a greaté treasure.

Alsó, to furnishé better his excuse,
　Ovid was banishéd for such a skill,
And many more whom I could induce;
　Juvenal was threat, pardee, for to kill [1]
　For certain invectives, yet wrote he none ill,
Saving he rubbéd some upon the gall;
It was not for him to abide the triall.

In general wordés, I say not greatly nay,
　A poet sometime may for his pleasure taunt,
Speaking in parables, how the fox, the gray,
　The gander, the goose, and the hugé elephaunt,
　Went with the peacock againé the pheasáunt;
The lizard came leaping, and said that he must,
With help of the ram, lay all in the dust.

Yet divers there be, industrious of reasón,
　Somewhat would gather in their conjectúre
Of such an endarkéd chapiter some seasón;
　Howbeit, it were hardé to construe this lecture;
　Sophisticated craftily is many a confecture;
Another man's mind diffusé is to expound;
Yet hardé is to make but some fault be found.

[1] i.e. for to be killed.

The QUEEN OF FAME *to* DAME PALLAS

Madam, with favour of your benign sufferance,
   Unto your grace then make I this motive;
Whereto made ye me him to advance
   Unto the room of laureate promotive?
   Or whereto should he have that prerogative,
But if he had madė some memorial
Whereby he might have a name inmortál?

To pass the time in slothful idleness,
   Of your royal palace it is not the guise,
But to do somewhat each man doth him 'dress:
   For how should Cato else be callėd wise,
   But that his bookės, which he did devise,
Record the same? or why is had in mind
Plato, but for that he left writingė behind

For men to look on? Aristotle alsó,
   Of philosophers callėd the principall,
Oldė Diogenes, with many other mo,
   Demosthenes, that orator royall,
   That gave Aeschines such a cordiall,
That banishėd was he by his propositíon,
Against whom he could make no contradictíon?

     DAME PALLAS *to the* QUEEN OF FAME

Soft, my good sister, and make there a pause.
   And was Aeschines rebukėd as ye say?
Remember you well, point well that clause;
   Wherefore then rasėd ye not away
   His name? or why is it, I you pray,
That he to your courtė is going and comíng,
Sith he is slanderėd for default of conníng?

     The QUEEN OF FAME *to* DAME PALLAS

Madame, your apposál is well inferrėd,
   And at your advantáge quickly it is

Touchéd, and hard for to be debarréd;
　　Yet shall I answer your grace as in this,
　　With your reformation, if I say amiss,
For, but if your bounty did me assure,
Mine argument else could not longé endure.

As touching that Aeschines is rememberéd,
　　That he so should be, meseemeth it fittíng,
Albeit great parté he hath surrenderéd
　　Of his honour, whose dissuasive in writíng
　　To encourage Demosthenes was much excitíng,
In setting out freshely his crafty persuasíon,
From whiché Aeschines had none evasíon.

The cause why Demosthenes so famously is bruted
　　Only proceeded for that he did outray
Aeschines, whiché was not shamefully confuted
　　But of that famous orator, I say,
　　Which passéd all other; wherefore I may
Among my recordés suffer him naméd,
For though he were vanquishéd, yet was he not shaméd

As Jerome, in his preamble *Frater Ambrosius*,[1]
　　From that I have said in no point doth vary,
Wherein he reporteth of the couragéous
　　Wordés that were much consolatory
　　By Aeschines rehearséd to the greaté glory
Of Demosthenes, that was his utter foe:
Few shall ye find or none that will do so.

Dame Pallas *to the* Queen of Fame

A thanké to have, ye have well deservéd,
　　Your mind that can maintain so apparently;
But a great parté yet ye have reservéd
　　Of that must follow then consequently,
　　Or else ye demeané you inordinately;

[1] The Epistle of Jerome to Paulinus, prefixed to the Vulgate, begins with these words.

For if ye laud him whom honour hath opprest,
Then he that doth worstè is as good as the best.

But whom that ye favour, I see well, hath a name,
   Be he never so little of substánce,
And whom ye love not ye will put to shame;
    Ye counterweigh not evenly your balánce;
    As well folly as wisdom oft ye do advance.
For reportè riseth many deverse ways.
Some be much spoken of for making of frays;

Some have a name for theft and bribery;
   Some be called crafty that can pick a purse;
Some men be made of for their mockery;
    Some careful cuckolds, some have their wivès curse;
    Some famous wittols,[1] and they be muchè worse;
Some litherons, some losels, some naughty packès;
Some facers, some bracers, some make great crackès;

Some drunken dastardès with their dry soulès;
   Some sluggish slovens, that sleep day and night;
Riot and Revel be in your court rollès;
    Maintenance and Mischief, these be men of might;
    Extortíon is counted with you for a knight;
These people by me have none assignèment,
Yet they ride and runnè from Carlisle to Kent.

But little or nothing ye shall hear tell
   Of them that have virtue by reason of conníng,
Which sovereignly in honour should excel;
    Men of such matters make but a mummíng,
    For wisdom and sadness be set out a-sunníng;
And such of my servantès as I have promoted,
One fault or other in them shall be noted.

[1] Tame cuckolds.

Either they will say he is too wise,
  Or else he can nought but when he is at school;
Prove his wit, saith he, at cardès or dice,
  And ye shall well findè he is a very fool!
  Twish, set him a chair, or reach him a stool,
To sit him upon, and read Jack-a-Thrum's bible,
For truly it were pity that he sat idle!

The QUEEN OF FAME to DAME PALLAS

To make repugnance against that ye have said
  Of very duty it may not well accord,
But your benigne sufferance for my discharge I laid,
  For that I would not with you fall at dischord;
  But yet I beseech your grace that good recórd
May be brought forth, such as can be found,
With laureate triumphè why Skelton should be crowned;

For else it were too great a derogatíon
  Unto your palace, our noble court of Fame,
That any man under supportatíon
  Without deserving shouldè have the best game.
  If he to the ample increasè of his name
Can lay any workès that he hath compiléd,
I am content that he be not exiléd

From the laureate senate by force of proscriptíon;
  Or elles, ye know well, I can do no less
But I must banish him from my jurisdiction,
  As he hath acquainted him with idleness;
  But if that he purpose to make a redress,
What he hath done, let it be brought to sight.
Grant my petitíon, I askè you but right.

DAME PALLAS to the QUEEN OF FAME

To your request we be well condescended.
  Call forth, let see where is your clarionar,

To blow a blasté with his long breath extended;
   Aeolus, your trumpet, that knowné is so far,
   That bararag bloweth in every martial war,
Let him blow now, that we may take a view
What poetés we have at our retinue;

To see if Skelton will put himself in press,
   Among the thickest of all the wholé rout.
Make noise enough, for clatterers love no peace!
   Let see, my sister, now speed you, go about;
   Anon, I say, this trumpet were found out,
And for no man hardely let him spare
To blow bararag till both his eyen stare.

SKELTON POETA

Forthwith there rose amongé the throng
A wonderful noisé, and on every side
They presséd in fast; some thought they were too long;
   Some were too hasty, and would no man bide;
   Some whisperéd, some rownéd, some spake, and some cried.
With heaving and shoutingé, have in and have out;
Some ran the nexté way, some ran about.

There was suing to the Queen of Fame;
   He pluckéd him back, and he went afore;
'Nay, hold thy tongue,' quod another, 'let me have the name!'
   'Make room,' said another, 'Ye press all too sore!'
   Some said, 'Hold thy peace, thou gettest here no more!'
A thousand thousand I saw on a plumpé;
With that I heard the noise of a trumpé,

That long time blew a full timorous blast,
   Like to the boreal windés when they blow,
That towers and townés and trees downé cast,
   Drove cloudés together like driftés of snow;
   The dreadful dinné drove all the rout on a row;
Some trembléd, some girnéd, some gaspéd, some gazéd,
As people half peevish, or men that were mazéd!

N

Anon all was whist, as it were for the nonce,
   And each man stood gazing and staring upon other.
With that there come in wonderly at once
    A murmur of minstrels, that such another
    Had I never seen, some softer, some louder;
Orpheus, the Thracian, harpéd melodiously
With Amphion, and other Muses of Arcady:

Whose heavenly harmony was so passing sure,
   So truèly proportionéd, and so well did agree,
So duly entunéd with every measúre,
    That in the forest was none so great a tree
    But that he dancéd for joy of that glee;
The huge mighty oaks themself did advance,
And leap from the hillès to learn for to dance.

In so much the stumpè, whereto I me leant,
   Start all at once an hundreth foot back!
With that I sprang up towardè the tent
    Of noble Dame Pallas, whereof I spake;
    Where I saw come after, I wot, full little lack
Of a thousand poetès assembléd together.
But Phoebus was foremost of all that came thither;

Of laurel leavès a coronal on his head,
   With hairès encrispéd yellow as the gold,
Lamenting Daphne, whom with the dart of lead
    Cupid hath striken so that she ne wold
    Consentè to Phoebus to have his heart in hold;
But, for to preserve her maidenhood clean,
Transforméd was she into the laurel green.

Meddléd with mourning the most part of his muse,
   O thoughtful heart, was evermore his song!
Daphne, my darling, why do you me refuse?
    Yet look on me, that lovéd you so long,
    Yet have compassion upon my painès strong!
He sang also how, the tree as he did take
Between his arms, he felt her body quake.

Then he assurded into this exclamatíon
   Unto Diana, the goddess immortall.
'O merciless madam, hard is your constellatíon,
   So close to keep your cloister virginall,
   Enharded adamant the cément of your wall!
Alas, what ails you to be so overthwart,
To banish pity out of a maiden's heart?

'Why have the gods shewéd me this cruelty,
   Sith I contrivéd first principals medicinable?
I help all other of their infirmity,
   But now to help myself I am not able;
   That profiteth all other is nothing profitable
Unto me; alas, that herbè nor grass
The fervent axes of love cannot repress!

'O fatal fortune! what have I offended?
   Odious disdain, why rayest thou me in this fashion?
But sith I have lost now that I intended,
   And may not attain it by no meditation,
   Yet, in remembrance of Daphne's transformation,
All famous poetès ensuing after me
Shall wear a garlandè of this laurel tree.'

This said, a great number followéd by and by
   Of poetès laureat [1] of many divers natíons;
Part of their namès I thinkè to specify.
   First, old Quintilian with his Declamatíons;
   Theocritus with his bucolical relatíons;
Hesiodus, the economicar,
And Homerus, the freshè historiar;

Prince of eloquence, Tullius Cicero,
   With Salusty against Lucius Cataline,

---

[1] *Poet laureat* meant a person who had taken a degree in grammar, including rhetoric and versification.   But the word *poet* was applied to a writer of prose as well as verse.

That wrote the history of Jugurta alsó;
    Ovid, enshrinéd with the Muses nine;
    But blessed Bacchus, the pleasant god of wine,
Of clusters engroséd with his ruddy floatės
These orators and poetės refreshéd their throatės!

Lucan, with Statius in Achilleidos;
    Persius presséd forth with his problemės diffuse;
Virgil the Mantuan, with his Aenidos;
    Juvenal satiric, that men maketh to muse;
    But blessed Bacchus, the pleasant god of wine,
Of clusters engroséd with his ruddy floatės
These orators and poetės refreshéd their throatės!

There Titus Livius himself did advance
    With decadės historious, which that he mingleth
With matters that amount the Romans in substance;
    Ennius that wrote of martial war at length;
    But blessed Bacchus, the potential god of strength,
Of clusters engroséd with his ruddy floatės
These orators and poetės refreshéd their throatės!

Aulus Gelius, that noble historiar;
    Horace alsó with his new poetry; [1]
Master Terence, that famous comicar,
    With Plautus, that wrote full many a comedy;
    But blessed Bacchus was in their company,
Of clusters engroséd with his ruddy floatės
These orators and poetės refreshéd their throatės!

Senec full soberly with his tragedies;
    Boyce,[2] recomforted with his philosophy;
And Maximian, with his maddė ditties,[3]
    How doting age would jape with youngė folly;
    But blessed Bacchus most reverent and holy,

[1] i.e. Horace's *Art of Poetry*.
[2] Boëthius.
[3] *Elegiarum liber* of Maximianus.

Of clusters engroséd with his ruddy floatès
These orators and poetès refreshéd their throatès!

There came John Bochas with his volumès great; [1]
   Quintus Curtius, full craftily that wrate
Of Alexander; and Macrobius that did treat
   Of Scipion's dream what was the true probate;
   But blessed Bacchus that never man forgate,
Of clusters engroséd with his ruddy floatès
These orators and poetès refreshéd their throatès!

Poggio alsó, that famous Florentine,
   Mustered there among them with many a mad tale; [2]
With a friar of France men call Sir Gaguine,
   That frownéd on me full angerly and pale;
   But blessed Bacchus, that bote is of all bale,
Of clusters engroséd with his ruddy floatès
These orators and poetès refreshéd their throatès!

Plutarch and Petrarch, two famous clerkès;
   Lucilius and Valerius Maximus by name;
With Vicentius *in Speculo*, [3] that wrote noble workès;
   Propertius and Pisander, poetès of noble fame;
   But blessed Bacchus, that mastries oft doth frame,
Of clusters engroséd with his ruddy floatès
These notable poetès refreshéd their throatès!

And as I thus sadly among them aviséd,
   I saw Gower, that first garnishéd our English rude,
And Master Chaucer, that nobly enterpriséd
   How that our English might freshely be enewéd;
   The monk of Bury then after them ensuéd,
Dan John Lydgate: these English poetès three,
As I imaginéd, repairéd unto me,

[1] Boccaccio's *De Genealogia*, and *De Casibus Virorum et Fe-
minarum Illustrium*, rather than the *Decamerone*.
[2] Poggio's *Facetiae*, then very popular.
[3] The *Speculum Majus* (1473) of Vincent of Beauvais.

Together in armés, as brethren, embracéd;
   Their apparel far passing beyond that I can tell;
With diamondés and rubies their tabards were traséd,
   None so rich stonés in Turkey to sell;
   They wanted nothing but the laurél; [1]
And of their bounty they made me goodly cheer,
In manner and form as ye shall after hear.

Master Gower *to* Skelton

Brother Skelton, your endeavourment
   So have ye done, that meritoriously
Ye have deservéd to have an employment
   In our collége above the starry sky,
   Because that ye increase and amplify
The bruted Britons of Brutus' Albion,
That well-nigh was lost when that we were gone.

Poeta Skelton *to* Master Gower

Master Gower, I have nothing deservéd
   To have so laudable a commendatíon:
To you three this honour shall be reservéd,
   Arecting unto your wise examinatíon
   How all that I do is under reformatíon,
For only the substánce of that I intend
Is glad to pleasé, and loth to offend.

Master Chaucer *to* Skelton

Counterweighing your busy diligence
   Of that we begané in the supplement,
Enforcéd are we you to recompense,
   Of all our whole college by the agreèment,
   That we shall bringé you personally presént
Of noble Fame before the Queenés grace,
In whose court appointed is your place.

---

[1] They were not poets laureate—like Skelton.

Poeta Skelton *answereth*

O noble Chaucer, whose polishéd eloquence
  Our English rude so freshely hath set out,
That bound are we with all due reverence,
  With all our strength that we can bring about,
  To owe to you our service, and more if we moght!
But what should I say? Ye wot what I intend,
Which glad am to pleasé, and loth to offend.

Master Lydgate *to* Skelton

So am I prevented of my brethren twain
  In rendering to you thankés meritory,
That well-nigh nothing there doth remain
  Wherewith to give you my regraciatory,
  But that I 'point you to be protonotory
Of Famé's court, by all our whole assent
Advancéd by Pallas to laurel permérnént.

Poeta Skelton *answereth*

So have ye me far passing my merits extolléd,
  Master Lydgate, of your accustomáble
Bounty, and so gloriously ye have enrolléd
  My name, I know well, beyond that I am able;
  That but if my workés thereto be agreeable,
I am elles rebukéd of that I intend,
Which glad am to pleasé, and loth to offend.

So finally, when they had shewéd their devise,
  Under the formé as I said tofore,
I made it strange, and drew back once or twice,
  And ever they presséd on me more and more,
  Till at the last they forcéd me so sore,
That with them I went where they would me bring,
Unto the pavilion where Pallas was sittíng.

Dame Pallas commanded that they should me convey
    Into the richè palace of the Queen of Fame;
There shall he hear what she will to him say
    When he is callèd to answer to his name.
    A cry anon forthwith she made proclaim,
All orators and poetès should thither go before,
With all the press that there was less and more.

Forthwith, I say, thus wandering in my thought,
    How it was, or elles within what hours,
I cannot tell you, but that I was brought
    Into a palace with turretès and towers,
    Engalleried goodly with hallès and bowers,
So curiously, so craftily, so cunningly wrought
That all the world, I trow, an it were sought,

Such another there could no man find;
    Whereof partly I purpose to expound,
Whiles it remaineth freshè in my mind.
    With turquoise and chrysolite enpavéd was the ground;
    Of beryl embossèd were the pillars round;
Of elephantès teeth were the palace gates,
Enlozengéd with many goodly plates

Of gold, entachéd with many a precious stone;
    An hundred steppès mounting to the hall,
One of jasper, another of whalèsbone;
    Of diamondès pointed was the rocky wall;
    The carpettès within and tapettès of pall;
The chambers hangéd with clothès of Arras;
Envaulted with rubies the vault was of this place.

Thus passéd we forth walking unto the pretory
    Where the postès were embullioned with sapphires
        Indy blue,
Englazéd glittering with many a clear story;
    Jacinths and smaragdès out of the florth they grew.
    Unto this place all poetès there did sue,
Wherein was set of Fame the noble Queen,
All other transcending, most richely beseen,

Under a glorious cloth of estate,
   Fret all with orient pearlès of garnate,
Encrownéd as empress of all this worldly fate,
    So royally, so richly, so passing ornate,
    It was exceeding beyond the common rate.
This house environè was a mile about;
If xii. were let in, xii. hundred stood without.

Then to this lady and sovereign of this palace
   Of pursuivants there pressèd in with many a diverse tale;
Some were of Poyle,[1] and some were of Thrace,
    Of Limerick, of Lorain, of Spain, of Portingale,
    From Naples, from Navern, and from Rouncevale,
Some from Flanders, some from the sea-coast,
Some from the mainland, some from the Frenchè host:

With, How doth the north? What tidings in the south?
   The west is windy, the east is meetly wele;
It is hard to tell of every mannès mouth;
    A slippery hold the tail is of an eel,
    And he halteth often that hath a kiby heel.
Some shewéd his safe-conduct, some shewéd his charter,
Some lookéd full smoothly, and had a false quarter;

With, Sir, I pray you, a little time stand back,
   And let me come in to deliver my letter!
Another told how shippès went to wrack;
    There were many wordès smaller and greater,
    With, I as good as thou! I' faith and no better!
Some came to tell truth, some came to lie,
Some came to flatter, and some came to spy.

There were, I say, of all manner of sortès,
   Of Dartmouth, of Plymouth, of Portsmouth alsó;
The burgesses and the bailiffs of the Cinque Portès,
    With, Now let me come! and, Now let me go!

[1] Apulia.

*N

And all time wandered I thus to and fro,
Till at the last these noble poetės three
Unto me said, Lo, sir, now ye may see

Of this high court the daily business.
From you must we, but not long to tarry.
Lo, hither cometh a goodly mistréss,
Occupation, Famės registary,
Which shall be to you a sovereign accessary,
With singular pleasures to drive away the time,
And we shall see you again ere it be prime.[1]

When they were passed and went forth on their way,
This gentlewoman, that calléd was by name
Occupation, in right goodly array,
Came toward me, and smiléd half in game;
I saw her smile, and I then did the same.
With that on me she cast her goodly look;
Under her arm, methought, she had a book.

OCCUPATION *to* SKELTON

Like as the lark, upon the summer's day,
When Titan radiant burnisheth his beamės bright,
Mounteth on high with her melodious lay,
Of the sunėshine engladed with the light,
So am I surpriséd with pleasure and delight
To see this hour now, that I may say
How ye are welcome to this court of array.

Of your acquaintance I was in timės past,
Of studious doctrine when at the port salu
Ye first arrivéd, when broken was your mast
Of worldly trust; then did I you rescúe;
Your storm-driven ship I repairéd new,
So well entackléd, what wind that ever blow,
No stormy tempest your barge shall overthrow.

[1] 9 a.m.

Welcome to me as heartily as heart can think,
  Welcome to me with all my whole desire!
And for my sake spare neither pen nor ink;
  Be well assuréd I shall requite your hire,
  Your name recounting beyond the land of Tyre,
From Sidony to the mount Olympian,
From Babel's Tower to the hillès Caspian.

SKELTON POETA *answereth*

I thankéd her much of her most noble offer,
  Affiancing her mine whole assuránce,
For her pleasúre to make a largè proffer,
  Imprinting her wordès in my remembrance,
  To owe her my service with true perséverance.
Come on with me, she said, let us not stand!
And with that word she took me by the hand.

So passéd we forth into the foresaid place,
  With such communication as came to our mind.
And then she said, Whiles we have time and space
  To walk where we list, let us somewhat find
  To pass the time with, but let us waste no wind,
For idle janglers have but little brain:
Words be swords, and hard to call again.

Into a fieldè she brought me wide and large,
  Enwalléd about with the stony flint,
Strongly embattled, much costious of charge.
  To walk on this wall she bade I should not stint.
  Go softly, she said, the stonès be full glint.
She went before, and bade me take good hold.
I saw a thousand gatès new and old.

Then questioned I her what those gatès meant;
  Whereto she answeréd, and briefly me told,
How from the east unto the occident,
  And from the south unto the north so cold,
  These gatès, she said, which that ye behold,

Be issues and portès from all manner of natíons;
And seriously she shewéd me their denominatíons.

They had writing, some Greekè, some Hebrew,
   Some Roman letters, as I understood;
Some were oldè written, some were written new,
   Some characters of Chaldy, some Frenchè was full good;
   But one gate specíally, whereas I stood,
Had graven in it of chalcedony a capital A.
What gate call ye this? And she said, Anglia.

The building thereof was passing commendable;
   Whereon stood a leopard, crownéd with gold and stonès,
Terrible of countenance and passing formidable,
   As quickly touchéd [1] as it were flesh and bonès,
   As ghastly that glarès, and grimly that groanès,
As fiercely frowning as he had been fightíng,
And with his former foot he shook forth this writíng.

Formidanda nimis Jovis ultima fulmina tollis:
Unguibus ire parat loca singula livida curvis
Quam modo per Phoebes nummos raptura Celaeno;
Arma, lues, luctus, fel, vis, fraus, barbara tellus;
Mille modis erras odium tibi quaerere Martis:
Spreto spineto cedant saliunca roseto. [2]

Then I me leant, and lookéd over the wall.
   Innumerable people presséd to every gate.
Shut were the gatès; they might well knock and call,
   And turn home again, for they came all too late.
   I her demanded of them and their estate.
Forsooth, quod she, they be haskardès and ribaldès,
Dicers, carders, tumblers with gamboldès.

Furtherers of love, with bawdry aquainted,
   Brainless blinkardès that blow at the coal,

[1] Executed as much to the life.
[2] I cannot make anything of this.

False forgers of money, for coinage attainted,
  Pope-holy hypocrites, as they were gold and whole,
  Pole-hatchets, that prate will at every ale-pole,
Riot, reveller, railer, bribery, theft,
With other conditions that well might be left.

Some feign themselves fooles, and would be called wise,
  Some meddling spies, by craft to grope thy mind,
Some disdainous dawcockes that all men despise,
  False flatterers that fawne thee, and curs of kind
  That speak fair before thee and shrewdly behind;
Hither they come crowding to get them a name,
But haled they be homeward with sorrow and shame.

With that I heard gunnes rushe out at ones,
  Bounce, bounce, bounce! that all they out cried;
It made some limp-legged and bruised their bones;
  Some were made peevishe, porishly pink-eyed,
  That ever more after by it they were espied;
And one was there, I wondered of his hap,
For a gun-stone, I say, had all to-jagged his cap:

Ragged and dagged, and cunningly cut,
  The blaste of the brimstone blew away his brain;
Mazed as a Marche-hare, he ran like a scut!
  And, sir, amonge all methought I saw twain,
  The one was a tumbler, that afterwards again
Of a dicer, a devil way, grew a gentleman,
Pierce Prater the second, that quarrels began;

With a pellet of peevishness they had such a stroke,
  That all the days of their life shall stick by their ribs!
Foo, foisty bawdias! some smelled of the smoke!
  I saw divers that were carried away thence in cribs,
  Dazing after dotterels, like drunkards that dribs.
These titivels with tampions were touched and tapped; [1]
Much mischiefe, I hight you, among them there happed.

[1] I suppose: These stupid fellows had stoppers put in their mouths.

Sometime, as it seemeth, when the mooné-light
  By meanés of a grisly endarkéd cloudé
Suddenly is eclipséd in the winter night,
    In like manner of wise a mist did us shroudé.
    But well may ye think I was nothing proudé
Of that aventuré, which made me sore aghast.
In darkéness thus dwelt we, till at the last

The cloudés gan to clear, the mist was rarified;
  In an herber I saw, brought where I was,
There birdés on the briar sang on every side;
    With alleys ensanded about in compáss,
    The banks enturféd with singular soláce,
Enrailéd with rosers, and vinés engrapéd;
It was a new comfort of sorrowés escapéd.

In the midst a conduit, that curiously was cast,
  With pipés of gold engushing out streams;
Of crystal the clearness these waters far past,
    Enswimming with roaches, barbellés, and breams,
    Whose scalés ensilveréd against the sun-beams
Englistered, that joyous it was to behold.
Then furthermore about me my sight I revol'd,

Where I saw growing a goodly laurel tree,
  Enverduréd with leavés continually green;
Above in the top a birdé of Araby
    Men call a phoenix; her wingés between
    She beat up a fire with the sparkés full keen
With branches and boughés of the sweet olíve,
Whose fragrant flower was chief preservative

Against all infectíons with rancour inflaméd,
  Against all baratous bruises of old.
It passéd all balmés that ever were naméd,
    Or gums of Araby so dearly that be sold.
    There blew in that gardené a soft pipling cold

Enbreathing of Zephyrus with his pleasant wind;
All fruitès and flowerès grew there in their kind.

Dryads there dancéd upon that goodly soil,
   With the nine Muses, Pierides by name;
Phyllis and Testalis, their tresses with oil
    Were newly enbibéd; and round about the same
    Green tree of laurel muchè solacious game
They made, with chapelets and garlandès green;
And foremost of all dame Flora, the queen

Of summer, so formally she footed the dance;
   There Cyntheus sat twinkling upon his harpè-strings;
And Iopas [1] his instrument did avance,[2]
    The poemès and stories, ancient inbrings [3]
    Of Atlas' astrology, and many noble things,
Of wandering of the moon, the coursè of the sun,
Of men and of beastès, and whereof they begun,

What thing occasionéd the showerès of rain,
   Of fire elementar in his supremè sphere,
And of that pole arctic which doth remain
    Behindè the tail of Ursa so clear;
    Of Hyades he preachéd with their drowsy chere,
Emoisturéd with misling and aye dropping eye,
And where the two Triones [4] a man should espy,

And of the winter days that hie them so fast,
   And of the winter nightès that tarry so long,
And of the summer days so long that do last,
    And or their short nightès; he brought in his song
    How wrong was no right, and right was no wrong.
There was countering of carols in metre and verse
So many, that longè it were to rehearse.

[1] The Carthaginian bard.
[2] Here, and for the next two stanzas, cf. Virgil, *Aeneid*, i. 740 ff.
[3] Tales brought from long ago.
[4] i.e. Ursa Major and Minor, the Wain.

Occupation *to* Skelton

How say ye? is this after your appetite?
   May this content you and your merry mind?
Here dwelleth pleasúre, with lust and delight;
   Continual comfort here ye may find,
   Of wealth and solace no thingė left behind;
All thing convenáble here is contrivéd,
Wherewith your spiritės may be revivéd.

Poeta Skelton *answereth*

Questionless no doubt of that ye say;
   Jupiter himselfė this life might endure;
This joy exceedeth all worldly sport and play;
   Paradise this place is of singular pleasúre:
   O well were him that hereof might be sure,
And here to inhabit and aye for to dwell!
But, goodly mistress, one thing ye me tell.

Occupation *to* Skelton

Of your demand shew me the contént,
   What it is, and whereupon it stands;
And if there be in it anything meant,
   Whereof the answer resteth in my hands,
   It shall be looséd full soon out of the bands
Of scrupulous doubt; wherefore your mind discharge,
And of your will the plainness shew at large.

Poeta Skelton *answereth*

I thank you, goodly mistress, to me most benign,
   That of your bounty so well have me assuréd;
But my request is not so great a thing
   That I ne force what though it be discuréd;
   I am not wounded but that I may be curéd;
I am not laden of liderness with lumpės,
As dazéd dotards that dreamė in their dumpės.

Occupation *to* Skelton

Now what ye mean, I trow I conject;
  God give you good year, ye make me to smile!
Now, by your faith, is not this the effect
  Of your question ye make all this while,
  To understand who dwelleth in yondé pile,
And what blunderer is yonder that played diddle diddle?
He findeth false measurés out of his fond fiddle.

Interpolata, que industriosum postulat interpretem, satira in
vatis adversarium.[1]

Tressis agasonis species prior, altera Davi:
Aucupium culicis limis dum torquet ocellum,
Concipit, aligeras rapit, appetit, aspice, muscas!
Maia quaeque fovet, fovet aut quae Jupiter, aut quae
Frigida Saturnus, Sol, Mars, Venus, algida Luna,
Si tibi contingat verbo aut committere scripto,
Quam sibi mox tacita sudant praecordia culpa!
Hinc ruit in flammas, stimulans hunc urget et illum,
Invocat ad rixas, vanos tamen excitat ignes,
Labra movens tacitus, rumpantur ut ilia Codro.[2]

17. 4. 7. 2. 17. 5. 18.
18. 19. 1. 19. 8. 5. 12.[3]

[1] An interpolated satire against the poet's adversary, which demands an industrious interpreter. (It certainly does!)

[2] The first kind is a twopenny-halfpenny groom, the second a Davus [i.e. a slave]. He strains at a gnat, turning his eye aslant and, look, he seizes, snatches at flies! Whatever Maia cherishes, or Jupiter, or cold Saturn, Sun, Mars, Venus, and the chill Moon, if you chance to put it in words or writing, how soon the heart begins to sweat with silent guilt! Hence he bursts into flames, stirs up this one and that, egging them on, yet only kindles ineffectual fires, muttering in silence—let Codrus [a poet hostile to Virgil] burst his lungs!

[3] Rogerous Statham. Deciphered by H. Bradley, *Academy*, 1 August 1896. (*See* lines to Mistress Gertrude Statham, page 381.)

His name for to know if that ye list,
    Envious Rancour truėly he hight:
Beware of him, I warn you; for an ye wist
    How dangerous it were to standė in his light,
    Ye would not deal with him, though that ye might,
For by his devilish drift and graceless provision
An whole realmė he is able to set at devision.

For when he speaketh fairest, then thinketh he most ill;
    Full gloriously can he glose, thy mind for to feel;
He will set men a-fighting, and sit himself still,
    And smirk, like a smithy cur, at sparkės of steel;
    He can never leave workė whilės it is weel;
To tell all his touches it were too great wonder;
The devil of hell and he be seldom asunder.

Thus talking we went in at a postern gate;
    Turning on the right handė, by a winding stair,
She brought me to a goodly chamber of estate,
    Where the noble Countess of Surrey [1] in a chair
    Sat honourably, to whomė did repair
Of ladies a bevy with all due reverence.
Sit downė, fair ladies, and do your diligence!

Come forth, gentlewomen, I pray you, she said,
    I have contrivéd for you a goodly wark,
And who can work bestė now shall be assayed.
    A coronal of laurel with verdurės light and dark
    I have deviséd for Skelton, my clerk;
For to his service I have suchė regard
That of our bounty we will him reward.

For of all ladies he hath the library,
    Their namės recounting in the court of Fame;

[1] Wife of Lord Thomas Howard and mother of the poet, Henry
Howard, to whom Skelton was tutor.

Of all gentlewomen he hath the scrutiny,
    In Fames court reportinge the same;
    For yet of women he never said shame,
But if they were counterfeits, that women them call,
That list of their lewdness with him for to brawl.

With that the tappettes and carpettes were laid,
    Whereon these ladies softly might rest,
The sampler to sew on, the laces to embraid;
    To weave in the stole some were full prest,
    With sleys, with tavelles,[1] with hiddles well drest;
The frame was brought forth with his weaving pin.
God give them good speed their work to begin!

Some to embroider put them in press,
    Well guiding their glowton to keep straight their silk,
Some pirling of gold their work to increase
    With fingers small, and handes white as milk;
    With, Reach me that skein of tuly silk!
And, Wind me that bottom of such an hue,
Green, red, tawny, white, black, purple, and blue.

Of broken workes wrought many a goodly thing,
    In casting, in turning, in flourishing of floweres,
With burres rough and bottons surfeling,
    In needle-work raising birdes in boweres,
    With virtue enbusied all times and houres;
And truly of their bounty thus were they bent
To work me this chaplet by good advisement.

OCCUPATION *to* SKELTON

Behold and see in your advertisement
    How these ladies and gentlewomen all
For your pleasure do their endeavourment,
    And for your sake how fast to work they fall:
    To your remembrance wherefore ye must call

[1] Silk-weaving instruments.

In goodly wordės pleasantly comprisėd,
That for them some goodly conceit be devisėd,

With proper captations of benevolence,
  Ornately polishėd after your faculty,
Sith ye must needs aforce it by pretence
  Of your profession unto humanity,
  Commencing your process after their degree,
To each of them rendering thankės commendable,
With sentence fructuous and termės covenable.

POETA SKELTON

Avancing myself some thankė to deservė,
  I me determinėd for to sharp my pen,
Devoutly arecting my prayer to Minerva,
  She to vouchsafe me to inform and ken;
  To Mercury also heartily prayėd I then,
Me to supportė, to help, and to assist,
To guide and to govern my dreadful trembling fist.

As a mariner that amazėd is in a stormy rage,
  Hardly bested and driven is to hope
Of that the tempestuous windė will assuage,
  In trust whereof comfortė his heart doth grope,
  From the anchor he cutteth the cable-rope,
Commiteth all to God, and letteth his ship ride,
So I beseech Jesu now to be my guide!

To the right noble COUNTESS OF SURREY

After all duly ordered obeisance,
  In humble wise as lowly as I may,
Unto you, madam, I make reconusance!
  My life enduring I shall both write and say,
  Recount, reportė, rehearse without delay
The passingė bounty of your noble estate,
Of honour and worship which hath the former date.

Like to Argia by just resemblánce,
  The noble wife of Polynices king;
Prudent Rebecca, of whom remembránce
  The Bible maketh; with whose chaste living
  Your noble demeanour is counterweighíng,
Whose passing bounty, and right noble estate,
Of honour and worship it hath the former date.

The noble Pamphila, queen of the Greekės land,
  Habiliments royal found out industriously;
Thamer [1] also wrought with her goodly hand
  Many devices passing curiously;
  Whom ye represent and exemplify,
Whos passing bounty, and right noble estate,
Of honour and worship it hath the former date.

As Dame Thamarys, which took the king of Percė,
  Cyrus by name, as writeth the story;
Dame Agrippina also I may rehearsė
  Of gentle corage and perfite memory;
  So shall your name endure perpetually,
Whose passing bounty, and right noble estate,
Of honour and worship it hath the former date.

To my Lady ELIZABETH HOWARD

To be your remembrancer, madam, I am bound,
  Like to Irene, maidenly of port,
Of virtue and conning the well and perfect ground;
  Whom dame Nature, as well I may report,
  Hath freshly embeautied with many a goodly sort
Of womanly features, whose flourishing tender age
Is lusty to look on, pleasant, demure, and sage.

Good Criseyde, fairer than Polexene,
  For to enliven Pandarus' appetite;

[1] Timarete, daughter to Mycon, the painter. (*See* Pliny, *Naś.
Hist.*)

Troilus, I trow, if that he had you seen,
    In you he would have set his whole delight.
    Of all your beauty I suffice not to write;
But, as I said, your flourishing tender age
Is lusty to look on, pleasant, demure, and sage.

To my Lady MURIEL HOWARD

My little lady I may not leave behind,
    But do her service needès now I must;
Benign, courteous, of gentle heart and mind,
    Whom Fortune and Fate plainly have dicust
    Long to enjoy pleasure, delight, and lust:
The embudded blossoms of roses red of hue,
With lilies white your beauty doth renew.

Compare you I may to Cydippe, the maid,
    That of Acontius, when she found the bill [1]
In her bosom, lord, how she was afraid!
    The ruddy shamefacedness in her visage fill,
    Which manner of abashment became her not ill.
Right so, madam, the roses red of hue
With lilies white your beauty doth renew.

To my Lady ANNE DACRE of the South

Zeuxis that empicturéd fair Elene the queen,
    You to devise his craftè were to seek;
And if Apelles your countenance had seen,
    Of portraiture which was the famous Greek,
    He could not devise the least point of your cheek!
Princess of youth, and flower of goodly port,
Virtue, conning, solace, pleasure, comfort.

Paregal in honour unto Penelope,
    That for her truth is in remembrance had;

[1] *Billet-doux.*

Fair Deianira surmounting in beautý;
  Demure Diana womanly and sad,
   Whose lusty looks make heavy heartės glad!
Princess of youth, and flower of goodly port,
Virtue, conning, solace, pleasure, comfort.

To Mistress Margery Wentworth

    With marjoram gentle,
     The flower of goodlihead,
    Embroidered the mantle
     Is of your maidenhead.
    Plainly I cannot glose;
     Ye be, as I devine,
    The pretty primrose,
     The goodly columbine.
    With marjoram gentle,
     The flower of goodlihead,
    Embroidered the mantle
     Is of your maidenhead.
    Benign, courteous, and meek,
     With wordės well devised;
    In you, who list to seek,
     Be virtues well comprised.
    With marjoram gentle,
     The flower of goodlihead,
    Embroidered the mantle
     Is of your maidenhead.

To Mistress Margaret Tylney

    I you assure,
     Full well I know
    My busy cure
     To you I owe;
     Humbly and low
    Commending me
    To your bounty.

As Machareus
    Fair Canace,[1]
So I, ywis,
    Endeavour me
    Your name to see
It be enrolled,
Written with gold.

Phaedra ye may
    Well represent;
Intentive aye
    And diligent,
    No time misspent;
Wherefore delight
I have to write

Of Margarite,
    Pearl orient,
Load-star of light,
    Much relucent;
    Madam regent
I may you call
Of virtues all.

To MISTRESS JANE BLENNERHASSET

What though my pen wax faint,
And hath small lust to paint?
Yet shall there no restraint
        Cause me to cease,
        Among this press,
        For to increase
        Your goodly name.

        I will myself apply,
        Trust me, intentively,
        You for to stellify;

[1] Their tale told by Gower, *Confessio Amantis.*

And so observe
That ye ne swerve
For to deserve
Immortal fame.

Sith Mistress Jane Hasset
Small flowers helped to set
In my goodly chapelet,
Therefore I render of her the memory
Unto the legend of far Laodamy.

To MISTRESS ISABEL PENNELL

By Saint Mary, my lady,
Your mammy and your daddy
Brought forth a goodly baby!

My maiden Isabel,
Reflaring rosabel.[1]
The fragrant camomel;
   The ruddy rosary,
The sovereign rosemary,
The pretty strawberry;
   The columbine, the nept,
The jelofer well set,
The proper violet:
   Ennewéd your colour
Is like the daisy flower
After the April shower;
   Star of the morrow gray,
The blossom on the spray,
The freshest flower of May;
   Maidenly demure,
Of womanhood the lure;
Wherefore I make you sure

[1] Odorous fair-rose.

It were an heavenly health,
It were an endless wealth,
A life for God himself,
  To hear this nightingale
Among the birdès smale
Warbeling in the vale,
    Dug, dug,
    Jug, jug,
      Good year and good luck,
      With chuck, chuck, chuck, chuck!

To MISTRESS MARGARET HUSSEY

Merry Margaret,
  As midsummer flower,
Gentle as falcon
Or hawk of the tower: [1]
With solace and gladness,
Much mirth and no madness,
All good and no badness;
    So joyously,
    So maidenly,
    So womanly
    Her demeaning
    In every thing,
    Far, far passing
    That I can indite,
    Or suffice to write
Of Merry Margaret
  As midsummer flower,
Gentle as falcon
Or hawk of the tower.
  As patient and still
And as full of good will
As fair Isaphill,[2]
Coriander,

[1] That towers aloft.   [2] Hypsipyle.

Sweet pomander,
Good Cassander,[1]
Steadfast of thought,
Well made, well wrought,
Far may be sought
Ere that ye can find
So courteous, so kind
As Merry Margaret,
    This midsummer flower,
Gentle as falcon
Or hawk of the tower.

To MISTRESS GERTRUDE STATHAM

Though ye were hard-hearted,
And I with you thwarted
With wordès that smarted,
    Yet now doubtless ye give me cause
    To write of you this goodly clause,
    Mistress Gertrude,
    With womanhood endued,
    With virtue well renewed.
I will that ye shall be
In all benignity
Like to dame Pasiphae;
    For now doubtless ye give me cause
    To write of you this goodly clause,
    Mistress Gertrude,
    With womanhood endued,
    With virtue well renewed.
Partly by your counsel,
Garnishéd with laurel
Was my freshè coronal;
    Wherefore doubtless ye give me cause
    To write of you this goodly clause,
    Mistress Gertrude,
    With womanhood endued,
    With virtue well renewed.

[1] Cassandra.

To MISTRESS ISABEL KNIGHT

But if I should requite your kindness,
    Else say ye might
That in me were great blindness
I for to be so mindless,
    And could not write
    Of Isabel Knight.

It is not my custom nor my guise
    To leave behind
Her that is both womanly and wise,
And specially which glad was to devise
    The means to find
    To please my mind

In helping to work my laurel green
    With silk and gold:
Galathea, the maid well beseen,
Was never half so fair, as I ween,
    Which was extoll'd
    A thousandfold

By Maro, the Mantuan prudent,[1]
    Who list to read!
But, an I had leisure competent,
I could shew you such a precedent
    In very deed
    How ye exceed.

OCCUPATION *to* SKELTON

Withdraw your handė, the time passes fast:
    Set on your head this laurel which is wrought;
Hear you not Aeolus for you bloweth a blast?
    I dare well say that ye and I be sought.
    Make no delay, for now ye must be brought

[1] i.e. Virgil (*See Ecl.* i and iii).

Before my lady's grace, the Queen of Fame,
Where ye must briefly answer to your name.

SKELTON POETA

Casting my sight the chamber aboutė,
  To see how duly each thing in order was,
Toward the door, as we were coming outė,
  I saw Master Newton sit with his compáss,
  His plummet, his pencil, his spectacles of glass,
Devising in picture, by his industrious wit,
Of my laurél the process every whit.

Forthwith upon this, as it were in a thought,
  Gower, Chaucer, Lydgate, these three
Before remembered, me courteously brought
  Into that place whereas they left me,
  Where all the said poetės sat in their degree.
But when they saw my laurel, richly wrought,
All other beside were counterfeit they thought

In comparison of that which I wear.
  Some praiséd the pearl, some the stonės bright:
Well was him that thereupon might stare!
  Of this workė they had so great delight,
  The silk, the gold, the flowerės fresh to sight,
They said my laurel was the goodliest
That ever they saw, and wrought it was the best.

In her estate there sat the noble Queen
  Of Fame.   Perceiving how that I was come,
She wonderéd, methought, at my laurel green;
  She lookéd haughty, and gave on me a glum.
  There was among them no wordė then but mum!
For each man hearkened what she would to me say;
Whereof in substance I brought this away.

The QUEEN OF FAME *to* SKELTON

My friend, sith ye are before us here presént,
  To answer unto this noble audience,
Of that shall be reasoned ye must be content;
  And, for as much as by the high pretence
  That ye have now thorough pre-eminence
Of laureate triumph, your place is here reservéd,
We will understand how ye have it deservéd.

SKELTON POETA *to the* QUEEN OF FAME

Right high and mighty princess of estate,
  In famous glory all other transcendíng,
Of your bounty the accustomable rate
  Hath been full often and yet is intendíng
  To all that to reason is condescendíng,
But if hastive credence, by maintenance of might,
Fortune to stand between you and the light.

But such evidence I think for to induce,
  As so largely to lay for mine indemnity,
That I trust to maké mine excuse
  Of what charge soever ye lay against me;
  For of my bookés part ye shall see,
Which in your recordés, I know well, be enrolled,
And so Occupation, your registrar, me told.

Forthwith she commanded I should take my place;
  Calliope 'pointed me where I should sit.
With that, Occupation presséd in apace;
  Be merry, she said, be not afeard a whit,
  Your discharge here under mine arm is it.
So then commanded she was upon this
To shew her book, and she said, Here it is.

The QUEEN OF FAME *to* OCCUPATION

Your book of remembrance we will now that ye read;
  If any recordés in number can be found

What Skelton hath compiléd and written indeed,
  Rehearsing by order, and what is the ground,
  Let see now for him how ye can expound;
For in our court, ye wot well, his name cannot rise
But if he write oftener than once or twice.

Poeta Skelton

With that of the book loosened were the claspés:
  The margent was illuminéd all with golden railés
And byse, empicturéd with gressops and waspés,
  With butterflies and freshé peacock tailés,
  Enfloréd with flowerés and slimy snailés;
Envived picturés well touchéd and quickly;
It would have made a man whole that had been right
  sickly

To behold how it was garnishéd and bound,
  Encovered over with gold of tissue fine;
The claspés and bullions were worth a thousand pound;
  With balasses [1] and carbuncles the borders did shine;
  With *aurum musaicum* [2] every other line
Was written.   And so she did her speed,
Occupatíon, immediately to read.

Occupation *readeth and expoundeth some part of* Skelton's *books and ballads with ditties of pleasure inasmuch as it were too long a process to rehearse all by name that he hath compiled, etc.*

  Of your orator and poet laureate
    Of England, his workés here they begin!
  In primis the Book of Honourous Estate;
    Item, the Book how men shouldé flee sin;
    Item, Royal Demeanance worship to win;
  Item, the Book to speak well and be still;
  Item, to learn you to die when ye will; [3]

[1] Rubies, found by Marco Polo in Balakhshan.   [2] Mosaic gold.
[2] A version, probably, of the same piece translated from the French by Caxton: *A lityll treatise, short and abridged, spekyng of the arte and crafte to knowe well to dye . . .* (1490).

Of Virtue also the sovereign interlude;
   The Book of the Rosiar; Prince Arthur's Creation;
The False Faith that now goeth, which daily is renewed;
   Item, his Dialogues of Imagination;
   Item, Automedon of Love's Meditation;[1]
Item, New Grammar in English compiléd;
Item, Bouge of Court, where Drede was beguiléd;

His comedy, Achademios calléd by name;
   Of Tully's Familiars the translation;[2]
Item, Good Advertisement, that brainless doth blame;
   The Recule against Gaguin of the French nation;
   Item, the Popinjay,[3] that hath in commendation
Ladyės and gentlewomen such as deservéd,
And such as be counterfeités they be reservéd;

And of Sovereignty a noble pamphelet;
   And of Magnificence a notable matter,
How Counterfeit Countenance of the new jet
   With Crafty Conveyance doth smatter and flatter,
   And Cloakéd Collusion is brought in to clatter
With Courtly Abusion; who printeth it well in mind
Much doubleness of the worldė therein he may find;

Of Mannerly Mistress Margery Milk and Ale,
   To her he wrote many matters of mirth;
Yet, though I say it, thereby lieth a tale,
   For Margery winchéd, and brake her hinder-girth;
   Lor, how she made much of her gentle birth!
With, Gingerly, go gingerly! her tail was made of hay;
Go she never so gingerly, her honesty is gone away!

Hard to make ought of that is naked nought;
   This fustian mistress and this giggish gase,

[1] Automedon, the charioteer of Ovid, *Ars amatoria*, 1, 5–8.
[2] Praised in Caxton's preface to *The Boke of Eneydos*, 1490.
[3] *Speak, Parrot?*

Wonder is to write what wrenches she wrought,
   To face out her folly with a midsummer maze!
   With pitch she patchéd her pitcher should not craze;
It may well rhyme, but shrewdly it doth accord,
To pick out honesty of such a potshord!

Patet per versus.

Hinc puer hic natus: vir conjugis hinc spoliatus
Jure thori; est foetus Deli de sanguine cretus;
Hinc magis extollo, quod erit puer alter Apollo;
Si quaeris qualis? meretrix castissima talis;
     Et ralis, et ralis et reliqualis.
     A good herring of these old tailès;
     Find no more such from Wanfleet to Walès!

Et reliquae omeliae de diversis tractatibus.

Of my lady's grace at the contemplatíon,
   Out of Frenchè into English prose,
Of Man's Life the Peregrinatíon,
   He did translate, interpret, and disclose;
   The Treatise of Triumphès of the Red Rose,
Wherein many stories are briefly containéd
That unremembered longè time remainéd;

The Duke of York's creancer when Skelton was,
   Now Henry the Eight, King of Englandè,
A treatise he deviséd and brought it to pass,
   Calléd *Speculum Principis*, to bear in his handè,
   Therein to read, and to understandè
All the demeanour of princèly estate,
To be our King, of God preordinate;

Also the Tunning of Elinour Rummíng,
   With Colin Clout, John Ive,[1] with Joforth Jack!
To make such trifles it asketh some conníng,

          [1] A heretic, *temp.* Edward IV.

o

In honest mirth pardee requireth no lack;
   The white appeareth the better for the black,
After conveyance as the worldè goes,
It is no folly to use the Welshman's hose;

The umbles of venison, the bottle of wine,
   To fair Mistress Anne that should have been sent,
He wrote thereof many a pretty line,
   Where it became, and whither it went,
   And how that it was wantonly spent;
The Ballad alsó of the Mustard Tart,
Such problemès to paint it 'longeth to his art;

Of one Adam all a knave, late dead and gone,—
   Dormiat in pace, like a dormouse!—
He wrote an Epitaph for his grave-stone,
   With wordès devout and sentence agerdouce,
   For he was ever against Goddès house,
All his delight was to brawlè and to bark
Against Holy Church, the priestè, and the clerk.

Of Philip Sparrow, the lamentable fate,
   The doleful destiny, and the careful chance,
Devisèd by Skelton after the funeral rate;
   Yet some there be therewith that take grievánce,
   And grudge thereat with frowning countenance;
But what of that! hard it is to please all men;
Who list amend it, let him set to his pen![1]

The grunting and the groigning of the gronning swine;[2]
   Also the Mourning of the Mapely-Root;
How the green coverlet suffered great pine,
   When the fly-net was set for to catch a coot,
   Struck one with a bird-bolt to the heart-root;

[1] There follow here in Dyce the lines known as 'an addition to *Philip Sparrow*.' As they appear on pp. 97–100 of this edition they are not repeated here.

[2] *Against Venomous Tongues* (perhaps).

Also a devouté Prayer to Moses' hornès,
Metrified merrily, meddeléd with scornès;

Of pageants that were playéd in Joyous Guard;
   He wrote of a mews [1] through a mud wall;
How a doe came tripping in at the rearward,
   But, lord, how the parker was wroth withall!
   And of Castle Angel the fenestrall,
Glittering and glistering and gloriously glazéd,
It made some men's eyen dazzled and dazéd;

The Repeat of the Recule of Rosamondès bower,
   Of his pleasant painè there and his glad distress
In planting and plucking a proper jeloffer flower;
   But how it was, some were too reckeless,
   Notwithstanding it is remediless;
What might she say? what might he do thereto?
Though Jack said nay, yet Mock there lost her shoe;

How then like a man he won the barbican
   With a saute of solace at the longè last;
The colour deadly, swart, blo, and wan
   Of Ixion, his limbès dead and past,
   The cheek and the neck but a shortè cast; [2]
In Fortune's favour ever to endure,
No man living, he saith, can be sure;

How dame Minerva first found the olive tree, *she read*,
   And planted it where never before was none; *unshred*
An hind enhurt, hit by casualty,   *not bled*
   Recovered when the forster was gone;   *and sped*
   The hartès of the herd began for to groan, *and fled*
The houndès began to yearn [3] and to quest; *and dread*
With little business standeth much rest;   *in bed*

---

[1] Opening.   [2] Referring to Ixion's position on the wheel,
perhaps.   MS. defective here.   [3] Give tongue.

His Epitomes of the miller and his joly make;
　　How her blee was bright as blossom on the spray,
A wanton wench and well could bake a cake;
　　The miller was loth to be out of the way,
　　But yet for all that, be as be may,
Whether he rode to Swaffham or to Soham,
The miller durst not leave his wife at home.

With, Woefully Arrayed, and shamefully betrayed;
　　Of his making devout meditatíons;
Vexilla regis he deviséd to be displayed;
　　With *Sacris solemniis*, and other contemplatíons,
　　That in them compriséd consideratíons;
Thus passeth he the time both night and day,
Sometime with sadness, sometime with play;

Though Galen and Dioscorides,
　　With Hippocrates and Master Avycen,[1]
By their physic doth many a man ease,
　　And though Albumasar can thee inform and ken
　　What constellations are good or bad for men,
Yet when the rain raineth and the goose winketh,
Little wotteth the gosling what the goose thinketh!

He is not wise against the stream that striveth;
　　Dun is in the mire——[2] dame, reach me my spur!
Needès must he run that the devil driveth;
　　When the steed is stolen, spar the stable-door!
　　A gentle hound should never play the cur;
It is soon espiéd where the thorn pricketh,
And well wotteth that cat whose beard she licketh;

With Marion clarion, sol, lucernè,
　　Grand juir, of this Frenchè proverb old,
How men were wont for to discernè

[1] Avicenna, the Arabian philosopher and physician of the eleventh century.

[2] A Christmas game, in which Dun (a cart-horse) is supposed to be stuck in the mud.

By Candlemas Day what weather should hold,
   But Marion clarion was caught with a cold cold,
      anglice a cuckold
And all overcast with cloudės unkind,
This goodly flower with stormės was untwined;

This jeloffer gentle, this rose, this lily floure,
   This primėrose peerless, this proper violet,
This columbine clear and freshest of colóur,
   This delicate daisy, this strawberry prettily set,
    With froward frostės, alas, was all to-fret!
But who may have a more ungracious life
Than a childės bird and a knavės wife?
          Think what ye will
          Of this wanton bill;
          By Mary Gipsy,
          Quod scripsi, scripsi:
          Uxor tua, sicut vitis,
          Habetis in custodiam,
          Custodite sicut scitis,
          Secundum Lucam, etc.[1]

Of the Bonhams of Ashridge beside Berkhamstead,[2]
   That goodly place to Skelton most kind,
Where the sang royal is, Christės blood so red,
   Whereupon he metrified after his mind,
    A pleasanter place than Ashridge is, hard were to find,
   As Skelton rehearseth, with wordės few and plain,
   In his distichon made on verses twain;

[1] What I have written, I have written [Vulgate, Joan. xix. 22].
Your wife, like a vine [Ps. cxxviii. 3], you have in your charge,
guard her as best you can, according to Luke, etc. ('Fear not . . .
thy wife Elizabeth shall bear thee a son').
[2] The college of the Bonhommes.   It was founded expressly in
honour of the blood of Jesus, which its founder, Edward, Earl of
Cornwall (*temp.* Henry III), is said to have brought to England.
(*See* Todd's *History of the College of Bonhommes*, 1823.)

Fraxinus in clivo frondetque viret sine rivo,
Non est sub divo similis sine flumine vivo; [1]

The Natíon of Foolès [2] he left not behindè;
   Item, Apollo that whirléd up his chair,
That made some to snur and snuf in the windè;
   It made them to skip, to stampè, and to stare,
   Which, if they be happy, have cause to beware
In rhyming and railing with him for to mell,
For dread that he learn them their A,B,C, to spell.

Poeta Skelton

With that I stood up, half suddenly afraid;
   Supplying to Fame, I besought her grace,
An that it would please her, full tenderly I prayed,
   Out of her bookès Apollo to rase.
   Nay, sir, she said, whatso in this place
Of our noble courtè is onès spoken out
It must needs after run all the world about.

God wot, these wordès made me full sad;
   And when that I saw it would no better be,
But that my petitíon would not be had,
   What should I do but take it in gre?
   For, by Jupiter and his high majestý,
I did what I couldè to scrape out the scrollès,
Apollo to rase out of her ragman rollès. [3]

---

[1] The ash-tree on the hill [or ridge] blooms and flourishes without
  a brook,
  There is not another like it under the sky without a living
    stream.

[2] Not the *Ship of Fools*, a few chapters of which were included
by mistake among Skelton's works. Perhaps this refers to the
lines in *Against a Comely Coistrown*, which begins: 'Of all nations
under the heaven, These frantic foolès,' etc.

[3] The collection of deeds in which the Scottish nobility and
gentry were compelled to subscribe allegiance to Edward I of
England—Rafman's Roll. Cf. Rigmarole.

Now hereof it irketh me longer to write;
　To Occupatíon I will again resort,
Which readè on still, as it came to her sight,
　Renderingè my devices I made in disport
　Of the Maiden of Kent callèd Comfórt,
Of lovers' testaments and of their wanton willès,
And how Jolas lovèd goodly Phillis;

Diodorus Siculus of my translatíon
　Out of fresh Latin into our English plain,[1]
Recounting commodities of many a strange natíon;
　Who readeth it once wouldè read it again;
　Six volumes engrosèd together it doth contain.
But when of the laurel she made rehearsal,
All orators and poets, with other great and small,

A thousand thousandè, I trow, to my dome,
　Triumpha, triumpha! they criéd all about!
Of trumpetès and clarions the noise went to Rome;
　The starry heaven, methought, shook with the shout;
　The ground groanèd and tremblèd, the noise was so
　　stout.
The Queen of Fame commanded shut fast the boke,
And therewith suddenly out of my dream I woke.

My mind of the greatè din was somedele amazéd,
　I wipéd mine eyen for to make them clear;
Then to the heaven spherical upward I gazéd,
　　Where I saw Janus, with his double chere,
　　Making his almanac for the new year;
He turnéd his tirikis, his volvèl ran fast:
Good luck this new year! the old year is past.

　　　Mens tibi sit consulta, petis? sic consule menti;
　　　Aemula sit Jani, retro speculetur et ante.[2]

[1] i.e. from the Latin of Poggio.
[2] Your mind must be consulted, you say?   Well, consult your
　　mind;
　　Let it emulate Janus, looking behind and before.

Skeltonis alloquitur librum suum.[1]

Ite, Britannorum lux O radiosa, Britannum
Carmina nostra pium vestrum celebrate Catullum!
Dicite, Skeltonis vester Adonis erat;
Dicite, Skeltonis vester Homerus erat,
Barbara cum Latio pariter jam currite versu;
Et licet est verbo pars maxima texta Britanno,
Non magis incompta nostra Thalia patet,
Est magis inculta nec mea Calliope.
Nec vos paeniteat rabiem tolerare caninam,
Nam Maro dissimiles non tulit ille minas,
Immunis nec enim Musa Nasonis erat.[2]

L'ENVOY

Go, little quair,
Demean you fair;
Take no despair,
Though I you wrate
After this rate
In English letter;
So much the better
Welcome shall ye
To some men be;
For Latin warkès
Be good for clerkès;
Yet now and then
Some Latin men
May haply look
Upon your book,
And so proceed

[1] Skelton addresses his own book.

[2] Go, radiant light of the Britons, make known our songs, your worthy British Catullus. Say Skelton was your Adonis; say Skelton was your Homer; though barbarous, you now run an equal race with Latin verse. And though the greater part is woven of British words, our Thalia is not too uncouth, nor my Calliope too unlearned. Nor should you be sorry to endure the attacks of mad dogs; for great Virgil bore the brunt of similar threats, and Ovid's muse was not exempt.

In you to read,
That so indeed
Your fame may spread
In length and bread.
But then I drede
Ye shall have need
You for to speed
To harness bright,
By force of might,
Against envý
And obloquý;
And wote ye why?
Not for to fight
Against despite,
Nor to derain
Battle again
Scornful disdain,
Nor for to chide,
Nor for to hide
You cowardly;
But courteously
That I have penn'd
For to defend,
Under the banner
Of all good manner,
Under protection
Of sad correction,
With toleration
And supportation
Of reformation,
If they can spy
Circumspectly
Any word defacéd
That might be raséd,
Else ye shall pray
Them that ye may
Continue still
With their good will.

*o

*Ad serenissimam Majestatem Regiam, pariter cum Domino
Cardinali, Legato a latere honorificatissimo, etc.*[1]

LAUTRE ENVOY

*Perge, liber, celebrem pronus regem venerare
Henricum octavum, resonans sua praemia laudis.
Cardineum dominum pariter venerando salutes,
Legatum a latere, et fiat memor ipse precare
Prebendae, quam promisit mihi credere quondam,
Meque suum referas pignus sperare salutis—
Inter spemque metum.*[2]

'Tween hope and dread
My life I lead,
But of my speed
    Small sikerness;
Howbeit I rede
Both word and deed
Should be agreed
    In nobleness.
Or else, etc.

EN PARLAMENT A PARIS

*Justice est morte,
Et Veryté sommeille;
Droit et Raison
Sont alez aux pardons:
Lez deux premiers
Nul ne les reveille;
Et lez derniers
Sont corrumpus par dons.*

[1] To the Most Serene Royal Majesty, likewise with the Lord
Cardinal, the most honourable legate *a latere*.

[2] Go, book, fall before the great King Henry VIII and worship
him, re-echoing his glories. Greet likewise, with reverence, the
great Cardinal, legate *a latere*, and may he be mindful to sue for
the prebend which he promised to entrust to me some day, and give
me ground to hope for his protection—between hope and fear.

OUT OF FRENCH INTO LATIN

Abstulit atra dies Astraeam; cana Fides sed
Somno pressa jacet; Jus iter arripuit,
Et secum Ratio proficiscens limite longo:
Nemo duas primas evigilare parat;
Atque duo postrema absunt, et munera tantum
Impediunt, nequeunt quod remeare domun.

OUT OF LATIN INTO ENGLISH

Justice now is dead;
Truth with a drowsy head,
As heavy as the lead,
Is lain down to sleep,
And taketh no keep:
And Right is over the fallows
Gone to seek hallows,
With Reason together,
No man can tell whither.
No man will undertake
The first twain to wake;
And the twain last
Be withhold so fast
With money, as men sayn,
They cannot come again.

A grant tort,
Foy dort.

How the Doughty

DUKE OF ALBANY [1]

Like a Coward Knight, ran away shamefully with an Hundred Thousand Tratling Scots and Faint-hearted Frenchmen, beside the Water of Tweed

REJOICE, England,
And understand
These tidings new,
Which be as true
As the gospél.
This duke so fell
Of Albany,
So cowardly,
With all his host
Of the Scottish coast,
For all their boast,
Fled like a beast;
Wherefore to jest
Is my delight
Of this coward knight,
And for to write
In the despite
Of the Scottès rank
Of Huntly-bank,[2]
Of Lothian
Of Loch Ryan,
And the ragged ray
Of Galloway.

[1] Regent of Scotland during James V's minority. This poem refers to his invasion of the borders in 1523.

[2] Skelton often uses Scottish names throughout the poem quite at random, as 'local colour.'

Dunbar, Dundee,
Ye shall trow me,
False Scots are ye:
Your hearts sore fainted,
And so attainted,
Like cowards stark,
At the castle of Wark,
By the water of Tweed,
Ye had evil speed;
Like cankered curs
Ye lost your spurs,
For in that fray
Ye ran away,
With, hey, dog, hey!

For Sir William Lyle
Within short while,
That valiant knight,
Put you to flight;
By his valiance
Two thousand of France
There he put back,
To your great lack,
And utter shame
Of your Scottish name.
Your chief chieftain,
Void of all brain,
Duke of all Albany,
Then shamefully
He recoiléd back,
To his great lack,
When he heard tell
That my Lord Admiral[1]
Was coming down
To make him frown
And to make him lour,

[1] i.e. Surrey

With the noble power
Of my lord cardinal,
As an hoste royál,
After the ancient manner,
With Saint Cuthbert's banner,
And Saint William's alsó;
Your capitain ran to go,
To go, to go, to go,
And brake up all his host;
For all his crake and boast,
Like a coward knight
He fled and durst not fight,
He ran away by night.

    But now must I
Your Duke ascry
Of Albany
With a word or twain
In sentence plain.
    Ye duke so doughty,
So stern, so stouty,
In short senténce
Of your pretence
What is the ground,
Briefly and round
To me expound,
Or else will I
Evidently
Shew as it is:
For the cause is this,
How ye pretend
For to defend
The young Scottish king,
But ye mean a thing,
An ye could bring
The matter about,
To put his eyes out
And put him down,

And set his crown
On your own head
When he were dead.
Such treachery
And traitory
Is all your cast;
Thus ye have compássed
With the Frenchè king
A false reckoníng
To invade England,
As I understand.
But our king royall,
Whose name over all,
Noble Henry the Eight,
Shall cast a bait,
And set such a snare
That shall cast you in care,
Both King Francis and thee,
That knowen ye shall be
For the most recrayd
Cowardès afraid,
And falsest forsworn,
That ever were born.

O ye wretched Scots,
Ye puant pisspots,
It shall be your lots
To be knit up with knots
Of halters and ropès
About your traitors' throatès!
O Scots perjuréd,
Unhappy uréd,
Ye may be assuréd
Your falsehood discuréd
It is and shall be
From the Scottish sea
Unto Gabione!
For ye be false each one,

False and false again,
Never true nor plain,
But fleer, flatter, and feign,
And ever to remain
In wretched beggary
And mangy misery,
In lousy loathsomeness
And scabbéd surfiness,
And in abomination
Of all manner of nation,—
Nation most in hate,
Proud and poor of state!
Twit, Scot, go keep thy den,
Mell not with Englishmen;
Thou did nothing but bark
At the castle of Wark.
Twit, Scot, yet again ones
We shall break thy bones,
And hang you upon poles,
And burn you all to coals;
With, twit Scot, twit Scot, twit!
Walk, Scot, go beg a bit
Of bread at each man's heck!
The fiend, Scot, break thy neck!
Twit, Scot, again I say,
Twit, Scot of Galloway,
Twit, Scot, shake thee dog, hey!
Twit, Scot, thou ran away!

We set not a fly
By your Duke of Albany;
We set not a prane
By such a drunken drane;
We set not a mite
By such a coward knight,
Such a proud palliard,
Such a skirgalliard,
Such a stark coward,

Such a proud poltroon,
Such a foul coistrown,
Such a doughty dagswain!
Send him to France again,
To bring with him more brain
From King Francis of France:
God send them both mischance!

Ye Scots all the rabble,
Ye shall never be able
With us for to compare;
What though ye stamp and stare?
God send you sorrow and care!
With us whenever ye mell,
Yet we bear away the bell,
When ye cankered knaves
Must creep into your caves
Your headès for to hide,
For ye darè not abide.

Sir Duke of Albany,
Right inconveniently,
Ye rage and ye rave,
And your worship deprave.
Not like Duke[1] Hamilcar,
With the Romans that made war,
Nor like his son Hanibal,
Nor like Duke Hastrubal
Of Carthage in Africa;
Yet somewhat ye be likè
In some of their conditions,
And their false seditions,
And their dealing double,
And their wayward trouble:
But yet they were bold,
And manly manifold,

[1] Duce, leader.

Their enemies to assail
In plain field and battail;
But ye and your host,
Full of brag and boast,
And full of waste wind,
How ye will bears bind,
And the devil down ding,
Yet ye dare do no thing
But leap away like frogs,
And hide you under logs,
Like pigs and like hogs,
And like mangy dogs!
What an army were ye?
Or what activity
Is in you, beggars, brawls,
Full of scabs and scawls,
Of vermin and of lice,
And of all manner vice?

Sir Duke, nay, Sir Duck,
Sir Drake of the Lake, Sir Duck
Of the Dunghill, for small luck
Ye have in feats of war;
Ye make nought but ye mar;
Ye are a false intruser,
And a false abuser,
And an untrue knight;
Thou hast too little might
Against England to fight.
Thou art a graceless wight
To put thyself to flight:
A vengeance and despite
On thee must needs alight,
That durst not bide the sight
Of my Lord Admiral,
Of chivalry the well,
Of knighthood the flower
In every martial shower,

The noble Earl of Surrey,
That put thee in suchè fray;
Thou durst no field derain,
Nor no battle maintain
Against our strong captain,
But thou ran home again
For fear thou should be slain,
Like a Scottish ketering
That durst abide no reckoning;
Thy heart would not serve thee:
The fiend of hell might sterve thee!

No man hath heard
Of such a coward,
And such a mad image
Carried in a cage,
As it were a cottage!
Or of such a mawment
Carriéd in a tent.
In a tent! nay, nay,
But in a mountain gay,
Like a great hill
For a windmill,
Therein to couchè still,
That no man him kill;
As it were a goat
In a sheep-cote,
About him a park
Of a maddè wark,
Men call it a toil.
Therein, like a royl,
Sir Duncan, ye dared,
And thus ye prepared
Your carcass to keep
Like a silly sheep,
A sheep of Cotswold,
From rain and from cold,
And from raining of raps,

And such after claps.
Thus in your cowardly castle
Ye decked you to dwell!
Such a captain of horse,
It made no great force
If that ye had ta'en
Your last deadly bane
With a gun-stone,
To make you to groan.
But hide thee, Sir Topas,
Now into the castle of Bass,
And lurk there, like an ass,
With some Scottish lass
With dugs, dugs, dugs!
I shrew thy Scottish lugs,
Thy munypins, and thy crag,
For thou cannot but brag
Like a Scottish hag.
Adieu now, Sir Wrig-wrag,
Adieu, Sir Dalyrag!
Thy melling is but mocking;
Thou mayst give up thy cocking,
Give it up, and cry creke,
Like an hoddipeke!

Whereto should I morė speak
Of such a farly freke,
Of such an hornė keke,
Of such a bold captain
That dare not turn again,
Nor durst not crack a word,
Nor durst not draw his sword
Against the Lion White,[1]
But ran away quite?
He ran away by night,
In the owlė flight,
Like a coward knight

[1] Surrey's badge.

Adew, coward, adew,
False knight, and most untrue!
I render thee, false rebel,
To the flingande fiend of hell.

   Hark yet, Sir Duke, a word,
In earnest or in bawd.
What, have ye, villain, forged,
And virulently disgorged,
As though ye would parbrake,
Your avaunts to make,
With wordès enbosèd,
Ungraciously engrosèd,
How ye will undertake
Our royal king to make
His ownè realm to forsake?
Such lewdè language ye spake,
Sir Duncan, in the devil way,
Be well ware what ye say.
Ye say that he and ye,—
Which he and ye? let see:
Ye mean Francis, French king,
Should bring about this thing.
I say, thou lewd lurdain,
That neither of you twain
So hardy nor so bold
His countenance to behold!
If our most royal Harry
List with you to varry
Full soon ye should miscarry,
For ye durst not tarry
With him to strive a stound;
If he on you but frowned,
Not for a thousand pound,
Ye durst bide on the ground,
Ye wouldè run away round,
And cowardly turn your backès,
For all your comely crackès,

And, for fear par case
To look him in the face
Ye would defile the place,
And run your way apace.
Though I trim you this trace
With English somewhat base,
Yet, *save voster grace*,
Thereby I shall purcháce
No displeasant reward,
If ye well can regard
Your cankered cowardness
And your shameful doubleness.

Are ye not frantic mad,
And wretchedly bestad,
To rail against his Grace
That shall bring you full base,
And set you in suché case
That betweené you twain
There shall be drawn a train
That shall be to your pain?
To fly ye shall be fain,
And never turn again.

What, would Francis, our friar,
Be such a falsé liar,
So mad a cordilar,
So mad a murmurer?
Ye muse somewhat too far,
All out of joint ye jar.
God let you never thrive!
Ween ye, dawcocks, to drive
Our king out of his ream?
Ge heme, rank Scot, ge heme,
With fond Francis, French king:
Our master shall you bring,
I trust, to low estate,
And mate you with checkmate!

Your brainès are idle;
It is time for you to bridle,
And pipe in a quibible;
For it is impossible
For you to bring about
Our king for to drive out
Of this his realm royal
And land imperial;
So noble a prince as he
In all activity
Of hardy martial actès,
Fortunate in all his factès.

And now I will me 'dress
His valiance to express,
Though insufficient am I
His Grace to magnify
And laud equivalently.
Howbeit, loyally,
After mine allegíance,
My pen I will advance
To extol his noble Grace,
Inspite of thy coward's face,
Inspite of King Francis,
Devoid of all noblesse,
Devoid of good coráge,
Devoid of wisdom sage,
Mad, frantic, and saváge;
Thus he doth disparáge
His blood with fond dotáge.
A prince to play the page
It is reckeless rage,
And a lunatic over-rage.
What though my style be rude?
With truth it is enewed.
Truth ought to be rescued,
Truth should not be subdued.

But now will I expound
What nobleness doth abound,
And what honour is found,
And what virtues be resident
In our royal regent,
Our peerless president,
Our king most excellent.

In martial prowess
Like unto Hercules;
In prudence and wisdom
Like unto Solomon;
In his goodly person
Like unto Absolon;
In loyalty and foy
Like to Hector of Troy;
And his glory to increase,
Like to Scipiades;
In royal majesty
Like unto Ptolemy,
Like to Duke Josuè,
And the valiant Machubè;
That if I would report
All the royal sort
Of his nobility,
His magnanimity,
His animosity,
His frugality,
His liberality,
His affability,
His humanity,
His stability,
His humility,
His benignity,
His royal dignity,
My learning is too small
For to recount them all.

What losels then are ye,
Like cowards as ye be,
To rail on his estate,
With wordès inordinate!

He rules his commonalty
With all benignity;
His noble baronage,
He putteth them in corage
To exploitè deeds of arms,
To the damage and harms
Of such as be his foes.
Wherever he rides or goes
His subjects he doth support,
Maintain them with comfort
Of his most princely port,
As all men can report.

Then ye be a knappish sort,
Et faitez à luy grand tort,
With your enbosèd jaws
To rail on him like daws.
The fiend scratch out your maws!

All his subjects and he
Most lovingly agree
With whole heart and true mind,
They find his Grace so kind;
Wherewith he doth them bind
At all hours to be ready
With him to live and die,
And to spendè their heart-blood,
Their bodies and their good,
With him in all distress,
Alway in readiness
To assist his noble Grace;
Inspite of thy coward's face,
Most false attainted traitor,
And falsè forsworn faitor.

Avaunt, coward recrayed!
Thy pride shall be allayed;

With Sir Francis of France
We shall pipe you a dance,
Shall turn you to mischance!
   I rede you, look about;
For ye shall be driven out
Of your landė in short space.
We will so follow in the chase
That ye shall have no grace
For to turn your face;
And thus, Saint George to borrow,
Ye shall have shame and sorrow.

LENVOY

Go, little quaire, quickly;
   Shew them that shall you read
How that ye are likely
   Over all the world to spread.
The false Scots for dread,
   With the Duke of Albany,
Beside the water of Tweed
   They fled full cowardly.
Though your English be rude,
   Barren of eloquence,
Yet, briefly to conclude,
   Grounded is your sentence
On truth, under defence
   Of all true Englishmen,
This matter to credence
   That I write with my pen.

SKELTON LAUREATE, *Obsequious et Loyal.*

A REPLICATION

Honorificatissimo, amplissimo, longeque reverendissimo in Christo patri, ac Domino, domino Thomae, etc., tituli sanctae Ceciliae, sacrosanctae Romanae ecclesiae presbytero, Cardinali meritissimo, et apostolicae sedis legato, a latereque legato superillustri, etc., Skeltonis laureatus, or. reg., humillimum dicit obsequium cum omni debita reverentia, tanto tamque magnifico digna principe sacerdotum, totiusque justitiae aequabilissimo moderatore, necnon praesentis opusculi fautore excellentissimo, etc., ad cujus auspicatissimam contemplationem, sub memorabili prelo gloriosae immortalitatis, praesens pagella felicitatur, etc.[1]

A REPLICATION AGAINST CERTAIN YOUNG SCHOLARS ABJURED OF LATE[2]

ARGUMENTUM

Crassantes nimium, nimium sterilesque labruscas,
Vinea quas Domini Sabaot non sustinet ultra
Laxius expandi, nostra est resecare voluntas.

[1] To the most honourable, most mighty, and by far the most reverend father in Christ and in the Lord, Lord Thomas, etc., of the title of the sacred Cecilian, presbyter of the Holy Roman Church, the most deserving cardinal, Legate of the Apostolic See, and the most illustrious legate *a latere*, etc., Skelton Laureate, *ora. reg.*, declares humble allegiance with all fit reverence due to such a great and magnificent Chief of Priests, most equitable moderator of all justice, and moreover the most excellent patron of the present little book, etc., at whose most auspicious contemplation, under the memorable seal of a glorious immortality, the present little treatise is commended [*or* devised—*see* Lenvoy].

[2] Thomas Bilney and Thomas Arthur, the two young Cambridge scholars who recanted their Lutheran Protestantism and carried their faggot of repentance at St. Paul's Cross on 29th September 1527.

Cum privilegio a rege indulto.

Protestation alway canonically prepensed, professed, and with good deliberation made, that this little pamphlet, called The Replication of Skelton Laureate, *ora. reg.*, remording divers recrayed and much unreasonable errors of certain sophisticate scholars and reckless young heretics lately abjured, etc., shall evermore be, with all obsequious readiness, humbly submitted unto the right discreet reformation of the reverend prelates and much noble doctors of our Mother Holy Church, etc.

Ad almam Universitatem Cantabrigensem.

EULOGIUM CONSOLATIONIS

Alma parens, O Cantabrigensis,
Cur lacrymaris?   Esto, tui sint
Degeneres hi filioli, sed
Non ob inertes, O pia mater,
Insciolos vel decolor esto.
Progenies non nobilis omnis,
Quam tua forsan mamma fovebat.
Tu tamen esto Palladis almae
Gloria pollens plena Minervae,
Dum radiabunt astra polorum:
Jamque valeto, meque foveto,
Namque tibi quondam carus alumnus eram.

How young scholars nowadays enbolned with the flyblown blast of the much vainglorious pippling wind, when they have delectably licked a little of the licorous electuary of lusty learning, in the much studious school-house of scrupulous Philology, counting themselves clerks excellently informed and transcendingly sped in much high conning, and when they have once superciliously caught

A little rag of rhetoric,
A less lump of logic,
A piece or a patch of philosophy,
Then forthwith by and by

They tumble so in theology,
Drownéd in dregs of divinity,
That they judge themself able to be
Doctors of the chair in the Vintry
At the Three Cranès,
To magnify their namès:
But madly it framès,
For all that they preach and teach
Is further than their wit will reach.
Thus by demerits of their abusíon,
Finally they fall to careful confusíon
To bear a faggot, or to be enflaméd:
Thus are they undone and utterly shaméd.

Ergo:

Licet non enclitice,
Tamen enthymematice,
Notandum imprimis,
Ut ne quid nimis.
Tantum pro primo.[1]

Over this, for a more ample process to be further related and continued, and of every true Christenman laudably to be employed, justified, and constantly maintained; as touching the sour theologisation of these demi-divines, and stoical students, and friskajolly younkerkins, much better baynéd than brainéd, basked and bathed in their wild burbling and boiling blood, fervently reboiled with the infatuate flames of their reckless youth and witless wantonness, embraced and interlaced with a much fantastical frenzy of their insensate sensuality, surmised unsurely in their perihermenial principles,[2] to prate and to preach proudly and lewdly, and loudly to lie; and yet they were but feebly informed in Master Porphiry's problems, and have waded but weakly in his three manner of clerkly works, analytical, topical, and logical. Howbeit they were puffed so full of vainglorious pomp and

[1] Therefore: . . . It must be noted in the first place that nothing may be in excess. So much for the first, *or* in the first place.
[2] Principles of interpretation.

arrogant elation, that popeholy and peevish presumption
provoked them to publish and to preach to people imprudent
perilously, how it was idolatry to offer to images of our
Blessed Lady, or to pray and go on pilgrimages, or to make
oblations to any images of saints in churches or elsewhere.

Against which erroneous errors, odious, orgulous, and
fly-blown opinions, etc.,

> To the honour of our Blessed Lady,
> And her most Blessed Baby,
> I purpose for to reply
> Against this horrible heresy
> Of these young heretics, that stink unbrent,
> Whom I now summon and convent,
> That lewdly have their timė spent
> In their study abominable,
> Our glorious Lady to disable,
> And heinously on her to babble
> With language detestable!
> With your lippės polluted
> Against Her Grace disputed,
> Which is the most clear crystál
> Of all pure cleanness virginal,
> That our Saviour bare,
> Which us redeemėd from care.

> I say, thou mad March hare,
> I wonder how ye dare
> Open your jangling jaws
> To preach in any clause,
> Like prating popping daws,
> Against her excellence,
> Against her reverence,
> Against her pre-eminence,
> Against her magnificence,
> That never did offence.

> Ye heretics recrayed,
> Wot ye what ye said

Of Mary, mother and maid?
With bawdry at her ye brayed;
With bawdy words unmeet
Your tongues were too fleet;
Your sermon was not sweet;
Ye were nothing discreet;
Ye were in a drunken heat.
Like heretics confettered,
Ye count yourselves well-lettered.
Your learning is stark nought,
For shamefully ye have wrought,
And to shame yourself have brought.

Because ye her misnaméd,
And would have her defaméd,
Your madness she attaméd;
For ye were worldly shaméd
At Paul's Cross openly,
All men can testify.
There, like a sort of sots,
Ye were fain to bear faggóts;
At the feast of her Conception
Ye suffered such correction.

Sive per aequivocum,[1]
Sive per univocum,[2]
Sive sic, sive not so,[3]
Ye are brought to, Lo, lo, lo!
See where the heretics go,
Witless, wandering to and fro!
With Te-he, ta-ha, bo-ho, bo-ho!
And such wanderings many mo.
Helas, ye wretches, ye may be woe!

Ye may sing well-a-way,
And curse both night and day
When ye were bred and born,

[1] Either through the equivocal.
[2] Or through the unequivocal.
[3] Or so or not so.

And when ye were priestès shorn,
Thus to be laughed to scorn,
Thus tattered and thus torn,
Thorough your own folly
Ye be blowen with the fly
Of horrible heresy.
Fain ye were to reny,
And mercy for to cry,
Or be brent by and by,
Confessing how ye did lie
In preaching shamefully.

Yourself thus ye discuréd
As clerkès unassuréd,
With ignorance obscuréd.
Ye are unhappily uréd.
In your dialectical,
And principles syllogistical,
If ye to remembrance call
How *syllogisari*
Non est ex particulari,
Neque negativis,
Recte concludere si vis,
Et caetera, id genus.[1]
Ye could not *corde tenus,*[2]
Nor answer *verbo tenus,*[3]
When prelacy you opposéd;
Your heartès then were hoséd,[4]
Your relations reposéd;
And yet ye supposéd
Respondere ad quantum.[5]
But ye were *confuse tantum,*[6]
Surrendering your suppositions,
For there ye missed your cushions.

[1] How to syllogize, it is not from the particular, nor from nega-
tives, if you want to conclude rightly, etc., in a case like this.
[2] In your heart.   [3] In your name.   [4] In your hose.
[5] To give your opinion.   [6] So much confounded.

Would God, for your own ease,
That wise Harpocrates [1]
Had your mouthès stoppéd,
And your tonguès croppéd,
When ye logic choppéd,
And in the pulpit hoppéd,
And foolishly there foppéd,
And porishly forth poppéd
Your schismaticate saws
Against Goddès laws,
And shewéd yourselves daws! [2]
Ye argued argumentes,
As it were upon the elenches,
De rebus apparentibus [3]
Et non existentibus; [4]
And ye would appear wise,
But ye were foolish nice!
Yet by meanès of that vice
Ye did provoke and 'tice,
Oftener than once or twice,
Many a good man
And many a good woman,
By way of their devotion
To help you to promotion,
Whose charity well regarded
Cannot be unrewarded.

I say it for no sedition,
But under patient tuition—
It is half a superstition
To give you exhibition [5]
To maintainè with your schools,
And to prove yourself such fools!

Some of you had ten pound,
Therewith for to be found

---

[1] Egyptian god of Silence.   [2] Simpletons.
[3] Concerning apparent things.   [4] And non-existent.
[5] A scholarship.

P

At the university,
Employed which might have be
Much better other ways.
But, as the man says,
The blind eateth many a fly.
What may be meant hereby
Ye may soonè make construction
With right little instruction;
For it is an ancient bruit,
Such apple-tree, such fruit.
What should I prosecute,
Or more of this to clatter?
Return we to our matter.

Ye soaréd over-high
In the hierarchy
Of Jovenian's heresy,
Your namès to magnify,
Among the scabbéd skies
Of Wyclif's fleshè-flies;
Ye stringéd so Luther's lute
That ye dance all in a suit
The heretics' ragged ray,
That brings you out of the way
Of Holy Church's lay,[1]
Ye shall *inter enigmata* [2]
And *inter paradigmata*,[3]
Markéd in your cradles
To bearè faggots for baubles.

And yet some men say
How ye are this day,
And be now as ill,
And so ye will be still,
As ye were before.
What should I reckon more?

[1] Law.   [2] Stumble among riddles.
                [3] Among paradigms.

A REPLICATION

Men have you in suspicion
How ye have small contrition
Of that ye have miswrought.
For, if it were well sought,
One of you there was
That laughed when he did pass
With his faggot in procession;
He counted it for no correction,
But with scornful affection
Took it for a sport,
His heresy to support;
Whereat a thousand gazéd
As people half-amazéd,
And thought in him small grace
His folly so to face.

Some judgéd in this case
Your penance took no place,
Your penance was too light;
And thought, if ye had right,
Ye should take further pain
To resort again
To places where ye have preachéd,
And your lollardy learning teachéd,
And there to make relation
In open predication,
And 'knowledge your offence
Before open audience,
How falsely ye had surmiséd,
And devilishly deviséd
The people to seduce,
And chase them through the mews
Of your naughty counsél,
To hunt them into hell
With blowing out your hornés,
Full of mockish scornés,
With chating and rechating,
And your busy prating.

Of the gospel and the 'pistles
Ye pick out many thistles,
And brimly with your bristles
Ye cobble and ye clout
Holy Scripture so about
That people are in doubt
And fear lest they be out
Of all good Christian order.
Thus all thing ye disorder
Throughout every border.

It had ben much better
Ye had never learned a letter,
For your ignorance is greater
(I make you fast and sure)
Than all your literature.
Ye are but lither *logici*,[1]
But much worse *isagogici*,
For ye have inducéd a sect
With heresy all infect.
Wherefore ye are well checked,
And by Holy Church correct,
And in manner as abjéct,
For evermore suspect,
And banishéd in effect
From all honest company,
Because ye have eaten a fly,
To your great villany,
That never more may die.

Come forth, ye popeholy,
Full of melancholy!
Your mad hypocrisy,
And your idiocy,
And your vainglory,
Have made you eat the fly,
Puffed full of heresy,

[1] Bad logicians.

To preach it idolatry
Whoso doth magnify
That glorious maid Marý;
That glorious maid and mother,
So was there never another
But that princéss alone,
To whom we are bound, each one,
The image of her grace
To reverence in every place.

I say, ye brainless beastés,
Why jangle you such jestés,
In your divinity
Of Luther's affinity,
To the people of lay fee,
Railing in your rages
To worship none imáges,
Nor do pilgrimages?
I say, ye devilish pages,
Full of such dotáges,
Count ye yourself good clerkés,
And snapper in such workés?

Saint Gregory and Saint Ambrose,
Ye have read them, I suppose,
Saint Jerome and Saint Austen,
With other many holy men,
Saint Thomas de Aquino,
With other doctors many mo,
Which *de latria* [1] do treat;
They say how *latria* is an honour great
Belonging to the Deity:
To this ye needs must agree.

But, I trow, yourself ye oversee
What 'longeth to Christ's humanity.

[1] Of worship.

If ye have read *de hyperdulia,*
Then ye know what betokeneth *dulia.*[1]
Then shall ye find it firm and stable,
And to our faith much agreeable
To worship images of saints.
Wherefore make ye no more restraints,
But mend your minds that are mazéd;
Or else doubtless ye shall be blazéd,
And be burnt at a stake,[2]
If further business that ye make.
Therefore I 'vise you to forsake
Of heresy the devilish schools,
And cry Godmercy, like frantic fools.

Tantum pro secundo.[3]

PERORATIO AD NUPER ABJURATOS QUOSDAM
HYPOTHETICOS HERETICOS, ETC.[4]

Audite, viri Ismaelitae, non dico Israelitae;
Audite, inquam, viri Madianitae, Ascalonitae;
Ammonitae, Gabaonitae, audite verba que loquar.[5]

Opus evangelii est cibus perfectorum;
Sed quia non estis de genere bonorum,
Qui caterisatis categorias cacodaemoniorum,

[1] i.e. If you have read of the very great adoration accorded to the Virgin—*hyperdulia*—then you know what worship is due to the saints—*dulia.*

[2] Bilney, one of these 'young scholars,' was burnt in 1531, two years after Skelton's death.

[3] So much for the second, *or* in the second place.

[4] The peroration against certain recently abjured hypothetical heretics.

[5] Hear, men of Ishmael, I do not say Israel; hear, say I, men of Madian, of Askalon, of Ammon, of Gabaon, hear the words I shall speak.

A REPLICATION 425

Ergo

Et reliqua vestra problemata, schemata,
Dilemmata, sinto anathemata!
Ineluctabile argumentum est.[1]

A confutation responsive, or an inevitably prepensed
answer to all wayward or froward altercations that can or
may be made or objected against Skelton Laureate, deviser
of this Replication, etc.

> Why fall ye at debate
> With Skelton Laureate,
> Reputing him unable
> To gainsay replicable
> Opinions detestable
> Of heresy execrable?
>
> Ye say that poetry
> May not fly so high
> In theology,
> Nor analogy,
> Nor philology,
> Nor philosophy,
> To answer or reply
> Against such heresy?
>
> Wherefore by and by,
> Now consequently,
> I call to this reckoning
> David, that royal king,
> Whom Hieronymus,
> That doctor glorious,
> Doth both write and call
> Poet of poetès all,
> And prophet principal.

[1] The Book of the Gospel is the food of the elect; but, because
you are not of the race of the good, you who 'caterize' [make
improper use of] the categories of the inspired, therefore also the
rest of your problems, schemata, dilemmas, may they be anathema!
It is an inescapable argument.

This may not be remorded,
For it is well recorded
In his epistle *ad Paulinum,*
Presbyterium divinum,[1]
Where word for word ye may
Read what Jerome there doth say.

David, inquit, Simonides noster, Pindarus, et Alcaeus, Flaccus
quoque, Catullus, atque Serenus, Christum lyra personat, et
in decachordo psalterio ab inferis excitat resurgentem. Haec
Hier.

THE ENGLISH

King David the prophet, of prophetės principal,
   Of poetės chief poet, Saint Jerome doth write,
Resembléd to Simonides, that poet lyrical
    Among the Greeks most relucent of light,
     In that faculty which shinéd as Phoebus bright:
Like to Pindarus in glorious poetry,
Like unto Alcaeus, he doth him magnify.

Flaccus nor Catullus with him may not compare
   Nor solemn Serenus, for all his harmony
In metrical muses, his harping we may spare;
    For David, our poet, harpéd so melodiously
     Of our Saviour Christ in his decachord psaltry,
That at his resurrection he harpéd out of hell
Old patriarchs and prophets in heaven with him to dwell.

    Return we to our former process.

        Then, if this noble king
        Thus can harp and sing
        With his harp of prophecy
        And spiritual poetry,
        As Saint Jerome saith,
        To whom we must give faith,
        Warbling with his strings
        Of such theological things,
        Why have ye then disdain

[1] Which is prefixed to the Vulgate. (*See* Hieronym *Opera*, i.
1011, ed. 1609.)

At poetės, and complain
How poets do but feign?

   Ye do much great outrage
For to disparage
And to discourage
The fame matriculate
Of poetės laureate.

   For if ye sadly look,
And wisely read the Book
Of Good Advertisement,[1]
With me ye must consent
And infallibly agree
Of necessity,
How there is a spiritual,
And a mysterial,
And a mystical
Effect energial,
As Greekės do it call,
Of such an industry,
And such a pregnancy,
Of heavenly inspiration
In laureate creation,
Of poets commendation,
That of divine miseration
God maketh his habitation
In poetės which excels,
And sojourns with them and dwells.

   By whose inflammation
Of spiritual instigation
And divine inspiration
We are kindled in such fashion
With heat of the Holy Ghost
(Which is God of mightės most),
That he our pen doth lead,
And maketh in us such speed
That forthwith we must need

[1] One of Skelton's lost poems.

*p

With pen and ink proceed,
Sometime for affection,
Sometime for sad direction,
Sometime for correction,
Sometime under protection
Of patient sufferance,
With sober circumstance,
Our mindès to advance
To no man's annoyance;
Therefore no grievance,
I pray you, for to take
In this that I do make
Against these frenetics,
Against these lunatics,
Against these schismatics,
Against these heretics,
Now of late abjuréd,
Most unhappily uréd:
For be ye well-assuréd
That frenzy, nor jealously,
Nor heresy will never die.

Dixi
iniquis, Nolite inique agere; et delinquentibus, Nolite exaltare
cornu.[1]

Tantum pro tertio.[2]

De raritate poetarum, deque gymnosophistarum, philosophorum,
theologorum, caeterorumque, eruditorum infinita numerositate,
Skel. L. epitoma.[3]

Sunt infiniti, sunt innumerique sophistae,
Sunt infiniti, sunt innumerique logistae,

[1] I said to the wicked, be not stubborn; and to evil-doers, Lift
not up the horn.

[2] So much for the third, *or* in the third place.

[3] About the rarity of poets, and the infinite abundance of gymno-
sophists, philosophers, theologians, and the rest of the learned, this
is Skelton Laureate's epitome.

Innumeri sunt philosophi, sunt theologique,
Sunt infiniti doctores, suntque magistri
Innumeri; sed sunt pauci rarique poetae.
Hinc omne est rarum carum: reor ergo poetas
Ante alios omnes divino flamine flatos.
Sic Plato divinat, divinat sicque Socrates;
Sic magnus Macedo, sic Caesar, maximus heros
Romanus, celebres semper coluere poetas.[1]

Thus endeth the Replication
of Skelton Laureate.

To My Lord Cardinal's Right Noble Grace, etc.

LENVOY

Go, little quaire, apace,
  In most humble wise,
Before his noble grace,
  That caused you to devise
  This little enterprise;
And him most lowly pray,
  In his mind to comprise
Those words his grace did say
Of an amice gray.
Je foy enterment en sa bone grace.[2]

---

[1] Infinite, innumerable are the sophists, infinite, innumerable are the logicians, innumerable are the philosophers and the theologians, infinite in number are doctors, and masters; but poets are few and rare. Hence all that is precious is rare. I think, then, that poets before all others are filled with the divine afflatus. So Plato thinks and so Socrates; so the great Macedonian, so Caesar, the greatest of Roman heroes, always honoured the renowned poets.

[2] I trust entirely in his good grace.

APPENDIX

Ad dominum properato meum, mea pagina, Percy,
Qui Northumbrorum jura paterna gerit;
Ad nutum celebris tu prona repone leonis
Quaeque suo patri tristia justa cano.
Ast ubi perlegit, dubiam sub mente volutet
Fortunam, cuncta quae malefida rotat.
Qui leo sit felix, et Nestoris occupet annos;
Ad libitum cujus ipse paratus ero.

TETRASTICHON [2] SKELTON. LAUREATI AD MAGISTRUM RUKSHAW,
SACRAE THEOLOGIAE EGREGIUM PROFESSOREM

Accipe nunc demum, doctor celeberrime Rukshaw,
Carmina, de calamo quae cecidere meo;
Et quanquam placidis non sunt modulata camenis,
Sunt tamen ex nostro pectore prompta pio.

Vale feliciter, virorum laudatissime.

CONTRA ALIUM CANTITANTEM ET ORGANISANTEM ASINUM, QUI
IMPUGNABAT SKELTONIDA PIERIUM, SARCASMOS

Praeponenda meis non sunt tua plectra camenis,
Nec quanium nostra fistula clara tua est:
Saepe licet lyricos modularis arundine psalmos,
Et tremulos calamis concinis ipse modos;
Quamvis mille tuus digitus dat carmine plausus,
Nam tua quam tua vox est mage docta manus;
Quamvis cuncta facis tumida sub mente superbus,
Gratior est Phoebo fistula nostra tamen.
Ergo tuum studeas animo deponere fastum,
Et violare sacrum desine, stulte, virum.

Qd Skelton, laureat.

---

[1] These lines appear before the Northumberland elegy in Marshe's
edition of Skelton's *Works*.

[2] These lines follow the Northumberland elegy in Marshe's edition.

431

I, LIBER, ETC.

I, liber, et propera, regem tu pronus adora;
Me sibi commendes humilem Skeltonida vatem:
Ante suam majestatem, (per caetera passim,)
Inclyta bella refer, gessit quae maximus heros
Anglorum, primus nostra de gente Ricardus,
Hector ut intrepidus, contra validissima castra
Gentis Agarenae; memora quos ille labores,
Quos tulit angores, qualesque recepit honores.
Sed
Chronica Francorum, validis inimica Britannis,
Saepe solent celebres Britonum compescere laudes.

SKELTONIS APOSTROPHAT [1] AD DIVUM JOHANNEM DECOLLATUM, IN
CUJUS PROFESTO FIEBAT HOC AUCUPIUM

O memoranda dies, qua, decollate Johannes,
Aucupium facit, haud quondam quod fecerit, intra
Ecclesiam de Dis, violans tua sacra sacrorum!
Rector de Whipstok, doctor cognomine Daucock,
Et dominus Wodcock; probat is, probat hic, probat haec hoc.

IDEM [2] DE LIBERA DICACITATE POETICA IN EXTOLLENDA PROBITATE,
ET IN PERFRICANDA IGNOBILITATE

Libertas veneranda piis concessa poetis
Dicendi est quaecunque placent, quaecunque juvabunt,
Vel quaecunque valent justas defendere causas,
Vel quaecunque valent stolidos mordere petulcos
Ergo dabis veniam.

Quod Skelton, laureat.

LAMENTATIO URBIS NORVICENSIS [3]

O lacrymosa lues nimis, O quam flebile fatum!
Ignibus exosis, urbs veneranda, ruis;
Fulmina sive Jovis sive ultima fata vocabant,
Vulcani rapidis ignibus ipsa peris.

---

[1] These lines follow *Ware the Hawk* in Marshe's edition.

[2] These lines follow *Ware the Hawk* in all editions.

[3] In April 1507 the city of Norwich was 'almost utterly defaced'
by two dreadful fires (Blomefield's *History of Norfolk*).

Ah decus, ah patriae specie pulcherrima dudum!
Urbs Norvicensis labitur in cineres.
Urbs, tibi quid referam? breviter tibi pauca reponam:
Prospera rara manent, utere sorte tua;
Perpetuum mortale nihil, sors omnia versat:
Urbs miseranda, vale! sors miseranda tua est.

Skelton.

IN BEDEL, QUONDAM BELIAL INCARNATUM, DEVOTUM EPITAPHIUM

Ismal, ecce, Bedel, non mel, sed fel, sibi des el!
Perfidus Achitophel, luridus atque lorell;
Nunc olet iste Jebal, Nabal. S. Nabal, ecce, ribaldus!
Omnibus exosus atque perosus erat;
In plateaque cadens animam spiravit oleto:
Presbyteros odiens sic sine mente ruit.
Discite vos omnes quid sit violare sacratos
Presbyteros, quia sic corruit iste canis.
Cocytus cui si detur per Tartara totus,
Sit, peto, promotus Cerberus huncque voret.
At mage sancta tamen mea Musa precabitur atros
Hos lemuresque eat sic Bedel ad superos;
Non eat, immo ruat, non scandat, sed mage tendat,
Inque caput praeceps mox Acheronta petat.

Bedel. Quanta malignatus est inimicus in sancto!

Ps. 74.

Mortuus est asinus,
Qui pinxit mulum:
Hic jacet barbarus;
The devil kiss his *culum!*   *Amen.*

Hanc volo transcribas, transcriptam moxque remittas
Pagellam; quia sunt qui mea scripta sciunt.
Redde { *Igitur quia sunt qui mala cuncta fremunt,*
{ *Igitur quia sunt qui bona cuncta premunt.*
Nec tamen expaveo de fatuo labio,
Nec multum paveo de stolido rabulo.

SALVE, ETC.

Salve plus decies quam sunt momenta dierum!
Quot generum species, quot res, quot nomina rerum,
Quot prati flores, quot sunt et in orbe colores,
Quot pisces, quot aves, quot sunt et in aequore naves,
Quot volucrum pennae, quot sunt tormenta gehennae,
Quot coeli stellae, quot sunt et in orbe puellae,
Quot sancti Romae, quot sunt miracula Thomae,
Quot sunt virtutes, tantas tibi mitto salutes.

ORATOR REGIUS SKELTONIS LAUREATUS IN SINGULARE MERITISSI-
MUMQUE PRAECONIUM NOBILISSIMI PRINCIPIS HENRICI SEPTIMI,
NUPER STRENUISSIMI REGIS ANGLIAE, HOC EPITAPHIUM EDIDIT,
AD SINCERAM CONTEMPLATIONEM REVERENDI IN CHRISTO PATRIS
AC DOMINI, DOMINI JOHANNIS ISLIPPAE ABBATIS WESTMONAS-
TERIENSIS OPTIME MERITI, ANNO DOMINI MDXII. PRIDIE DIVI
ANDREAE APOSTOLI, ETC.

Tristia Melpomenes cogor modo plectra sonare;
    Hos elegos foveat Cynthius ille meos.
Si quas fata movent lacrymas, lacrymare videtur
    Jam bene maturum, si bene mente sapis.
Flos Britonum, regum speculum, Salomonis imago,
    Septimus Henricus mole sub hac tegitur.
Punica, dum regnat, redolens rosa digna vocari,
    Jam jam marcescit, ceu levis umbra fugit.
Multa novercantis fortunae, multa faventis
    Passus, et infractus tempus utrumque tulit.
Nobilis Anchises, armis metuendus Atrides,
    Hic erat; hunc Scottus rex timuit Jacobus.
Spiramenta animae vegetans dum vescitur aura,
    Francorum populus conticuit pavidus.
Immensas sibi divitias cumulasse quid horres?
    Ni cumulasset opes, forte, Britanne, luas.
Urgentes casus tacita si mente volutes,
    Vix tibi sufficeret aurea ripa Tagi.
Ni sua [1] *te probitas consulta mente laborans*
    Rexisset satius, vix tibi tuta salus.
Sed quid plura cano? meditans quid plura voluto?
    Quisque vigil sibi sit: mors sine lege rapit.
Ad Dominum, qui cuncta regit, pro principe tanto
    Funde preces quisquis carmina nostra legis.

---

[1] Used for *ejus*.

Vel mage, si placeat, hunc timuit Jacobus,
  Scottorum dominus, qui sua fata luit;
Quem Leo Candidior [1] *Rubeum necat ense Leonem,* [2]
  Et jacet usque modo non tumulatus humo.

Refrigerii sedem, quietis beatitudinem, luminis habeat
  claritatem. Amen.

EULOGIUM PRO SUORUM TEMPORUM CONDITIONE, TANTIS PRIN-
  CIPIBUS NON INDIGNUM, PER SKELTONIDA LAUREATUM, ORA-
  TOREM REGIUM.

Huc, pia Calliope, propera, mea casta puella,
  Et mecum resona carmina plena deo.
Septimus Henricus, Britonum memorabilis heros,
  Anglica terra, tuus magnanimus Priamus,
Attalus hic opibus, rigidus Cato, clarus Acestes,
  Sub gelido clausus marmore jam recubat.
Sic honor omnis, opes, probitas, sic gloria regum,
  Omnia nutabunt mortis ad imperium.
Anglia, num lacrymas? rides; lacrymare quid obstas?
  Dum vixit, lacrymas: dum moritur, jubilas.
Canta, tamen penses, dum vixerat, Angligenenses
  Vibrabant enses, bella nec ulla timent.
Undique bella fremunt nunc, undique proelia surgunt:
  Noster honor solus, filius, ecce, suus!
Noster honor solus, qui pondera tanta subire
  Non timet, intrepidus arma gerenda vocat;
Arma gerenda vocat, (superi sua coepta secundent!)
  Ut quatiat Pallas aegida saepe rogat.
Sors tamen est versanda diu, sors ultima belli:
  Myrmidonum dominus Marte silente ruit;
Et quem non valuit validis superare sub armis
  Mars, tamen occubuit insidiis Paridis.
Nos incerta quidem pro certis ponere rebus
  Arguit, et prohibet Delius ipse pater.
Omnia sunt hominum dubio labentia fato,

---

[1] i.e. Earl of Surrey; reference to his badge.
[2] Rubeum Leonem, i.e. King James IV; the royal arms of
Scotland.

Marte sub incerto militat omnis homo.
    Omne decus nostrum, nostra et spes unica tantum,
        Jam bene qui regnat, hunc Jovis umbra tegat!
Ut quamvis mentem labor est inhibere volentem,
        Pauca tamen liceat dicere pace sua:
Pace tua liceat mihi nunc tibi dicere pauca,
        Dulce meum decus, et sola Britanna salus.
Summa rei nostrae remanet, celeberrime princeps,
        In te praecipuo, qui modo sceptra geris.
Si tibi fata favent, faveant precor atque precabor,
        Anglia, tunc plaude; sin minus, ipsa vale.

Polychronitudo basileos.

TETRASTICHON VERITATIS

Felix qui bustum formasti, rex, tibi cuprum; [1]
    Auro si tectus fueras, fueras spoliatus,
Nudus, prostratus, tanta est rabiosa cupido
    Undique nummorum: rex, pace precor requiescas.
        Amen.

CHORUS DE DIS CONTRA SCOTTOS CUM OMNI PROCESSIONALI FESTIVITATE
SOLEMNISAVIT HOC EPITOMA XXII DIE SEPTEMBRIS, ETC.

Salve, festa dies, toto resonabilis aevo,
    Qua Scottus Jacobus, obrutus ense, cadit.
Barbara Scottorum gens, perfida, plena malorum,
    Vincitur ad Norram, vertitur inque fugam.
Vasta palus, sed campestris, (borei memoratur
    Branxton Moor), *Scottis terra perosa fuit.*
Scottica castra fremunt Floddun sub montibus altis,
    Quae valide invadens dissipat Angla manus.
Millia Scottorum trusit gens Anglica passim;
    Luxuriat tepido sanguine pinguis humus:
Pars animas miseri miseras misere sub umbras,
    Pars ruit in foveas, pars subiit latebras.
Jam quid agit Jacobus, damnorum germine cretus?
    Perfidus ut Nemroth, lapsus ad ima ruit.
Dic modo, Scottorum dudum male sane malorum
    Rector, nunc regeris, mortuus, ecce, jaces!

---

[1] i.e. *cupreum.*

Sic Leo te rapidus, Leo Candidus,[1] *inclytus ursit,*
Quo Leo tu Rubeus[2] *ultima fata luis.*
Anglia, duc choreas; resonent tua tympana, psallas;
Da laudes Domino, da pia vota Deo.
   Haec laureatus Skeltonis, regius orator.

CHORUS DE DIS, ETC. SUPER TRIUMPHALI VICTORIA CONTRA GALLOS,
   ETC. CANTAVIT SOLEMNITER HOC ELOGIUM IN PROFESTO DIVI
   JOHANNIS AD DECOLLATIONEM [3]

Salve, festa dies, toto memorabilis aevo.
   Qua rex Henricus Gallica bella premit.
Henricus rutilans Octavus noster in armis
   Tirwinnae gentis moenia stravit humi.
Sceptriger Anglorum bello validissimus Hector,
   Francorum gentis colla superba terit.
Dux armis nuper celebris, modo dux inermis,
   De Longville modo dic quo tua pompa ruit?
De Clermount clarus dudum dic, Galle superbe,
   Unde superbus eris? carcere nonne gemis?
Discite Francorum gens caetera capta, Britannum
   Noscite magnanimum, subdite vosque sibi.
Gloria Cappadocis, divae milesque Mariae,[4]
   Illius hic sub ope Gallica regna reget.
Hoc insigne bonum, divino numine gestum,
   Anglica gens referat semper, ovansque canat.
      Per Skeltonida laureatum, oratorem regium.

ELEGIA IN SERENISSIMAE PRINCIPIS ET DOMINAE, DOMINAE MARGARETAE
   NUPER COMITISSAE DE DERBY, STRENUISSIMI REGIS HENRICI
   SEPTIMI MATRIS, FUNEBRE MINISTERIUM, PER SKELTONIDA
   LAUREATUM, ORATOREM REGIUM, XVI. DIE MENSIS AUGUSTI,
   ANNO SALUTIS MDXVI.

Aspirate meis elegis, pia turma sororum,
   Et Margaretam collacrymate piam.

---

[1] i.e. Earl of Surrey.   [2] i.e. royal arms of Scotland.
[3] This poem celebrates the Battle of the Spurs, 16th August 1513,
in which the Duke of Longueville, Clermont, etc., were made
prisoners. Thérouanne surrendered on the 22nd of the same month.
[4] i.e. St. George, before termed 'Our Lady's knight.'

Hac sub mole latet regis celeberrima mater
  Henrici magni, quem locus iste fovet;
Quem locus iste sacer celebri celebrat polyandro,
  Illius en genitrix hac tumulatur homo!
Cui cedat Tanaquil (Titus [1] *hanc super astra reportet),*
  Cedat Penelope, carus Ulixis amor:
Huic Abigail, velut Hester, erat pietate secunda:
  En tres jam proceres nobilitate pares!
Pro domina, precor, implora, pro principe tanta
  Flecte Deum precibus, qui legis hos apices.
Plura referre piget, calamus torpore rigescit,
  Dormit Maecenas, negligitur probitas;
Nec juvat, aut modicum prodest, nunc ultima versu
  Fata recensere (mortua mors reor est).
Quaeris quid decus est? decus est modo dicier hircus;
  Cedit honos hirco, cedit honorque capro.
Falleris ipse Charon; iterum surrexit Abyron, [2]
  Et Stygios remos despicit ille tuos.
Vivitur ex voto: mentis praecordia tangunt
  Nulla sepulcra ducum, nec monumenta patrum;
Non regum, non ulla hominum labentia fato
  Tempora, nec totiens mortua turba ruens.
Hinc statuo certe periturae parcere chartae, [3]
  Ceu Juvenalis avet eximius satirus.

  Distichon execrationis in phagoloedoros.
Qui lacerat, violatve rapit praesens epitoma,
  Hunc laceretque voret Cerberus absque mora!

  Calon, agaton, cum areta. Re. in pa.
Hanc tecum statuas dominam, precor, O sator orbis,
  Quo regnas rutilans rex sine fine manens!

---

[1] Livy, who gives an account of Tanaquil, wife of Tarquinius Priscus. See his *Hist.* i. 34.

[2] Abiram. See Numbers, xvi. [3] Juvenal, *Sat.* i. 18.

CALLIOPE

LATINUM CARMEN SEQUITUR

Cur tibi contexta est aurea Calliope?

RESPONSIO EJUSDEM VATIS

Candida Calliope, vatum regina, coronans
Pierios lauro, radiante intexta sub auro!
Hanc ego Pierius tanto dignabor honore,
Dum mihi vita manet, dum spiritus hos regit artus:
Quamquam conficior senio marcescoque sensim,
Ipse tamen gestare sua haec pia pignora certo,
Assensuque suo placidis parebo camenis.
Inclyta Calliope, et semper mea maxima cura est.

Haec Pierius omni Spartano liberior.

CALLIOPE

Musarum excellentissima, speciosissima, formosissima, heroicis praeest
versibus.

ADMONET SKELTONIS OMNES ARBORES DARE LOCUM VIRIDI LAURO
JUXTA GENUS SUUM

Fraxinus in silvis, altis in montibus ornus,
Populus in fluviis, abies, patulissima fagus,
Lenta salix, platanus, pinguis ficulnea ficus,
Glandifera et quercus, pirus, esculus, ardua pinus,
Balsamus exudans, oleaster, oliva Minervae,
Juniperus, buxus, lentiscus cuspide lenta,
Botrigera et domino vitis gratissima Baccho,
Ilex et sterilis labrusca perosa colonis,
Mollibus exudans fragrantia thura Sabaeis
Thus, redolens Arabis pariter notissima myrrha,
Et vos, O coryli fragiles, humilesque myricae,
Et vos, O cedri redolentes, vos quoque myrti,
Arboris omne genus viridi concedite lauro!

[1] *Prenez en gré.   The Laurelle.*

GLOSSARY

GLOSSARY

Abolete, antiquated, abolished

Advertisement, consideration

Aforce, attempt

Again, against

Agerdouce, bitter-sweet

Agrise, shudder

Algife, although

Animosity, spiritedness

Apposal, posing question

Appose, to question, examine

Arect, raise

Ascry, shout

Aspect, planetary relation

Assurd, exclaim

Astonied, astonished

Axes, paroxysms, fits

Ba, bas, buss, kiss

Baile, a call to combatants to engage

Bale, sorrow

Ban, curse

Barlichood, fit of drunkenness

Basnet, cap

Bate, debate, strife

Baud, jest

Baudeth, befouls

Bayard, bay horse

Begare, adorn

Bet, better; beaten

Birle, pour out

Ble, complexion

Bless, bliss, wound

Blinkard, blear-eyed

Blo, livid

Blother, babble

Blowbowl, drunkard

Bote, remedy

Bots, worms

Bourne, burnished

Bowsy, boozy

Brace, brag, boast

Braid, at a, at a pinch, suddenly

Brent, burnt

Bribance, plundering

Brimly, fiercely

Brothel, worthless man or woman

Budge, lamb-skin

Bullions, bosses, studs

Bushment, ambush

Busk, prepare

By and by, at once

Bydene, together

Byse, azure

Callet, lewd woman

Calstock, cabbage stalk

Cammock, crooked stick

Camuse, flat

Cantel, piece, portion

Captations, compliments

Carp, sing

Cavel, horse

Chaffer, merchandise

Chase, a piece of dung

Check, taunt; turn against (a hawking term)

Chevisaunce, booty

Clifte, fork
Clinchard, miser
Cocket, pertness
Cock's, corruption of God's
Coistrel, varlet
Coistrown, scullion
Colation, comparison
Colour, ornament of style or diction
Conceit, opinion
Condescend, agree
Conning, learned
Contribute, lay under tribute
Copyus, wearing a cope or cape
Corage, affection
Cordilar, Franciscan friar
Covenable, suitable, fitting
Counter, sing
Coy, haughty, disdainful
Crag, neck, throat
Craze, break
Creanser, tutor, guardian
Crow, arrow
Crowch, a piece of money
Cue, half a farthing
Culerage, piles
Cure, care
Curtal, horse with docked tail
Cut, nag; *to keep one's cut*, to be on one's best behaviour

Dag, clotted with dirt
Dagswane, lit. a rough coverlet; a term of abuse
Dare, terrify, to lurk or lie hid (a hawking term)
Daw, *dawcock*, jackdaw, simpleton

Deinte, pleasure
Demi, vest
Derain, contest
Diffuse, difficult
Discure, *discrive*, reveal, discover
Diser, scoffer
Divendop, didapper, dabchick
Dome, opinion
Dought, to fear
Dow, pigeon
Draff, brewer's lees
Draughte, a move at chess
Drift, device
Drivel, term of contempt

Eisel, vinegar
Embose, foam at the mouth
Enbolned, swollen, puffed up
Encheason, cause
Endew, digest (a hawking term)
Engrose, enrich
Enhached, inlaid, adorned
Enharped, edged
Ennewed, tinted
Ensaymed, purged of grease (a hawking term)
Exploit, expel

Face, outface, boast
Fain, sing
Faitor, scoundrel, impostor
Fang, seize
Farly, strange
Favel, flattery
Fawchin, cut
Faytor, dissembler
Feat, neat

Fet, fetched
Fetis, graceful
Fiest, fart
Fizgig, floozy
Flocket, cloak with sleeves
Florth, wall
Fode, trickster, deceiver
Foison, abundance
Fon, fool
Fond, foolish
Force, fors: I ne force, I do not care; *no force*, no matter
Frain, ask; refrain
Frame, succeed
Frete, devour
Frithy, woody
Frounce, hawk's distemper

Gader, gather
Galls, sore spots
Gambaudes, gambols
Gar, make
Garde, trimming
Gaud, jest
Gaure, glare, stare
Geets, finery
Gery, giddy
Geson, scanty, rare
Glair, slime
Glaze, shine
Gle, squint
Glede, glowing coal, kite
Glent, glancing
Glint, slippery
Glose, flatter
Glowton, needle, bodkin
Gnar, snarl

Gong, privy
Grame, anger
Gray, badger
Gre, take in, take in good part
Groat, coin worth 4*d.*
Groyne, grunt
Gryl, rough, fierce
Guise, fashion

Hackney, whore
Haft, swindle
Hake, idle loiterer, whore
Hallows, saints
Halsed, embraced round the neck
Hap, luck, chance
Haras, stud
Hardely, boldly
Harre, hinge, joint
Hastard, dirty fellow
Haut, lofty, haughty
Hayne, haynard, low fellow
Heal, health
Heck, hutch
Heckle, hackle, flax-comb
Hent, seized
Herber, enclosed garden
Hodipeke, term of abuse
Hofte, head
Hook, rogue
Huckle, hip

Irous, angry
Isagogical, introductory

Jangle, prattle, chatter
Januays, Genoese
Javel, knave
Jelofer, gillyflower

Jet, strut; fashion; stick out
Jollivet, reveller

Keep, care, reck
Kibe, blister
Kind, nature
Kith, show
Knack, toy
Knuckleboneyard, contemptible person

Layne, conceal
Lazars, lepers
Leman, sweetheart
Lere, complexion, learn, teach
Lese, lose
Lesings, lies
Let, hinder, stop, forbear
Lewd, ignorant, poor, worthless
Lither, *liddrous*, wicked, lazy
Lorel, *losel*, knave
Lowt, bow down
Luge, lodge, abode
Lugs, ears
Lumbreth, plays clumsily
Lurdain, clown
Lust, pleasure, delight
Lyerd, learned
Lynde, linden-tree

Make, mate, wife
Maker, poet
Male, purse, wallet
Mammocks, scraps
Manticore, human-headed tiger
Mapely, maple
Marmol, inflamed sore

Maunchet, small white loaf
Mawmet, *maument*, false god, puppet (Mahomet)
Meing, gang
Mell, mingle, meddle
Miting, sweetheart, darling
Morrel, black horse
Munypins, mouth-pins, teeth
Muss, mouth
Muted, dunged
Mutton, whore
Mych, much

Nappy, heady
Nept, cat-mint
Next, nearest
Nice, saucy
Nis, is not
Nisot, lazy jade

Occupy, make use of
Orbicular, circle
Ornacy, ornate diction
Ouch, jewel
Ounces, small pieces
Overthwart, perverse

Paint, pretend
Pall, fine cloth
Palliarde, rascal
Paltock, patch
Parbrake, vomit
Paregal, equal
Partlet, neckerchief
Pass, excel
Paves, shield
Pawtenar, scrip, wallet
Pendugum, penguin
Pilch, furred garment

Pill, peel, strip bare
Pilled, bald, mangy
Pillion, skull-cap
Plenarly, fully
Polehatchet, blockhead
Polling, plundering
Pomander, ball of perfume
Popping, blabbing
Pose, rheum in the head
Pounced, perforated
Prane, prawn
Pranked, set in order
Preke, vomit
Prest, ready, neat
Pretory, praetorium
Prevent, anticipate
Prick-song, counterpoint
Pring, prank
Proper, clean, handsome
Puant, stinking

Race, pierce
Railles, borders, marginal decorations
Ramage, wild (of a hawk)
Rase, bruise
Ream, realm
Reasty, rancid
Rebibe, old woman
Rechate, to call hounds together in hunting
Reclaimed, tamed (a hawking term)
Recrayed, recreant, cowardly
Recule, collection of writings
Rede, counsel
Redeless, unavailing
Reflare, scent

Remorde, find fault with
Remotes, remote places
Reny, refuse
Report, refer
Resset, a resting place for those following the hounds on foot
Rock, distaff
Rocket, smock-frock
Ropy, viscid
Rosiar, rose-bush
Rough, *rout*, belch
Rounces, nags
Royl, lout or hoyden
Ruddies, ruddy colour in cheeks
Rutter, gallant
Rue, pity

Sack, wine imported from Spain and the Canary Islands
Sad, serious, discreet, firm
Saute, assault, leap
Scath, harm
Scut, hare; coin worth 3s.
Sentence, meaning
Shale, stumble
Shrew, rascal
Shule, shovel
Sib, akin
Sickerness, security
Silly, simple
Skirlgalliard, rascal
Skit, hasty
Slo, slay
Soho, huntsman's cry on seeing the hare
Snite, snipe

Somedele, somewhat
Sort, company
Sound, swoon
Souse, tripes
Sow (of lead), a large lump
Sowter, cobbler
Spere, stripling
Spill, destroy
Sporn, look scornfully
Stale, decoy
Steep, brilliant (of eyes)
Stercory, dung
Stevin, voice
Stith, anvil
Stound, instant
Stow, falconer's cry to bring hawk back to his fist
Supply, supplicate
Surfle, embroider
Swinker, labourer

Tapet, tapestry
Tavel, instrument for silk-weaving
Tewly, from Toulouse
Thees, thighs
Three, thrive
Threte, threaten
Titivel, rascal
To- (prefix), very
Tonnel, little tun, bottle
Tool, pen
Toolman, penman
Toot, peep
Train, deceit
Tretys, well-made
Tunning, brewing, brew
Twible, double-headed axe

Uncouths, strange matters
Undergrope, spy out
Unkind, unnatural
Unlust, unsavouriness
Unneth, scarcely
Untwine, undo, destroy
Urchin, hedgehog
Ure, luck, fortune
Ured, disposed, fortuned
Utter, away, outside

Varry, fall at variance
Vauntperler, one who is too ready to speak, thruster
Vilyard, old man

Walter, tumble
Wanhope, despair
Warre, worse
Waterlag, water-carrier
Weasand, gullet
Wed, pledge
Ween, wend, think
Werrin, hinder, ward off
Wery, worry, devour
Wharrow, whorl of a spindle
Whinyard, short sword
Wite, blame
Won, dwell
Wood, mad
Worts, vegetables
Wose, ooze
Wrench, deceit
Wrest, to tune, tuning-key
Wroken, avenged, satiated

Yark, lash with a whip
Yaw, yew, hew, cut down
Yede, went
Y-wis, certainly, indeed